SEXUALITY
SUBORDINA

Sexuality and Subordination uses the insights of a range of disciplines to examine the construction of gender in nineteenth century Britain and France. With contributions from history, literature, sociology, and philosophy, its interdisciplinary approach demonstrates the extent to which a common focus can illuminate problems inaccessible to any single discipline.

'Victorianism' is generally understood to mean sexual double standards, hypocrisy, and prudery among the middle classes. But, as this collection shows, the representation of sexuality in the nineteenth century was more diverse and complex than is sometimes realized. Both art and literature point to the deployment of sexual metaphors and imagery, and the language of educated public opinion was shaped by the dichotomy between mind and matter, between rationality and sexuality. The contributors to this volume explore how women, in questioning their subordination, had to challenge a construction of femininity which imposed sexual ignorance. As they did this, women claimed admission to a wider world of knowledge and experience, and came to construct an ideology of their own, a framework of thinking about sexual relationships and masculine power in a new way.

With its new research presented within a unified collective framework, this book will be an indispensable text for women's studies courses. It will also appeal to students of nineteenth-century history, philosophy, literature, art history, and political theory.

Susan Mendus is Lecturer in Philosophy and Morrell Fellow in Toleration and Jane Rendall is Lecturer in History, both at the University of York. At the time of writing, the editors and contributors were all teaching on an interdisciplinary women's studies course at the University of York.

SEXUALITY AND SUBORDINATION

Interdisciplinary studies of gender in the nineteenth century

Edited by
SUSAN MENDUS
and
JANE RENDALL

R
ROUTLEDGE
London and New York

First published in 1989 by
Routledge
11 New Fetter Lane, London EC4P 4EE
29 West 35th Street, New York NY 10001

Set in Baskerville by Columns of Reading
and printed in Great Britain by The Guernsey Press, Guernsey

British Library Cataloguing in Publication Data
Sexuality and subordination : interdisciplinary studies of gender in the
nineteenth century.
1. Great Britain. Sex roles, 1800–1900
I. Mendus, Susan   II. Rendall, Jane
305.3′0941

Library of Congress Cataloging in Publication Data
Sexuality and subordination.
Includes index.
1. Sex role—Great Britain—History—19th century.
2. Sex role—France—History—19th century.
3. Women—Great Britain—Socialization—History—
—19th century. 4. Women—France—Socialization—
History—19th century.   5. Sex differences (Psychology)—
History—19th century.   I. Mendus, Susan.
II. Rendall, Jane, 1945–
HQ1075.5.G7S49   1988   305.3   88–18274

ISBN 0–415–01368–2
ISBN 0–415–01369–0 (pbk.)

CONTENTS

CONTENTS

ACKNOWLEDGEMENTS

All contributors to this volume were members of staff at the University of York when, in October 1984, the first students were admitted to the newly established MA in Women's Studies. One component of the MA is an interdisciplinary course on Victorianism, and this book arises out of the collective experience of those who were involved in putting on that course. It reflects the difficulties inherent in adopting an interdisciplinary approach, but we hope it also exhibits the benefits.

Chief among the debts of gratitude which we, as editors, are happy to acknowledge is the debt to our fellow contributors. The precise shape and content of the book was formed during workshop sessions at which both individual contributions and overall structure were discussed. These sessions were particularly helpful in enabling us to see more clearly what we wanted to aim for.

Thanks are also due to the students of York, who have encouraged us to rethink and integrate our teaching, and who have invariably been constructive and good-natured about our failings.

Mary Maynard, as Co-ordinator of Women's Studies, has fostered an energetic and supportive atmosphere, which has encouraged collective enterprises such as this. The Routledge reader offered helpful and constructive criticisms for which we are very grateful.

Jane Rendall would like to thank the Mistress and Fellows of Girton College, Cambridge, for permission to quote from the Parkes papers.

Finally, we extend our thanks to Jacqueline Morgan and Pamela Dowswell for their assistance in typing parts of the final manuscript.

SUSAN MENDUS
JANE RENDALL

INTRODUCTION

SUSAN MENDUS and JANE RENDALL

The papers in this volume examine aspects of the construction of gender through the representation of women in two western societies, Britain and France, in that quintessentially 'Victorian' period *c.*1840–1900. The papers themselves cover a variety of topics and are written from within different disciplines. Yet they are united by a common concern with the twin themes of sexuality and subordination. They concentrate on a comparatively short historical period and, within that period, on a single but increasingly dominant section of society, the middle classes. In emphasizing the themes of sexuality and subordination our aims are twofold. First we wish to examine more closely the received wisdom that 'Victorianism' means sexual double standards, hypocrisy, and prudery. That these qualities existed is not in doubt, but concentrating on this aspect alone can obscure other features of Victorian life which are equally important. Historically it can serve to disguise the fact that in the private realm much has simply been assumed about Victorian sexuality (or lack of it). Politically, it may deny the extent to which Victorian women themselves sought to transform the language of sex, and with it the force of sexuality. Philosophically it underestimates the importance of the dichotomy between rationality and sexuality – mind and matter. In brief, it overlooks the existence of 'a multiplicity of discourses' about sexuality in nineteenth-century western society.[1] By adopting a multidisciplinary approach we hope to reveal this multiplicity: to show how, in different contexts (religious, philosophical, literary, medical), different languages of sexuality operated. And these different languages present a more subtle and complex representation of Victorian attitudes than can the simple equation of 'Victorian' with 'prudish'.

1

Our second aim is to draw attention to the relationship between sexuality and political and economic subordination. The sexual innocence deemed mandatory for middle-class women in our period was (and was seen to be) closely associated with political ignorance and impotence. To question their subordination women had also to challenge different discourses of sexuality, and constructions of femininity.[2] In the nineteenth-century debate on the position of women, both feminists and anti-feminists related women's demands for political and economic power to their claims to knowledge and experience: terms which did not imply crude sexual freedom, but admission to a world of sexual reality, and recognition of themselves as sexual agents. In that continuing dialogue, feminists began to construct an ideology of their own, a framework of thinking about sexual relationships and masculine power.

Our two themes (sexuality and subordination) are thus connected one with another. But the connection is not simple or straightforward. It can be understood only through examining more closely the changing boundaries of gender in the nineteenth century.

From the late eighteenth century onwards, in Britain and other countries of western Europe, gender definitions were sharpened and heightened as a result of social and industrial change. New forms of production, new class relationships, and the emergence of an international market economy involved changes in the experience of all women: these shifts marked out new boundaries of gender. The spheres of women and of men, of public worlds and private lives, of political economy and domestic morality, of experience and innocence, were increasingly more carefully distinguished. Gendered polarities were of course not new, but they were gradually to take a novel form: in the nineteenth century their form is most characteristically associated with the growth, assertiveness, and self-definitions of the middle ranks.

The relationship between class awareness, gender identity, and racial consciousness is a complex one. Institutionally, in state and church, the nineteenth-century middle classes challenged existing patterns of political authority, still resting with the landed classes. In that challenge, those same middle ranks also offered their own distinctive structures of *order*, inside and outside the family, within and beyond their own national boundaries. The boundaries of gender were an essential part of that order, incorporating the particular qualities attributed to masculinity – authority, rationality, force – and to femininity – domesticity, innocence, weakness. Such distinguishing characteristics defined the middle classes both in their political demands and, later, also in their claims to regulate the lives of the working population. For by the later part of the century those notions of female sexuality and subordination generated in a middle-class milieu were reflected, paralleled, and reproduced elsewhere. The lives of working-class women too came to be shaped by the cultural dominance of such values in a variety of ways: through their adoption of the ideals of domesticity and sexual propriety, through the exercise of middle-class philanthropy, through the intervention of the state. The dominance of these patterns of gender difference, clearly established by the later nineteenth century, was challenged in the same years, as middle-class women began from their experience to analyse their separate situation, and the structure of masculine privilege.

Historians have suggested that by mid-century the British middle classes had significantly expanded as a proportion of the population, in 1851 to between 20 and 30 per cent, though in France the growth of a powerful middle class with a significant base in new wealth was slower.[3] The range of incomes was considerable, encompassing both the poorest junior clerks, and London merchants and brokers who were millionaires, like the merchant banker James Morrison, who left £5 million on his death in 1857. We would certainly conventionally include major manufacturers, such as the Lancashire cotton manufacturers, of whom Mrs Gaskell's John Thornton in *North and South* was one, and those professional classes represented by the heroine of the novel, the poor clergyman's daughter Margaret Hale, and the clever young London barrister whom she might have married. British manufacturers had their counterparts in France in the manufacturing dynasties of the French textile towns in the north and in Alsace. There were rural industrialists and many small employers, the tradesmen and shopkeepers of urban life in France and England. The ranks of the bourgeoisie could incorporate varying degrees of wealth and different political opinions. In France the bourgeoisie might include both leading bankers of 1830, like Ferdinand Du Tillet, described in Nicole Ward Jouve's study of *A Daughter of Eve*, and radical republicans like Armand Carrel, who was to fight the July monarchy. There were Whigs and Tories, Anglicans, Methodists, and Unitarians, republicans, Orleanists, and legitimists. There were metropolitan and provincial tensions. The London intelligentsia – utilitarians, Christian Socialists, bureaucratic reformers – might share yet criticize dominant values; and a lively provincial middle-class culture rooted in Leeds, Birmingham, and Manchester equally felt free to criticize metropolitan mores.

What characterized the family lives of the middle classes during this time was that separation of spheres which has been so generally observed. Yet the separation of work and home, though a material reality, should not obscure the fact that both home and work were equally embedded in a complex network of economic and political relationships. The recent work of Leonore Davidoff and Catherine Hall has brought into focus some essential elements of the nineteenth-century family. The middle-class family remained the basis for most economic activity well into the first half of the century, adapted to expansion through the extensive use of partnership agreements, linking kin and friends. Such a basis was only slowly overtaken by the coming of limited liability, from 1856 onwards legally possible in England, and from the 1860s more extensively used in France. Women were an essential part of such linked structures: in France their marriages could still be arranged in the family interest.[4]

At the same time the economic functions of the middle-class household were also transformed, as women of that class withdrew from personal participation in the family enterprises. They made themselves responsible for the daily consumption of the household, on the suburban estate, in the semi-detached villa or the terraced house. Yet domesticity was not simply a private matter. The demands of the consuming middle-class household were essential to the continuing well-being of manufacturing industry – textiles, furniture, glass, carpets. The demands of the domestic world had far wider dimensions, not only for the continuing economic strength of European economies. British formal and informal empire already extended to the Middle East, China, India, South America, the southern United States, and beyond. Expanding trade, sometimes supported by imperial authority, fed the developing wealth and demands of that domestic market: for cotton goods, tea, sugar, fashions.

Nevertheless the most popular view of the Victorian family remains that associated with the term 'Victorianism', used as a cliché to express sexual repression and masculine hypocrisy. Setting aside sensational approaches, a few historians have been able to chart the public aspects of this apparent silencing of sexuality. What were emerging were new and powerful ways of ordering the disruptive forces of sexuality, not by legislation or ecclesiastical penalties, but through the qualities appropriated to masculinity and femininity. New kinds of sexual order were embedded within the family, within the separate worlds of men and women. The appropriate ordering of family life did not lie in the following of aristocratic patterns of fashion, and freer sexual morality, nor in the customary obligations and communal assumptions surrounding the courtship, marriage, and childbearing of different communities of labouring people. Rather, the bourgeois family was distinguished by the values of order, frugality, and propriety. One side of this lay in the refinement of manners, the adoption of patterns of gentility, always contrasted with the rougher manners of an earlier age, and associated with the civilizing and moralizing influence of women. Another side lay in the silencing of sexuality in public.[5]

In Britain, there is much evidence to suggest a significant reduction in public frankness about sex well before the accession of Queen Victoria. It was in 1798 that Mrs Grundy was first introduced on to the English stage and in 1818 that Dr Bowdler published his Family Shakespeare for the young. The *Choix de lettres édifiantes* (1809) by the abbé de Montmignon, highly edited extracts from literature for the use of young girls, were a French counterpart in the same period. By the 1830s and 1840s the bawdiness of the Regency print had entirely given way to more sober and domesticated periodicals like *Punch*. In France, among the legitimist and Catholic aristocracy of the restoration, a new emphasis on domesticity and maternal responsibility, to be directed against the forces of revolution, replaced the frivolous and anticlerical world of the eighteenth-century salon. The strength of the forces of religious revival brought even aristocratic families in England and in France to make some acknowledgement of changing styles: the outward appearance of the behaviour of the upper circles shifted, as Queen Victoria's court set a tone for the public life of the nineteenth century.

Yet it must be said that, though we know something about the public representations of sexuality, very little indeed is known about the private sexual lives of middle-class men and women, inside and outside marriage. Propriety undoubtedly set the bounds of behaviour specifically of women, whose responsiblity lay in defining the territory of the home against the encroachments of disorder and the hazards of the external world. The disorder represented by the sexual appetite was still perceived and feared, however inaccurately, in the corruption and licence of the rich, and the apparent sexual freedom of the poor. It might be contained within the middle-class home, through the agency of women, imposing new degrees of moral order. In the recognition and mapping of sexuality – first as a silent yet latent presence within the middle-class marriage, second as a potentially disruptive external force – lay new possibilities for the exploration of the erotic, the disturbing, the alien. There is much to suggest that the recognition was not confined to the distant and the exotic. Yet, for lack of appropriate evidence, Davidoff and Hall's exhaustive study of the family lives of men and women of the British middle classes of the first half of the nineteenth century tells us little of such private worlds.[6]

Historians have not been able to explore such themes: the absence of source materials has meant that much has simply been assumed about the 'passionlessness' imposed upon the nineteenth-century woman. Even women's memoirs and journals underwent a complex self-censorship. Still, there has been uneasiness about the picture presented, of a sexually repressive and morally hypocritical society.[7] Very occasionally source materials have allowed a glimpse of something different. Patricia Jalland's study of the papers of aristo-cratic and middle-class families brought to light relationships like that of Molly and Charles Trevelyan, which rested on mutual sexual fulfilment.[8] Peter Gay has described in the famous journals of the American Mabel Loomis Todd a world of erotic interest.[9] And Carl Degler has used the famous Mosher survey of the 1890s to point to a far wider, presumed, discrepancy between prescription and reality.[10] Clearly we should not see the rhetoric of repression alone as characterizing the sexual lives of Victorian women and men; nor can a programme of Freudian recovery offer us a truly differentiated and historical portrait of nineteenth-century sexuality. Equally we cannot rely on occasional revelation through the survival of written records.

To uncover the ways in which Victorian culture constructed and interpreted the force of sexuality, other disciplines must be invoked. As mentioned earlier, Michel Foucault has argued for the existence of a 'multiplicity of discourses' about sexuality in nineteenth-century western society, and in this volume we look at the construction of innocence, through the pursuit of rationality in philosophy and in science, and through religious discipline. But we stress also the possibility of reading the meanings of textual and visual representations of women, by women and by men. For such representations provide a unique way of understanding the construction of gender boundaries. It is argued that the understanding of sexuality is central to the political relationships, the masculine ideologies, of western societies. And women and men were, in the second half of the century, engaged in combative dialogue through the variety of means offered by such discourses, in challenges to and reassertions of masculine power.

The ninteenth century saw new definitions of the quality of innocence. Virginity in women had been valued and continued to be valued for the security it gave to the dynastic transmission of property. Innocence offered a greater security, an internalized security, in a world more vulnerable to political and economic disorder. For upper- and middle-class French and English women, innocence meant knowing nothing about sex: the very etymology of the word – non-nocere (not to do harm) – suggests that knowledge of sexuality was harmful. Within the nineteenth-century debate, the duality of the term 'to know' became apparent: 'You will be like Gods, knowing good and evil', 'Adam knew Eve'. In these biblical sentences 'to know' functions in two different ways. In the first sentence it refers to intellectual/moral knowledge; in the second to love-making. That duality, that equation of sexual experience and of knowledge, through which the full subjecthood of the adult might be attained, is one which pervades nineteenth-century discourses of gender. One of the few historians to have pursued the political implications of such a duality, Susan Kingsley Kent, has, following Foucault, noted of the late nineteenth-century suffrage movement: 'to be recognized as individuals qualified to participate in political life, suffragists had, necessarily, to challenge and overturn cultural constructions of femininity and female sexuality.'[11] And the categories of different discourses which sought to order sexuality were used, reordered, and reversed by feminists in their own demands for access to power.

The language of western philosophy since the time of Descartes is the language of dualism. Descartes's original distinction between mind and matter was central, but brought in its train a whole range of other

7

dichotomies and dualisms, many of which are relevant to our discussion of the themes of sexual innocence and even ignorance. It is tempting to construe this as merely a manifestation of a quite general Victorian prudery. This, however, would be a mistake. Woman's sexual innocence was not simply part of the folklore or mythology of the Victorian era, but an almost inevitable consequence of a quite general philosophical view of the world, and of man's place in it, which demanded that women be construed in this way. In this connection, it is salutary to recall that throughout the sixteenth and seventeenth centuries women were thought, far from being sexually innocent and passive, to be capable of giving and enjoying sexual pleasure, even voracious and insatiable.[12]

The move from woman as whore to woman as angel was paralleled by, and not unconnected with, the growth of scientific rationalism, which involved the division of the world into mind and matter, and the recognition of the possibilities of human control of nature via the essential inertness of matter. Crudely put, a move was made from the belief that the world was a strange, mysterious, uncontrollable collection of supernatural forces and divine or demonic interventions, to the belief that the world was composed of inert stuff whose operations were governed by scientifically discoverable and regular laws of nature. Human beings (especially men) appropriated nature in this period, and the appropriation was a consequence of the hypothesis of a dualism of mind and matter. In this dualism, however, rationality became a supreme value and a value associated exclusively with men. Women by contrast were consigned to the matter part of the dichotomy, along with beasts of nature, and members of the working classes and other races.

The appropriation of nature was thus the fruit of rationality; mind dominated and controlled matter, and intellect – the scientific pursuit of truth – was the means by which man's ascendancy over nature would become complete. At this stage, you did not need an argument to prove that woman's rationality was less than man's. Assertion was sufficient. The Secretary of the Royal Society was quick to observe that the New Philosophy was 'Masculine Philosophy' and the model was not simply a model of mind opposed to matter, but of the essential inertness of matter until influenced by motion. Body and motion were explicitly claimed to be female and male respectively.[13] Man was associated with mind; woman with matter. But the belief that matter was inert itself provided the philosophical underpinning for the image of women as passive, innocent, sexually inactive, and malleable. *Just as* matter, woman was possessed of these qualities. *Just as* body, she was inert, incapable of activity until influenced by male motion. The ground was thus laid for those representations of innocence and passivity which so dominated the Victorian era.

Of course it would be a mistake to imply that this model was the only one in operation at the time. Victorian philosophical thought was influenced not only by the scientific rationalism of the Royal Society, but also (and even further back in history) by Aristotelian essentialism and its concomitant doctrine of natural kinds. Mill's *System of Logic* included a discussion of natural kinds, and the guiding thought here was that man is a natural kind separated from the kind animal by the specific determinants of rationality and having a certain external form. Mill remarked that natural kinds which reflect specific distinctions in this way are 'parted off from one another by an unfathomable chasm instead of a mere ordinary ditch with a visible bottom'.[14] Just as the philosophy of the seventeenth century had urged man's separateness from and control over nature, so here a distinction was drawn between the natural kind man and the natural kind animal. What separated man from the beasts of the field was precisely his possession of rationality. The possibility of perfection therefore consisted in the development of this and the suppression of the 'animal instincts', chief among which was the sexual appetite. Gender divisions and class divisions both became confused into a quite general claim (not made by Mill, but common among Victorian thinkers) that women and members of the working classes generally were prone to weak rationality and strong sexual appetite. Despite the fact that the perfect Victorian lady was construed as passionless, the 'low and vulgar' Victorian woman was perceived as retaining the animal's sexual voraciousness.

The pursuit of rationality was thus part both of a mind/matter distinction, which dictated the possibility of control over the natural world, and of a man/animal distinction, which dictated the necessity of suppressing sexual appetite in order to achieve a fully human existence. Both these dualisms had consequences for the representations of women which coexisted in uneasy disharmony in Victorian times. The mind/matter distinction generated a picture of women as sexually inert, innocent, and ignorant: the man/animal distinction generated a picture of both women and men as potentially bestial. But, in so far as it urged the supremacy of rationality in the pursuit of

SUSAN MENDUS AND JANE RENDALL

perfection, it made women of necessity more akin to the animal than to the essentially human. If the model was a model of choice between human elements and animal elements, and if it was conceded, as it readily was, that woman's capacity for rationality was less than man's, then the image of woman as sexually innocent and passionless became not a truth of nature but a social and moral necessity. To free women from their passivity was now construed as socially dangerous – a threatening and morally damaging unleashing of animal instincts of the most base sort. John Stuart Mill claimed for women an equal humanity in the pursuit of rationality, yet, as Susan Mendus argues, did so only at the cost of the suppression of human sexuality, and only for those women and men who could aspire to a particular model of intellectualized and companionate marriage.

Yet there were circumstances under which forms of spiritual equality might create different models of innocence in the language of nineteenth-century religious practice. The religious impetus of evangelicalism, and the force of a newly generated Catholic revivalism in the early part of the century, offered a particular message to women. For not only did such an impetus offer the rationale of a separate sphere of duty and separate qualities of womanhood. In France, the imagery and the symbolism of a church increasingly responsible for the education of girls was directed towards the maintenance of innocence and sexual purity.[15] The Catholic Church throughout the century still retained an important hold over the education of girls, as it clearly had over the education of the de Granville sisters in Balzac's *A Daughter of Eve*. That hold was reinforced with the passing of the 'loi Falloux' in 1851, and was seriously challenged only when, in the 1880s, Catholic influence over girls' education became a target for the anticlerical leadership of the Third Republic. Religious belief was most likely to be transmitted by the women of the family: the women of the Parisian bourgeoisie were far more likely to participate in the activities of the church than their anticlerical husbands and fathers. Similarly the well-to-do bourgeois women of Lille in the second half of the century found in the church the rituals, the symbolism, the worship which explained and ordered their own lives – though their husbands saw such faith as reactionary and anachronistic. The strength of devotion to Mary, seen in the church's pronouncement of the doctrine of the Assumption of the Virgin Mary in 1854, was clearly developing among women of all classes; for the middle-class woman it offered a theology of direct relevance to the life of the family.[16]

The Christian message, whether that of evangelical Protestantism or nineteenth-century Catholic piety, stressed purity and innocence as intrinsic to female morality. Women, assumed to be more emotional and affectionate than men, could also be assumed to be closer to God. That message has an important nineteenth-century genealogy, from Sarah Lewis, who in *Woman's Mission* (1839) could claim 'The moral world is ours', to Ellice Hopkins, who in 1877 wrote that 'the woman is the conscience of the world'.[17] One element in that latent moral superiority lay in the adoption of the language of 'passionlessness', a language which could be turned to different purposes, to the 'rescue' of those fallen into impurity. To undertake such 'rescue' work, women like Josephine Butler had to claim the right to a *knowledge* of that impurity, the right to enter public debate on such issues, and eventually the right to participate in legislation which might control the force of male sexuality. Such a language might ultimately be translated too into the late nineteenth-century feminist assertion of a more spiritual sexuality, into the command to 'banish the brute' of masculine sexuality and selfishness, as 'feminists as well as anti-feminists sacrificed the idea of women as inherently passionate'.[18] Where Mill pursued the ideal of rationality, and the suppression of sexuality, many late nineteenth-century feminists like Josephine Butler urged restraint through the imposition of a single moral standard. As Mary Maynard has illustrated, their arguments, while having comparable political force, spring from very different analyses. Some women were to urge the transformation of the force of sexuality. Margaret Shurmer Sibthorp, editor of the periodical *Shafts*, wrote:

> Woman is not free from passion . . . only *more* free having put her foot on the further track which, developing the maternal, leaves the passional some paces behind. Eventually passion must cease and give place to the God-like love, universal . . . but *wholly* of the spirit. . . . With the death of passion will cease all desire on the part of man to dominate over woman.[19]

Yet the language which focused more clearly and positively on the sexuality of women from the late eighteenth century onwards was, as

Foucault suggests, that of medicine. The medical profession turned its attention to the charting of women's sexuality, a knowledge to which few women had access. It was a field of knowledge concerned above all with drawing the boundaries of difference between men and women. Women's very identity was to be conceived in terms of their difference, as reproductive beings. As Anne Digby suggests, the profession was creating 'a new female atlas ... in which provisional frontiers of new countries of frailty, disease, and nervous instability were charted'. But the topography of those countries, though ostensibly mapped scientifically, was to be perceived and understood only through the subjective deployment of cultural assumptions. Biology could serve to rationalize gender differentiation, but its terms could also be used in different directions. As Thomas Laqueur has recently argued, the study of menstruation in the nineteenth century could also be used to point the comparison between women and the animal kingdom, to liken women's sexual potential, thinly covered by civilized behaviour, to that of an animal on heat. On the other hand, it could also be used by a feminist such as Mary Putnam Jacobi not to portray a woman tied to a future of reproduction, but to suggest precisely the opposite: the separation of the reproductive instinct from the sexual. For her the quality of female sexual difference lay not in periods of heat or nervous tension but in 'the quiet processes of nutrition', not incompatible with the pursuit of rationality.[20] For the majority of the medical profession, the acceptance of the orthodox view would have meant the preservation of the world of the intellect for men, while women retained their 'biological straitjacket'.

It is important to note that recently historians have argued that even the medical and scientific works of the nineteenth century cannot be understood without a recognition of the importance that language and metaphor play in the depiction of sexuality. The artist's engagement with metaphor and language, and with visual represen-tation, offers a significant route towards the reconstruction of nineteenth-century sexuality. The representation of women may have its part in a cultural symbolism in which women are not the representers, or those who possess knowledge. Rather, as Lévi-Strauss described, they are the objects, not the agents, of matrimonial exchange; and they are a means of communication, not themselves communicators – in language, art, science.[21] Those who read Balzac or looked at the paintings of Delacroix and Ingres saw not merely 'images of women' but 'signs' which pointed towards the continuing discourses of sexuality. The weakness of the term 'images of women' is that it points merely toward the reproduction in a painting or a text of socially produced categories; but a painting or a text may offer representations which are neither totally independent of social reality nor reducible to it. Deborah Cherry and Griselda Pollock have written of the notion of 'woman as sign':

> art history is treated as a system of representations, a signifying system, a point of production of definitions and meanings which can be seen both in their particularity and in their relations to other mutually reinforcing discursive and institutional practices across whose varying processes woman/femininity and man/masculinity are produced, renegotiated and fixed in relative hierarchies.[22]

In this volume Joanna de Groot shows how the commonplace vocabulary of literary and artistic orientalism may be deployed, both in explicit treatments of the Middle East and in other work, to place and explore the contradictory hierarchies of gender and of race. Similarly, Karen Hodder shows how analysing the Victorians' selection of medieval imagery may contribute to an understanding of how sexuality was represented in mid-nineteenth-century England.

Nevertheless women writers did themselves engage the theme of sexuality in nineteenth-century France and England, in spite of the limitations of their knowledge and experience. We have charted the pursuit of rationality in philosophical and social terms. Yet clearly writers and artists of the early nineteenth-century worked in the context of romantic inspiration, of spontaneous self-expression, of the depiction of passion and heroism. In such a context the conventions surrounding the representation of sexuality in the French and English literary worlds were very different: evangelical standards of propriety were irrelevant to the writings of Stendhal, Balzac, and George Sand, though middle-class French life might still maintain such standards. French writers of the early nineteenth-century recognized the sexual potential and awareness of women; yet bourgeois standards sought equally to order and control that awareness. The result was a complex struggle and indirectness in writing, to be found in the work of some of the greatest women writers of the period. For instance, in Charlotte Brontë's *Villette* (1853), Lucy Snowe's most direct statement of passion is through her *observation* of the actress Vashti. Lucy, herself torn between 'the dry stinting check of Reason' and 'the full, liberal impulse of Feeling', is confronted with a performance of tragic power, conveying a strength which ran through the experience of human emotions, a passion born of experience, but also devilish.

> Wicked perhaps she is, but also she is strong: and her strength has conquered Beauty, has overcome Grace, and bound both at her side, captives peerlessly fair, and docile as fair. Even in the uttermost frenzy of energy is each maenad movement royally, imperially, incedingly upborne. Her hair, flying loose in revel or war, is still an angel's hair, and glorious under a halo. Fallen, insurgent, banished, she remembers the heaven where she rebelled. Heaven's light, following her exile, pierces its confines, and discloses their forlorn remoteness.[23]

Lucy has claimed the right to a contemplation of such experience, as she desired the freedom to contemplate the portrait of a naked Cleopatra. For Lucy the dry rationality with which a Dr Bretton could watch such a performance allowed no place at all to 'what was wild and intense, dangerous, sudden and flaming' in human existence. The novel explored a claim for emotional independence through Lucy's passage to serenity; but it was a passage which eventually found a love to be distinguished from passion, as 'furnace-tried by pain, stamped by constancy, consolidated by affection's pure and durable alloy, submitted by intellect to intellect's own tests'.[24] There was a sense of danger in passion, a danger which women too might and should confront and – always – control, through mature knowledge and understanding.

The setting of *Villette* was significant. English women writers looked beyond England and especially to France for an understanding and exploration of sexual feeling. They recognized and accepted Madame de Staël's view of a kind of desexualized England, to be contrasted with France.[25] The impact of George Sand on Victorian writing was considerable – on the Brontës, on Elizabeth Barrett Browning, and on many minor writers. They sought to portray that sexual feeling which they recognized in themselves and in the work of their contemporaries, and in so doing they staked a claim to forbidden knowledge and forbidden territories – though their commitment to moral order might not allow them to endorse, as Barrett Browning noted, 'the dangerous point in George Sand . . . the *irresistible* power she attributes to human passion'.[26] Out of all Bessie Rayner Parkes's early writing, it was her reference to the desirability of young women reading George Sand in

14

AA

11111111111111AAA

her pamphlet *Remarks on the Education of Girls* (1854) which most enraged both paternal and critical opinion.

For George Sand represented to Bessie Rayner Parkes the claim both to knowledge and to power:

Ignorance is the curse of God,
Knowledge the wing wherewith we fly to heaven   *Henry VI Pt II*
(Frontispiece, *Remarks on the Education of Girls*)

It was a demand echoed throughout the rest of the century by feminists. As an embryonic feminist ideology, analysed in this volume by Mary Maynard, was constructed, an understanding was emerging of the close relationship between masculine sexuality and women's subordination. From that knowledge came the demand for a new single sexual standard, to be observed by men as well as by women. Late nineteenth-century middle-class feminists sought both to protect women and to control and channel the power of sexuality in certain ordered ways: new definitions of sexuality might be appearing, though within the confines of heterosexual monogamy. Innocence might be challenged, but the new feminist analysis set itself the task of a different ordering of sexual experience not without its own contradictions.

NOTES

1   The outstanding theoretical discussion used here is M. Foucault, *The History of Sexuality*, tr. Robert Hurley, 2 vols, London, Allen Lane, 1979, 1986.
2   For an important reading of the relationship between sexuality and subordination, see Sherry B. Ortner and Harriet Whitehead, 'Introduction: accounting for sexual meanings', in Ortner and Whitehead (eds), *Sexual Meanings: The Cultural Construction of Gender and Sexuality*, Cambridge, CUP, 1981.
3   The most significant recent work on the family lives of the early Victorian middle classes is Leonore Davidoff and Catherine Hall, *Family Fortunes: Men and Women of the English Middle Class 1780–1850*, London, Hutchinson, 1987. Also used here are: W. D. Rubinstein, 'The Victorian middle classes: wealth, occupation and geography', *Economic History Review*, 2nd series, 30, 1977, 602–23, and 'Wealth, elites and the class structure of modern Britain', *Past and Present*, 76, 1977, 99–127; G. Crossick, 'Urban society and the petty bourgeoisie in nineteenth century Britain', in D. Fraser and A. Sutcliffe (eds), *The Pursuit of Urban History*, London, Edward Arnold, 1983; Jane Lewis (ed.), *Labour and Love: Women's Experience of Home and Family, 1850–1940*, Oxford, Basil Blackwell, 1986.

On France, see A. Daumard, *La Bourgeoisie parisienne 1815–48*, Paris, SEVPEN, 1963; L. Bergeron, *Les Capitalistes en France 1780–1914*, Paris, Gallimard-Julliard, 1978; B. Gille, *Recherches sur la formation de la grande entreprise capitaliste, 1815–48*, Paris, SEVPEN, 1959. Helpful discussions in English include: G. Palmade, *French Capitalism in the Nineteenth Century*, tr. G. M. Holmes, Newton Abbot, David & Charles, 1972; Adeline Daumard, 'Wealth and affluence in France since the beginning of the nineteenth century', in W. D. Rubinstein (ed.), *Wealth and the Wealthy in the Modern World*, London, Croom Helm, 1980; Christopher Johnson, 'The revolution of 1830 in French economic history', in John Merriman (ed.), *The Revolution of 1830*, New York, New View Points, 1975; Roger Price, *A Social History of Nineteenth Century France*, London, Hutchinson, 1987, 121–42.

4   Davidoff and Hall, op. cit., 200–1; Palmade, op. cit., 101–2, 139; B. Smith, *Ladies of the Leisure Class: The Bourgeoises of Northern France in the Nineteenth Century*, Princeton, NJ, Princeton University Press, 1981, 57–62. On France, see also R. Wheaton and Tamara Hareven (eds), *Family and Sexuality in French History*, Philadelphia, University of Pennsylvania Press, 1980; Theodore Zeldin, *France 1848–1945*, 2 vols, Oxford, OUP, 1973, 1977, vol. 1: *Ambition, Love and Politics*.

5   Davidoff and Hall, op. cit., chs 3 and 9; N. Cott, 'Passionlessness: an interpretation of Victorian sexual ideology, 1790–1850', *Signs*, 4, 1978, 219–36; Margaret H. Darrow, 'French noblewomen and the new domesticity, 1750–1850', *Feminist Studies*, 5, Spring 1979, 41–65; Barbara Corrado Pope, 'Maternal education in France 1815–48', *Proceedings of the Third Annual Meeting of the Western Society for French History, 4–6 December 1975*, ed. B. D. Gooch, Austin, Texas, 1976, and 'Revolution and retreat: upper class French women after 1789', in Carol R. Berkin and Clara M. Lovett (eds), *Women, War and Revolution*, New York, Holmes & Meier, 1980.

6   Davidoff and Hall, op. cit., 401–3.

7   This uneasiness was well expressed in F. Barry Smith, 'Sexuality in Britain 1800–1900: some suggested revisions', in Martha Vicinus (ed.), *A Widening Sphere: Changing Roles of Victorian Women*, Bloomington, Indiana University Press, 1977.

8   Pat Jalland, *Women, Marriage and Politics 1860–1914*, Oxford, Clarendon Press, 1986, 120–1.

9   See Peter Gay, *The Bourgeois Experience: Victoria to Freud*, vol. 1: *Education of the Senses*; vol. 2: *The Tender Passions*, New York and London, OUP, 1984, 1986. This work has excellent bibliographies on the subject.

10 Carl Degler, 'What ought to be and what was: women's sexuality in the nineteenth century', *American Historical Review*, 79, 5, December 1974, 1467–90.

11 Susan Kingsley Kent, *Sex and Suffrage in Britain 1860–1914*, New York, OUP, 1987.

12 See, for instance, Angus Maclaren, *Reproductive Rituals: The Perception of Fertility in England from the Sixteenth Century to the Nineteenth Century*, London, Methuen, 1984, esp. ch. 1.

13 Brian Easlea, *Witch-Hunting, Magic and the New Philosophy*, Brighton, Harvester, 1980, 241–52.

14 John Stuart Mill, *A System of Logic, Collected Works*, vol. 8, Toronto, University of Toronto Press, 1973, 123.

15 Françoise Mayeur, *L'Education des filles en France au XIXe siècle*, Paris, Hachette, 1979; R. D. Anderson, *Education in France 1848–70*, Oxford, Oxford University Press, 1975, chs 6,7, and 9; James F. McMillan, *Housewife or Harlot: The Place of Women in French Society, 1870–1940*, Brighton, Harvester, 1981, 46–55.

16 Daumard, op. cit., 366–8; B. Smith, op. cit., chs 5 and 6; for more general discussion of this point, see Hugh Macleod, *Religion and the People of Western Europe, 1789–1970*, Oxford, OUP, 1981, 28–35, and Martine Segalen, *Love and Power in the Peasant Family: Rural France in the Nineteenth Century*, Oxford, Basil Blackwell, 1983, 148–50.

17 Sarah Lewis, *Woman's Mission*, 2nd ed, London, 1839, 128–9; Ellice Hopkins, *Work in Brighton; or, Woman's Mission to Women* (1877), 40–1, quoted in F. K. Prochaska, *Women and Philanthropy in Nineteenth Century England*, Oxford, Clarendon Press, 1980, 204.

18 Lucy Bland, 'The married woman, the "New Woman" and the feminist: sexual politics of the 1890s', in Jane Rendall (ed.), *Equal or Different: Women's Politics 1800–1914*, Oxford, Basil Blackwell, 1987, 156; Thomas Laqueur, 'Orgasm, generation, and the politics of reproductive biology', in Thomas Laqueur and Catherine Gallagher (eds), *The Making of the Modern Body: Sexuality and Society in the Nineteenth Century*, Berkeley and Los Angeles, University of California Press, 1987, 41.

19 Quoted in Bland, op. cit., 157.

20 Laqueur, op. cit., 27–35.

21 Claude Lévi-Strauss, *The Elementary Structures of Kinship*, rev. edn, tr. James Harle Bell and John Richard von Sturmer, ed. Rodney Needham, London, Eyre & Spottiswoode, 1969.

22 Deborah Cherry and Griselda Pollock, 'Woman as sign in Pre-Raphaelite literature: a study of the representation of Elizabeth Siddall', *Art History*, 7, 1984, 206–27; see also Griselda Pollock, 'What's wrong with images of women?', in Roszika Parker and Griselda Pollock (eds), *Framing Feminism: Art and the Women's Movement 1970–1985*, London, Pandora, 1987.

23 Charlotte Brontë, *Villette*, Harmondsworth, Penguin, 1979, 340. Useful critical readings include Susan Gilbert and Susan Gubar, *The Madwoman in the Attic: The Woman Writer and the Nineteenth Century Literary Imagination*, New Haven and London, Yale University Press, ch. 12; Mary Jacobus, 'The buried letter: feminism and Romanticism in *Villette*' in Mary Jacobus (ed.), *Women Writing and Writing about Women*, London, Croom Helm, 1979.

24 Brontë, *Villette*, 567.

25 Cora Kaplan, 'Introduction' to Elizabeth Barrett Browning, *Aurora Leigh and Other Poems*, London, Women's Press, 1978; *Aurora Leigh*, 50.

26 Quoted in Patricia Thomson, *George Sand and the Victorians: Her Influence and Reputation in Nineteenth Century England*, London, Macmillan, 1977, 49.

REPRESENTATIONS OF SEXUALITY

INTRODUCTION

Our first group of essays explores the representation of sexuality by male writers and artists in nineteenth-century France and England. New representations of womanhood and of masculinity could be crude, didactic, and oppressive; they might also rest on the imaginative and creative apprehension of experience, through unique textual patterns of metaphor and narrative. Nicole Ward Jouve's study of Balzac's *A Daughter of Eve* suggests the ambivalence of Balzac's writing on the theme of innocence. In his work, women are exchanged in marriage. They are the objects of masculine contracts made to advance the interests, the wealth, and the political standing of husbands and fathers. Innocence remained perhaps the most appropriate preparation for marriage: it was an innocence and a passivity which mirrored the role which the people might play in the political order, yet also distinguished the bourgeois woman from the woman of the people. Innocence had manifold implications; but it was only one element in the layers of meaning which Balzac's text conveys to us, one element in the impossible requirements imposed upon the two sisters, the two Maries – who, once married, are expected to fulfil the requirements of society, to demonstrate their capacity for 'impertinence', for maturity, even for appropriate kinds of adultery. Yet at the same time Balzac condemned the education of the de Granville sisters as bigoted and repressive of feeling, offering an expectation of release only through marriages arranged for them. He looks for happiness through the unity of love and marriage, suggesting the possibility of women as subject, not merely as an object. Yet, as Nicole Ward Jouve has suggested, Balzac's text goes beyond the possible experience of the female reader – even the educated and autonomous female reader – in its portrayal of the courtesan Florine,

21

who *knows* the Bohemian world of dirt and passion. Innocence and knowledge are irreconcilable.

One way of exploring concepts of femininity and masculinity, and of sexuality, lay in the construction of an alien world, of past or present, into which difference and ambivalence might be projected without contravening social taboos. In such worlds erotic attraction and fantasy could be explored, contrasted silently though implicitly with the bourgeois household, ordered in emotions and lifestyle, in which women within a domestic setting might claim an influence through individual, domestic, and religious morality. Different relationships of dominance and submission, different requirements of fantasy and need, could appear safely masked in medieval or orientalist imagery.

The medievalist revival in England and in France clearly had such implications for the study of gender, for the construction of both masculinity and femininity. Nineteenth-century medievalism, as Mark Girouard has illustrated, provided one way of defining a new kind of Christian manliness – in which men chivalrously protected and respected women of their class and quality, yet retained a common masculine fellowship. In the contemporary poetry of Coventry Patmore and Alfred Tennyson is to be found both an exaltation of certain kinds of womanhood, and an ambivalence towards masculine sexuality, and its association with aggression and action.[1]

As Karen Hodder has stressed in her study of *The Lady of Shalott*, Tennyson's choice of source and image, his specific rendering of Malory's story, is not merely a study in purity and innocence, but one in which Tennyson raised for his contemporaries an enchantress, 'a fairy lady' weaving a 'magic web'. This theme was one recognized by Pre-Raphaelite artists, who created a powerful system of representations through which the sexual ambivalence of the Lady of Shalott became increasingly apparent. There was a continuing fascination with such enchantresses as Sir Frederick Sandys's *Morgan le Fay* or Frank Cadogan Cowper's *La Belle Dame*. Their attractions were undoubtedly erotic, but Tennyson's choice of Arthurian imagery may also express a projected concern with those qualities which were a part of redefined manliness: gentleness, humility, renunciation. Later interpretations by Tennyson, Holman Hunt, and other artists, which stressed a moralistic reading of the poem, suggest how diverse tensions can be understood through focusing on such a single poem.

Moral and romantic interpretations coexisted. It is significant that in *The Princess* in 1848 Tennyson constructed a world of fantasy in which he was able to play upon the horrors, yet also the fascination, of a female separatism which brought access to forbidden knowledge.[2] The liberal compromise of that poem – the marriage between Ida, rescued from delusions of separatism and autonomy, and Psyche – celebrated the complementary nature of the couple, 'the two-celled heart beating'. It might be compared to John Stuart Mill's ideal of marriage, and his distrust of human sexuality, as expressed twenty years later.

Pre-Raphaelite painters both in their lives and in their work could choose the imagery of medievalism to hint at the erotic, even the sexually suggestive. As Joanna de Groot suggests, the projection of gender difference into different cultural worlds might also provide an unchallenged means of portraying sexual dominance. It was equally a language through which a more general superiority of the dominant over the weak, of colonizers over colonized, of one race over others, might be expressed. Such a theme had roots in the assertion of cultural hierarchies common to many eighteenth-century writers, a part of which lay in the assertion of the superiority of the relationship between the sexes in western European civilizations. As the formal and informal empires of the west expanded, such claims to superiority were gradually to become more rigid, as anthropologists and biologists contributed to the study of racial difference. In particular, the Orient was defined in terms rooted in western and masculine power: it was that Other terrain in which the intimate and complex relationship between sexuality and subordination might be explored. The superiority of the west to other peoples could be inferred from the implicit superiority of its monogamous domesticity. Yet middle-class western men found in the appeal of the female imagery of the harem, the slave market, the Middle Eastern peasant, ways not only of pointing the inferiority of different cultures, but also of expressing most clearly their own fantasies of sexual domination, their own desires and needs for access to the erotic and the intimate. The interplay between race and gender in western representations of the Orient most clearly illustrates how changing definitions of gender were integral to an expanding imperialism.

PART I

NOTES

1   Mark Girouard, *The Return to Camelot: Chivalry and the English Gentleman*, New Haven and London, Yale University Press, 1981; Carol Christ, 'Victorian masculinity and the angel in the house', in Martha Vicinus (ed.), *A Widening Sphere: Changing Roles of Victorian Women*, Bloomington, Indiana University Press, 1977.
2   See John Killham, *Tennyson and 'The Princess': Reflections of an Age*, London Athlone University Press, 1958.

Chapter One

BALZAC'S *A DAUGHTER OF EVE* AND THE APPLE OF KNOWLEDGE

NICOLE WARD JOUVE

Natural Law and the Code are enemies, and we are the field on
which they do battle.   (Balzac's young bride)[1]

. . . in the [Hegelian] scheme of recognition, there is no place for
the other, for an equal other, for a whole and living woman. . . .
Everything takes place as if, in a split second, man and being had
propriated each other. And as if his relationship to woman was still
at play as the possibility – though threatening – of the not-proper,
not-clean, not mine; desire is inscribed as the desire to reappro-
priate for himself that which seems able to escape him.
                                (Hélène Cixous, *The Newly Born Woman*)[2]

Women are different. Or so the 'Avant-Propos' to the *The Human
Comedy* asserts (1842). The model Balzac had found for his great work
was zoology, the science which Buffon, Cuvier, and Geoffroy Saint-
Hilaire had recently developed. The different milieux in which man's
action is deployed make as many men as there are varieties in Nature.
But Society goes further than Nature in its capacity for differentiation:

When Buffon depicted the lion, he sketched the lioness in a few
sentences; but in Society woman is not always the female of the
male. There can be two perfectly dissimilar beings inside a couple.
The wife of a merchant is sometimes worthy to be that of a prince.
. . . The Social State has hazards which Nature does not permit
itself, for it is Nature plus Society. The description of the Social
Species therefore had to be at least twice that of the Animal Species,
if you considered but the two sexes.[3]

The need to give women the representation and importance which
their difference required, and the feeling that the difference arose from

their *marriageable status*, were there early in Balzac. His first major work is *La Physiologie du mariage* (*The Physiology of Marriage*). He began it when he was 23, in 1822, and he completed and published it in 1829. He meant later to place it as the coping-stone of the final architectural structure of *The Human Comedy*. It was soon after completing the *Physiology* that, in the early 1830s, he embarked on the novels that were to become part of the *Scènes de la vie privée* (*Scenes from Private Life*).

Exploring women in society, Balzac felt he was doing something new. '*The Thousand and One Nights* of the West' is what he calls *The Human Comedy* in the Introduction to *A Daughter of Eve* (1838). In the Arabian tales there is no 'Society', for woman only appears 'by accident and always locked up'. 'Their "merveilleux" is wholly inspired by the seclusion of women.' France, Balzac goes on to say, is the most socially 'fecund' modern western country for a novelist because of the position of the women in it. Autocratic power and a small privileged class oppress and restrict Russia. Germany is full of confusion, the struggle of new conventions against old ones. England, though it has vigorous 'modern doctrines', is hampered by customs, bowed down under 'the empire of duty'. Italy is not as free as France, and anyway the only possible Italian novel has been written by Stendhal: *La Chartreuse de Parme* (*The Charterhouse of Parma*).[4]

It is significant that Balzac (here talking of 'freedom') should have started with a 'physiology' of *marriage* – marriage, not love. Stendhal, who, like Balzac, spent his life endlessly in love with women, wrote *De l'amour* before he launched into fiction. Stendhal was frankly subversive. In his quest for the absolute he had no time for the powers of the structures that be. His novels are never concerned with marriage as a happy ending or a social reality with which the pursuit of the ideal should in some way be conciliated. Stendhal is quite clear that love and marriage do not mix, that the ideal and the real cannot be reconciled. Balzac was not so sure; indeed, he passionately wished otherwise.[5] He had fallen in love in 1835, when he was 36, with a pen-admirer, a Polish lady called Madame Hanska. She was married to an older man. He waited for her all his life. Marriage to her became a millennial horizon, something to be striven for. In the face of increasing disillusionment and waning strength, he had to keep alive the possibility that marriage might work. But even before his meeting with Eve Hanska, when he was writing the *Physiology*, he had endorsed Rousseau's demand: marriage is nothing without love.

26

Novels like *A Daughter of Eve* sprang from the dream that the two could be combined.

Balzac takes stock of the antagonism between morals and the law where the fate of women in society is concerned. Even Bonaparte and Portalis had noted it when they wrote the article 'divorce' of the *Civil Code*, and Madame de Staël kept passionately denouncing it in novels such as *Delphine* and *Corinne*. How can marriage, regarded as of public utility, and demanding of women the sacrifice of their freedom and ambition, be compatible with their happiness? Don't they, as human beings, have a right to happiness? Corinne says she might as well kill herself, since Society, requiring that she sacrifice her faculties to the accomplishment of duty, is willing her to kill herself morally. Balzac will echo her: one of his young brides exclaims that laws have been made by old men and austere philosophers and that Society takes as its supreme law the sacrifice of Woman to the Family.[6] *The Scenes From Private Life* tirelessly denounce the failures and miseries of marriage such as it is. The 'amiable and honest' woman with whom several are concerned, the fruit of a rich and elaborate civilization, is shown to be delivered over to the temptation of adultery by her social prestige, beauty, and idleness. She labours and sometimes breaks under shackles and a sense of violation. But unlike the Saint-Simonians and George Sand, with whom he was engaged in endless debate, Balzac neither wants to do away with marriage nor to reinforce the practice of divorce. His idea is slowly to correct and alter morals, collective mentalities.[7]

Girls see marriage as a promise of happiness. But, Balzac answers, 'marriage can be considered in political, civil, and moral terms, as a law, a contract, and an institution'; however, 'neither reproduction nor property nor children constitutes happiness'.[8] To make things worse, no one knows how to cultivate happiness. Yet this would help. To this end there must be a school for wives, but also a school for parents, and a school for husbands. Molière, to whose *School for Husbands* and *School for Wives* everyone is appealing in the period, including Balzac, is immensely relevant.[9]

Husbands were in much need of the tact which the *Physiology*, an *ars amoris* and an *ars erotica* rolled into one, tried to teach them. 'Never begin marriage with a rape': crude as this sounds, it was a necessary piece of advice if we are to believe George Sand and Marie Capelle.[10] There was no shortage of cavalier, brutal, or cynical attitudes among bridegrooms, but even the nice ones must have had something of a problem on their hands, given the ignorance, passivity, and some-times terror of their brides. Upper-class young girls received no instruction, sexual or otherwise, which might fit them for their future roles. There was continuing reference in the period to the liberal ideas of Molière and Fénelon, Rousseau and Laclos, on the part of would-be reformers, ranging from the radical Saint-Simonians to 'bourgeois feminists' such as Madame de Genlis, Madame Guizot, and Madame de Rémusat: they asked that girls be given a practical education, taught their rights as well as their duties.[11] Siding with the Saint-Simonians, Balzac boldly asks that they also be given some experi-ence of men – but (by contrast with the Saint-Simonians) so that they will thereafter knowingly and virtuously accept the married state:

> Do you want to know the truth? Open Rousseau, for there isn't one important question of public morality that he hasn't anticipated. . . . 'Among moral people, girls are promiscuous and wives virtuous'. . . . Perish the virtue of ten virgins, rather than the sanctity of morals, the crown of honour which a mother must wear![12]

Balzac as a youth had suffered from his mother's infidelity to his father. The early part of the *Physiology* suggests that for him the Fall is connected with woman's adultery. Interestingly, though, the novels do not bear out what the *Physiology* preaches. I cannot think of any occasion when the virtue of an upper-class young girl perishes (whereas it happens repeatedly in Stendhal, and it doesn't matter). But many of Balzac's wives and mothers gleefully wear the scarlet letter (and not a few of those who wear the crown of honour, like Adeline Hulot in *La Cousine Bette*, turn out to be bloody fools, at least as far as worldly existence is concerned).

Balzac was the historian of nineteenth-century society, not the writer of a utopia. Some of the fictions, however, adumbrate the possibility of a happier state of things, and offer meditations on how education could fit young girls for a successful married relationship.[13] *A Daughter of Eve* is doubly revealing in this context. It shows how dangerous an education in ignorance is, thus posing the question of what the right kind *of education* might be. It also offers itself as a school for husbands, prolonging the preoccupations of the *Physiology*. It is a novel of reprieve, in which the tragedy of adultery is avoided thanks to the tactful intervention of the husband. A lesson in fact, you might say.

THE SCHOOL FOR HUSBANDS

A Daughter of Eve opens in a heaven-coloured 'boudoir', all blue and white, all elegance and luxury. The two women in it, who are confiding in each other, are in hell. They are sisters with heavenly names, both called Marie. The daughters of a magistrate, the Count de Granville, they have been brought up in the most despotic fashion by a bigot of a provincial bourgeois mother, to know next to nothing and marry the first man that offered. The elder sister, Marie-Angélique, is married to Félix de Vandenesse, a man committed to the fortunes of the Bourbons. The marriage took place in 1829, before their overthrow in 1830. It is now early 1835. The Granvilles have bought Vandenesse's title and position (higher than their own) in exchange for a large dowry. They have then used the second daughter, Marie-Eugénie, to compensate for the extra expenditure involved in the settlement of the elder. Parvenu banker Du Tillet, a supporter of the July Monarchy, glad to get a prize lamb from the upper classes, has recognized a large non-existent dowry to Marie-Eugénie in the marriage contract. Now both sisters are equally unhappy. Marie-Eugénie is treated like a slave by her husband. He bullies her sexually, keeps her under surveillance, exerts all sorts of petty tyrannies over her. He keeps her penniless but buys her splendid furniture, jewellery, and carriages. He has made her into an unwilling, innocent, and touching Mrs Merdle, a 'bosom' on which the husband's wealth is displayed, as in Dickens's *Little Dorrit*.

Marie-Angélique has been luckier. Félix de Vandenesse, world-weary and older than herself, has wisdom and tact. He is the hero of the 'school for husbands' side of the story. He has a loaded past, which has yet to be told within the framework of *The Human Comedy*: in *Le Lys dans la vallée*. In the Introduction to *A Daughter of Eve* Balzac justifies having things the wrong way round by saying he is seeking a mosaic rather than a chronological effect. He is dealing with present, not past history: in the present you often hear of a man's past after you have met him in his mature state. Only what is genuinely over allows for chronological telling. The technique applies to the narration of most of his novels, including *A Daughter of Eve*, in which the stories of the sisters are told retrospectively, to explain their disconsolate state, a crisis-point in their life, at the opening of the novel. The reader who is meant to read and *reread* the totality of *The Human Comedy* is free, however, to feed (or not) *Le Lys dans la vallée* into the character of Félix.

If she does, she will know that he is one of the protagonists who is very close to Balzac's heart, and she may also know that Félix is close to Balzac autobiographically: his wretched childhood is modelled on Balzac's, his great love for Madame de Mortsauf, an older woman, on Balzac's love for Madame de Berny, his stormy affair with Lady Dudley on Balzac's passion for Countess Bolognini-Visconti, born Sarah Lowell. At any rate, all passion spent, Félix de Vandenesse has decided to be a model husband, and make his wife happy. He has initiated her with art and patience, he has formed her for society, completed her education, they have a child, he has indeed created an 'Eden' for her, a 'paradise' in the Faubourg Saint-Honoré where they live, rue du Rocher, street of the Rock.

Félix is a mixture of God and Adam. Apparently all-powerful and wise, he has failed to perceive the 'serpent' threatening his Eve, which is boredom, and with it the curiosity to know passion. A splendid, many-coloured serpent turns up in the person of Raoul Nathan, a Romantic poet, a jack of all trades also, a Bohemian, unkempt, dirty, flamboyant, a brilliant talker. Marie-Angélique meets him in the winter of 1833–4, when the first salons reopen after the upheavals of the July Revolution and the takeover of Louis-Philippe, the bourgeois king. Nathan has decided to go into politics through journalism, and is looking for an aristocratic, powerfully placed young woman to help him in his social ascent. Marie fits the bill: as pure and beautiful, she can be his Ideal, his Beatrix; as aristocratic and influential, she can help his career. What begins as an infatuation with love and poetry on Marie's part, and as a calculated mixture of ambition and flattered vanity on Raoul's, develops into an absorbing passion. Raoul has to deploy a prodigious activity, to hold his sundry enterprises afloat and to keep up with the relentless rituals of the rich so he can pay his court to Marie. This makes him keen. Marie discovers the herculean labours and devotion he is putting at her feet and worships him for it. What she does not know is that Nathan has a mistress, actress Florine, for whom he writes plays and who gives him money to help in his ventures.

A crisis occurs. Nathan has had to sign *lettres de change*, to borrow money on short-term credit to keep his newspaper alive. The bills have become due and he cannot cover them. He does not know that the secret lender is Du Tillet, Marie-Eugénie's husband, who plans to discredit and ruin Nathan, a dangerous rival for the electoral college he is plotting to occupy with fellow bankers. At bay, threatened with dishonour and prison, Nathan attempts to asphyxiate himself. Marie-Angélique finds him, revives him. She promises to find the money for him, has thoughts of running away with him. With two days in which to find the 40,000 francs, she has come to her sister for help, but neither of them has any money. Du Tillet, eavesdropping, is suspicious.

Energized by her sister's despair, Marie-Eugénie finds an ingenious relay of lenders and endorsers of the *lettres de change* to save Raoul. But she also decides to tell Félix, fearing ruin and social ostracism for her sister. There was a famous example of such ruin, which the novel refers to. Marie d'Agoult, née Marie de Flavigny, a wife and mother, had eloped with the musician Lizst. She was all the more on Balzac's mind as at the time he was writing *A Daughter of Eve* he was also completing *Béatrix*, which is centred on a character very like Marie d'Agoult. The 'real-life' Marie had suffered from the way in which society had cast her off after her elopment, and from the state of financial insecurity she had brought upon herself.

Félix responds to Marie-Eugénie's revelation as a model husband. He blames himself. He sets about repairing the damage. He buys back the *lettres de change*. He teases his wife with the tale of Nathan's relationship with Florine, but kindly, and in such a way that she decides to own up, gives him Nathan's letters, which he burns; she might not forgive him later for having read them. He engineers a salvage operation of Marie's compromising letters to Nathan by meeting both Nathan and Florine at the masqued ball of the opera, and revealing to Florine under disguise that Nathan is being unfaithful to her. She is furious. He gets her to find Marie's letters in Nathan's portfolio and exchanges them for the *lettres de change*. Confronted with all the marks of Nathan's duplicity and his intimacy with Florine, the countess experiences a revolution of feelings. Félix's diplomacy is vindicated. Nathan, who was already full of compromise, ends the novel politically compromised as well, a finished man. The count and countess riding in their carriage pass by Florine and Nathan on foot, scruffy and shabby-looking. The countess wonders how she could ever have loved such a man.

Thus Eve is saved from the serpent. The apple of adultery is gently removed from her hand just as she was about to take the fatal bite. The husband gains her a reprieve, ensuring a happy ending, keeping her in the earthly paradise of what she now comes to appreciate as a happy marriage. It is not a usual fictional situation in the nineteenth century. Indeed, I can think of no other novel, in France or in England, in which the *husband* is the saviour of his wife. Darcy saves Lydia Bennett by getting Wickham to marry her, in *Pride and Prejudice*; Louisa Gradgrind is saved from elopement with Harthouse by Sissy Jupes in *Hard Times*; Natasha, in *War and Peace*, from elopement with Anatol Kuragin, by Pierre, who at that time is not even her fiancé – Prince André is. *A Daughter of Eve* offers an unusual happy ending which is neither the prospect of an idyllic marriage (as at the end of all Austen novels) nor the fulfilment of desire, but the *avoidance* of adultery. The heroine realizes that happiness is here and now. Happiness is both negative (not doing it) and conservative. That it should be found inside the married state shows how important that was for Balzac as the place where the ideal and the real could be conciliated. He is aware that he is producing something close to a utopia, however. The Introduction tries to cater for the possible disappointment of readers who might expect tragedy, the triumph of violent passions, as appropriate. This is a tale about youth, a merciful, tender tale, Balzac says. He certainly had a right to it, if you think how many of the *Scenes from Private Life* do have tragic endings.

In Félix, Balzac is providing a justification for the views of Bonald, whom he much admired. Bonald's ethics of the family derived from a political mysticism of power. In the circle of domestic life, he argued, the father, like the king in the state, embodied divine power: this may be why Félix is in the position of God as well as of Adam in the elaborate imagery of marriage as Eden, adultery as the Fall. Woman, for Bonald, appears as the minister of the power of the husband-and-father, the children as its subjects. Although bound up with legitimism and the Restoration, Bonald's views were gaining enhanced prestige in the July monarchy, the bourgeoisie seeing in the family, as the *Memoirs of Two Young Brides* state, 'the only possible social unit'[14]. But you could also read the religious parable as a sign of the growing 'secularization of the sacred' which is taking place in the period[15]. This was brought forcibly across to me when, meditating on *A Daughter of Eve*, I came across the following verses in a hymn by Newman:

> O loving wisdom of our God
> when all was sin and shame
> a second Adam to the fight
> and to the rescue came.

O wisest love! that flesh and blood
which did in Adam fail
should strive afresh against the foe
should strive and should prevail

If you put Félix in the place of Christ (the second Adam), this is most appropriate. Félix is also the first Adam. He has had tragic or erotic affairs; he is fallen in the flesh a first time. He says himself to Marie: 'Wouldn't we men be absurd, when we have been behaving foolishly for twenty years, to want you not to be imprudent once in your entire life?' (376). Falling, Félix has acquired a knowledge of *good and evil* (which makes him merciful). His fault is a happy fault. *Felix culpa.* That must also be why he is called Félix. As the first Adam, he has put his wife in paradise, has almost lost her to the serpent. As the second Adam, he saves her. The Old Testament and the New are rolled into one in the novel, which must be the reason why Marie is called Marie, not Eve. But salvation does not go very far. Man Félix cannot redeem the world, he can only protect his wife: 'I am indulgent; but Society is not, it avoids a woman who has caused a scandal . . . but if I cannot reform the world it is at least within my power to protect you against yourself' (376). Félix's power to do good, in moral and religious terms, has been reduced to the domestic sphere. Let us note in passing, for we are moving towards the question, that, for him to be given the chance, the woman must remain in the situation of a child, an innocent, one who does not know. Marie does not even know that Nathan has Florine.

To do good at all, Félix needs his wife – the more so as he cannot reform the world politically either. His class lost power in 1830. Having two couples in the story, placing Marie-Eugénie's fate at the hands of the banker Du Tillet next to that of Marie-Angélique and the aristocratic Vandenesse, Balzac is making a point about which class, and which brand of the monarchy, he would prefer to see as the rulers of France. He first thought of the novel in 1832, two years after the July Revolution. He makes the novel take place in 1833–5, when things were still in flux, as Nathan's journalistic and political ventures make clear (he does not quite know which party to back, which is the winning horse). Yet it was becoming clear that the Orléans dynasty and the moneyed bourgeoisie with it were consolidating their power. The bankers Du Tillet and Nucingen have got into the electoral college by the end of the novel. Félix, however, points out to Baroness

Nucingen, whom he promises favours to in exchange for the *lettres de change* should he be returned to power, that political regimes are highly unstable in France. There was a hope of the return of the Bourbons even as late as 1838. Contrasting Vandenesse's enlightened, tolerant, adroit, and fatherly performance as a husband who knows how to control his wife without wounding her pride or alienating her affections with Du Tillet's vulgar, slave-driving, reifying treatment of his, Balzac is saying, 'which ruler would you rather have?' The wife is placed in the position of the nation to be governed, and the reader invited to reflect on what makes for good government. It is in the interest of the political as well as the religious and moral lesson that the novel teaches that the wife remain *this* side of knowledge: passive. The position in which, according to Hélène Cixous, culture eternally places woman.[16] Taking stock of this, the reader is bound to wonder where this leaves Balzac's condemnation of girls' ignorance.

THE SCHOOL FOR WIVES

Indeed, you could say that Marie's education has been devised to place her in the very position society requires her to occupy.

With his customary flair Balzac is wonderfully accurate in his account of the upbringing of these upper-class sisters. His tone is both compassionate and sarcastic; you might think he is overdoing it, but studies such as Isabelle Bricard's *Saintes ou pouliches* quite confirm what he describes.[17]

There were three possible courses for parents. They could place their daughters behind the railings of a convent-school. New ones were being founded or reopened in Paris under the Restoration: the Sacré-Cœur, the 'Dames Anglaises' (where George Sand spent some time), L'Abbaye-aux-Bois, or Les Oiseaux. Girls could also be sent to one of the new lay schools, which Madame Campan had pioneered with the Légion d'honneur under the patronage of the emperor. Or they could be brought up at home. This was supposed to be the ideal thing: Fénelon among others had recommended it. Convent schools were imitating mothers in wanting to bring girls up on 'the knees of the church'. Mothers, especially since Rousseau, who did much to make motherhood fashionable and promote breastfeeding, were supposed to have the intuitive genius that would enable them to develop the specific 'feminine essence'[18] that was requisite. Women

have 'more soul than man' (Monseigneur Dupanloup). According to
the novelist Barbey d'Aurevilly, they have much less intellect –
neither the 'creative faculty of invention' nor the 'synthesizing power
of generalization'; they only have 'convulsive strength' (presumably
meaning hysteria).[19] 'They lack the male faculties as radically as the
Venus de Milo lacks the organism of Hercules.' Joseph de Maistre
offers women a consolation prize:

> They have made neither the Iliad nor the Aeneid, nor Saint Peter
> nor the Medici Venus. . . . They have invented neither algebra nor
> telescopes . . . but they do something greater than any of this: it is on
> their knees that the most excellent thing in the world is formed: an
> honest man and an honest woman.[20]

How a mother who herself has been given very little instruction can
accomplish the prodigy of so roundly educating her children is never
explained. It comes with the milk: 'a mother alone knows or rather
feels what her daughter needs, and any food that comes to the young
girl's mind without going through the motherly channel is singularly
suspect.'[21]

Like the real-life Marie d'Agoult, the two Maries have been
educated at home by their mother. What in terms of the Rousseauist
ideology has made that upbringing a parody is that their mother has
no milk of human kindness. She is a bigot, a censor. The girls'
curriculum has been a reduced version of what was taught in convent
schools: 'grammar, the French language, history, geography, and the
little arithmetic necessary for women' (276).[22] History and geography
for girls consisted in memorizing names, dates, chronology. It was
similar to what was being taught in England, if we are to believe
Jane Austen's comic *History*, which has one king die to be succeeded
– surprise, surprise – by his son.[23] Literature and morals have been
filtered by the Christmas *Leçons de littérature* and the inept *Choix de
lettres édifiantes* by the abbé de Montmignon, whom Balzac seems to
have particularly detested.[24] Any other reading has been suppressed,
even Fénelon's *Télémaque*, regarded as 'dangerous'. The entire drive of
the education of the two Maries has been to make them as ignorant of
men and sexual matters as possible. Their only walks have been in the
garden; they have never been to the theatre, only to church. Their
only company has been the bigots and elderly priests of their mother's
circle. Their female tutors have been watched over by their mother's
confessor (and they have conceived a strong distaste for religion).

Drawing has been taught them by a 'spinster', and their notions of anatomy are such that they would have 'feminized' the 'Farnese Hercules himself'. There is a nice tautology there, when you reflect that women's lack of 'Hercules' organism' was for Barbey d'Aurevilly the sign of their imbecility, but that somehow it must be carefully hidden from them that such an organism exists. To make sure they do not know their own organism exists either, and nobody else knows, the sisters have had to sleep their entire life next to their mother's bedroom with the door left open. They have had to wear clothes that went down to their feet and up to their chins, even at the few balls they attended when they were of age. The only thing of quality that has been judged innocuous enough for them to learn has been music, the confessors having decided it was a 'Christian art'.[25] They have had an old male piano master, a German exile and musical genius, devoted, comical, one of life's true innocents. Under Schmucke's guidance they have become expert pianists, pouring their whole soul into music.

In *Albert Savarus*, accusing the 'University of France' to have quite ditched the problem of girls' education, Balzac suggests that the legislator in this case is between the devil and the deep blue sea: either you make girls knowledgeable, and they risk turning into Célimènes (the coquette of *Le Misanthrope*); or you repress their sensibilities, but you risk an explosion of the kind Molière portrayed in his Agnès in *L'Ecole des femmes*.[26] Are we to suppose that music has made the two Maries dangerously susceptible, preparing the ground for Marie-Angélique's infatuation with a poet – or has it been the outlet which has stopped them from going mad? Balzac's position is unclear. He is lyrical about the music, the girls being 'Saint Cecilias'; he is also sentimental about the beauty of their being 'hidden flowers' brought up away from the eyes of the world in the 'thorny bushes' of a mother's vigilance. He twice concedes, in odd phrases, that it is 'the first duty' of a mother to preserve her daughter's innocence. Has he forgotten Rousseau's 'Perish the virtue of ten virgins . . '? It is difficult to know whether he is being ironic, temporarily swayed by the rhetoric of innocence, or just pretending to assent to consensus opinion. That the text cannot make up its mind is interesting in itself: perhaps Balzac knows no better than the 'University of France' how to cut the Gordian knot.

It may be appropriate to talk, as Arlette Michel does, of a 'Balzacian feminism' in the sense that he repeatedly protests against repressiveness and bigotry in girls's education, and genuinely pleads for a humane and tender school for daughters and wives. But his attitude is more ambivalent than Michel is prepared to recognize. For, given the world as it is, hasn't Marie-Eugénie, for instance, had the best education possible to prepare her to be the wife of Du Tillet? You can try, as Balzac was doing, to reform mentalities through writing. But, until the Du Tillets of this world cease to have the power, how can you ensure that a Marie's best equipment for marriage won't be to know how to endure? The less developed a woman's faculties, the more repressed her spirits, the less pain she will have to bear. Perhaps the 'right' type of education is unthinkable until you have reformed the institutions themselves? Isabelle Bricard ends her book wondering that, with all the idiocy of the education girls were given, the century should have produced such sensible, charming, literate, and even happy women. It is true, however, that the most remarkable women were those who had a totally idiosyncratic upbringing, like Madame de Staël, who was given licence by an exceptional father, or George Sand, whose father was dead, and who was allowed to roam the library by an eighteenth-century-style grandmother. Balzac was forever arguing against George Sand, who did not believe in the institution of marriage such as it stood. His inability to produce effective suggestions for an education of girls for marriage, the fact that within the parameters he had chosen he could critique but not propose, shows that logic, at least, was on the side of the woman writer.[27]

IMPOSSIBLE CONTRADICTIONS

> You bring them up like saints, and sell them like fillies.
>
> (George Sand)

What I have said Balzac is saying is by no means the whole story. A piece of fiction is a weave, made up of many strands, crossed and twisted. Or, to use his own simile, it is a mosaic, in which thousands of different pieces are juxtaposed. Only when you see the whole do you see the pattern. Extracting an intelligible narrative and a moral and political parable from it is rather like following lines, or the variations of a colour in it. For them to have their meaning, you have to pay attention to what else there is.

It is an impossible task. Roland Barthes has shown how huge is the complexity of a Balzac text by producing some 300 pages of analysis of a story thirty pages long, *Sarrasine* in his *S/Z. A Daughter of Eve* is 130 pages. To do anything like justice to it I would need several volumes. But I can at least suggest the direction which such an analysis would follow. In a volume comprised of essays from different disciplines, it might be useful to show how literary criticism establishes its object. The choice of a particular piece of language as the place of significance, and the decision to treat everything in it as significant, and potentially of equal weight, make it specific. It entails a distinctive treatment of ideas, lessons, political positions, and so on. That Balzac should have chosen to deal with issues like marriage and the education of girls through novels, not treatises, after the *Physiology*, means that his purpose is different, more complete or less abstract. You maim his creation if you use it to extract ideological positions from it. There are positions, but they are inseparable from the network in which they are caught: if you pull, the whole fabric should come also.

Thus, having stated that the western woman, unlike the oriental one, is allowed to go out, Balzac the novelist fully accepts the consequences, even while he appears to half negate them. He does have 'Scenes from *private* life', meant to contrast with 'Scenes from *Parisian* (=*public*) life'. But the narrative pattern he has devised for *The Human Comedy* negates the distinction between public and private: he is a very anti-Victorian writer, an effective if not theoretical subverter of the domestic bourgeois ethos. *A Daughter of Eve* is the inside life of one (or two, or three) couple(s). But the fortunes of Marie, Félix, Nathan, and Florine (not to mention Marie-Eugénie and Du Tillet) are mixed with the fortunes of the larger Parisian world, flow in and out of the *Scenes from Parisian Life*. When Balzac wrote the novel, he was elaborating the 'return of the characters' from one book to the next, which is the distinguishing feature of his collection, what binds it together and makes it into one society (the thing, he said, that was lacking in Scott). And so the future minister Rastignac (from *Le Père Goriot, La Maison Nucingen* ...), the banker Nucingen (from 'What Love Costs Old Men' in *A Harlot's Progress*), Baroness Nucingen, Madame d'Espard (from *L'Interdiction*), Nathalie de Manerville (from *Le Contrat de mariage, Le Lys dans la vallée*), and many more, people the salons and devise the intrigues in which Marie and Raoul are caught. Indeed, Balzac emphasizes this in the Introduction, where he actually produces Rastignac's pedigree and history as it can be culled from the other novels in which he figures, and he also explains who some of the other characters are. Furthermore, the year in which Balzac wrote *A Daughter of Eve* (1837; published 1838) is one of his most prolific periods. He had just finished *Béatrix*, and he was working on *Le Curé de village*, *Le Cabinet des antiques*, and the sequel to *Les Illusions perdues (Lost Illusions)*, in which Nathan appears, several years younger, with Florine, and where his journalist friends Blondet and Lousteau also figure. Revising the proofs of *A Daughter of Eve*, he altered the names of some of the characters, like Blondet, who had taken shape in the intervening writing.

The effect of all the salon life, the political and journalistic intrigues, in *A Daughter of Eve*, is to half contradict the demand that the good aristocratic husband keep his wife within the boundaries of marriage. The wife is meant to be for the family only, a case of 'she for God in him'. She should not have lovers, let alone elope. Yet not only would there be no novel unless the wife at least threatened to take a lover (this signals she is different); but also by its format an aristocratic marriage requires that the wife should circulate socially, and should pretend by her costume and wit to be sexually available. This marks her out as different from a bourgeoise. Vandenesse's first task after his marriage is to educate an ill-formed young wife for Society. That means wearing *décolletés*, looking alluring, flirting, having her own independent relationships. Thus she falls, unprotected, into the company of seemingly friendly upper-class bitches like Madame d'Espard and Nathalie de Manerville, who want to take their revenge against Félix and – another figure of the serpent – push Marie towards adulterous love. All these high-society women, in effect, have affairs, every one of them: Moïra de Saint-Héren (*La Femme de trente ans*), the Countess of Montcornet (*Les Paysans*), Mesdames d'Espard and de Manerville, Baroness Nucingen (with Rastignac). The rules of the eighteenth-century aristocratic marriage still prevail in this society: it is perfectly allowed for the wife to have affairs provided she keep up appearances; provided, above all, that she does not run away with her lover. Honest passion damns you in that world. One of the paradoxes Balzac is arraigning in the education of the two Maries is that they have been given no equipment to deal with this. That Marie should be genuinely naïve, fresh in her feelings, given over to passion, exposes her to the risk of open elopement, therefore social damnation. Society is cruel, as Félix says. He could have added that it is also immoral. In that sense, a moral education ill fits you for it.

Indeed, taken seriously, the moral education incapacitates you. An earlier novel, about Marie's parents and their disastrous marriage, had spelt this out: *Une Double Famille*. The Count de Granville marries an angelic-looking provincial bourgeoise, Angélique Bontemps (hence the daughter Marie-Angélique's name). She is in the pockets of the 'Congregation' of repressive and ambitious priests, the Tartuffes of the nineteenth century, who poison her with excessive devotion, persuade her that religious virtue is incompatible with the demands her husband and society make upon her wifehood. She runs her house like a convent, refuses to go out *décolletée* to balls she regards as devilish (in this there were many authorities of the period with her, and even under the Second Empire the question of whether a young girl should waltz was hotly disputed; Madame Bovary's entranced waltz in the arms of the viscount caused a sensation). Angélique treats sex as if it were a 'duty', not a pleasure. She places a symbolic crucifix between her husband's bed and her own, whose ivory, the narrator said, is no colder than their life, and which bears the body of the 'crucified husband'. The husband gets a mistress, has a second family, then disaster strikes. It is made clear in the process that a husband needs a wife who will accept the values of society if he is to have a social existence himself.

In this system, wives are subject to a series of impossibilities (and it may be because they have to square the circle that they turn out to be so clever in the end). Brought up to believe everything they have been taught by convent schools or devout mothers till the day they are married, or till the day they hit the market (and then the shorter they are in it, the better their chances of a good marriage, since being unexposed and undamaged goods is of the essence of marriageability), from the day they are married they suddenly have to become the reverse. They are told by their mothers to be docile, and are soon expected by their husbands to be expert at love. They suddenly have to show all, or almost all – transparent veils under the Empire, deep *décolletés* under the Restoration and July monarchy – this, after they have not even been allowed to undress when they were washing (they even had to wear a nightgown to have a bath) in their schoolgirl days. They have had to be submissive and show no understanding of anything a bit 'risqué' when they were maidens; now they're meant to be witty, independent, cutting, even: it is a sign of class. Du Tillet reproaches his wife for her lack of impertinence – how bourgeois it is, he says – though he does not like it when she finally finds a tongue at his expense. The demand that girls, through the simple operation of a marriage contract and ceremony, should be transformed from one thing into its reverse is enough to drive anybody mad. One of Balzac's heroines, Honorine, actually runs away.

They are asked to be virtuous, on a religious/monarchical model. But they are also *not to believe* what religion says. Having been taught so much about renouncing the world and placing God above all things, they must now make their husband into an idol, a god, otherwise they are 'crucifying' him. Angélique Bontemps's bigotry, unlovely as it is, makes perfect sense. She's simply being consistent with what she's been brought up to believe.

A further impossibility is that, within the existing structure, a young woman must both apply a bourgeois morality (be faithful, devote herself to her children) *and* seek for an aristocratic type of fulfilment. Balzac rightly saw that aristocratic marriage, based on a 'chivalrous ideal, inscribed in history and meant to pass on a name and a race', was on the wane, and bourgeois marriage, meant 'to pass on property, and seeking sometimes to associate personal feelings with utility', was on the ascent.[28] Woman had fallen victim to the clash between the ancient 'Christian and chivalric ideal' and the new 'principles of reason and justice' advocated by the French Revolution, which it had, however, failed to extend to women.[29] There was no space in which to work out how women fitted in. As the values of bourgeois marriage were flourishing, yet in the upper circles the courtly ideal still floated, etiolated, almost ghostly. The only way left to a woman who wanted to conciliate the two was to pretend: to play, through clothes, wit, flirtation, with the possibilities of courtly love, i.e. adultery – but not *do* it. The wife must be religious but not believe what religion tells her, be sexy but not sexual, appear available but not be so. This is all the more difficult as there is a *real* role, a political and social role, for aristocratic women in that society. The return of the characters shows this. We know perfectly well that Madame de Nucingen has made Rastignac's fortune through clever advice and use of her husband. Blondet has his entries into the salons that count, thanks to his affair with Madame de Montcornet: she's giving him his chance. Nathan is looking for a similar chance. What woman could resist the lure of actually counting for something, doing something? For, if the husband has access to social existence through the wife, the wife has access to a *real* social existence only by taking a lover.

That Balzac should choose to have Félix rescue Marie through a masquerade shows not only that the rescue half belongs to the world of fantasy, but also that in a sense the wife is being pulled back into the world of make-believe, the world of pretence, which is the only one she is allowed to inhabit. This pulls against the other lessons and happy parables that are being offered.

CIRCULATIONS: WOMEN, LETTERS, MONEY

Balzac is not contradicting himself. He is creating situations which are full of contradictions because they are so in life. I can read what I do because the text is giving it to me. How much or how clearly the author intends this to happen is another question. So it is with the contradiction between women's position as objects of exchange and their evident ability to do the exchanging.

Women pass on from fathers to husbands – from Granville to Vandenesse and Du Tillet. Elaborate marriage contracts are involved, the rationale of which is written both in French history and in the Code Napoléon. The two husbands have married into the Granville family, the one because he needed money and the other because he needed the social prestige; the Granvilles have given away their daughters for the converse reasons: 'The Bank has mended the breach made into the Judiciary by Nobility.' An equivalence is created between the fate of the young women and their dowries, all the more so as the one with a large dowry (Marie-Angélique) is the one who is treated kindly by her husband, and the one with a non-existent dowry is treated by hers as a 'slave'. Yet for the two Maries the financial end-result is identical: both husbands are rich; neither of the wives has a penny. Marie-Angélique can neither sell her diamonds (she will be found out) nor apply to brother, father or mother (though the latter remains a possibility). The only woman they find to help them out is Baroness Nucingen, herself an adulteress (Rastignac's mistress). She has a certain leeway because she closes her eyes to her banker husband's misdemeanours. She herself, however, is afraid of being given away by her husband's cashier: she is not that free.

Marie does not have the power to sign the *lettres de change*. Civil existence and effective literacy are denied her. Yet she can sign what gives others power over her. She does not get imprisoned, unlike Pamela by her noble boss Mr B., nor Clarissa by her parents, then by Lovelace, nor Emily by Montoni in Mrs Radcliffe's *The Mysteries of*

Udolpho, nor the girl with the golden eyes by her possessive lover in Balzac's story of that name. But her letters get imprisoned in her place. Baroness Nucingen puts Marie's acknowledgement of debt in a secret drawer. Nathan keeps Marie's love letters in a secret portfolio with a refined safety lock. When Félix knows all, his first task is to retrieve both the *lettres de change* and Marie's letter from the baroness. He then exchanges the *lettres* signed by Nathan for the love letters by playing upon Florine's jealousy. Retrieving the compromising trail of letters left by his wife, Félix is both freeing her from symbolic\gaols (the secret drawers, the possibility of blackmail and exposure) *and* removing her from circulation. He signals that from now on she will remain in his possession.

What form of education would ensure that a woman, once she has passed from the father to the husband, will circulate no more? Again the thought comes to me that the passivity and timidity instilled into the sisters answers very well. Indeed, you could argue that making them literate at all is a mistake. In Molière's *The School for Wives* Agnès has been brought up to be as ignorant as can be by her tutor Arnolphe so he will not be cuckolded by her when he marries her. Arnolphe comes to regret bitterly that she has been taught to read and write at all when he finds out that Agnès can both read the love letters she receives from Horace, a young man who has seen her on her balcony, and reply to them.

You could also say that if Marie could neither read nor write she could neither fall in love with a poet (as Lady Caroline Lamb did with Byron) nor enter into correspondence with him. Here is yet another contradiction between the demand that an aristocratic lady be highly cultivated, and the demand that she be unresponsive to the consequences of literacy.

These consequences are double. Reading literature fosters feelings, but also the desire to apply those feelings, to act upon them, or to imitate them (as Madame Bovary does). But it also develops a dual consciousness, something akin to the knowledge of good *and* evil. Marie's access to double meaning is by way of Poetry. She falls in love with poetry through a Poet, as in Dante the courtly couple *par excellence*, Paolo and Francesca, have fallen in love by reading together about the love of Lancelot and Guinevere. Marie, who has been formed by music, is led to passion through the delights of Imagination and metamorphosis. Courtly love and the poet's capacity to alter reality come to her both at once:

43

The countess had been seized by ideas worthy of the times of knights, but quite modernized. . . . What a sweet thought! . . . to be the secret creator of great fortune, to help a man of genius struggle with fate and tame it, to embroider his sash for the joust, to get arms for him, give him the amulet against evil spells and balm for his wounds! . . . The least things in life now appeared charming to her. . . . *Toilette*, the magnificent poetry of feminine life, . . . reappeared endowed with a magic she had not perceived before. It became for her what it is for all women, a constant manifestation of intimate thought, a language, a symbol. (327–8)

True, she fails to see through Nathan, who has seduced her with talk all white and blue, all angelic virtue and forget-me-nots, luring her with the thought she could be Rebecca to his Ivanhoe. But she knows she is courting danger; the narrator says that like all women she cannot resist the temptation to play with Blue-Beard's bloody key. And if in the above passage the only poetry that she can make is that of *toilette* (she can *be*, not write, a poem), still her writing-box is also illuminated by love now, she can write letters – and for the first time in her life she responds to the magic of the salons around her.

As the novel goes on, with a contradictoriness which the reader must by now be accustomed to expect, she actually *becomes* the poet. 'Love was explaining Nature to the countess, as it had already explained Society to her' (341). She becomes a visionary philosopher: 'Marie only lived for the life whose circles are intertwined like those of a sphere and at the centre of which lies the world' (348).

I suggested earlier that the novel functioned according to the law of patriarchy, with the narrator as God/Adam, placing his main male character also in that position. Perhaps I was wrong. Lévi-Strauss defines women as the objects of exchange, what enables the symbolic, and culture as a collection of symbolic systems, to function.[30] On one level, Balzac's placement of Marie in relation to matrimonial rule and language/literacy verifies Lévi-Strauss. She *is* the object of exchange, the letter that circulates, not the one who does the exchanging. *And yet* she is also shown to be one who *can* know: she creates a language (*toilette*), rediscovers all by herself the world of symbols and the intertwined circles of the sphere. True, she does not actively become a poet, nor a philosopher, nor even a musician, though we are told that Mozart, Beethoven, and others have 'developed in [the sisters] a thousand feelings that did not go beyond the chaste precincts of their veiled hearts but penetrated Creation where they flew on wide wings' (280). It is clearly social constraints, not native incapacity, that makes feelings *and* mysticism the only realms of knowledge open to them: the vertical world is strangely open, it does not take them out of the precincts (*enceinte*), the closure of their hearts. Woman can only know the absolute from inside home or convent. But Balzac's Marie verifies what Catherine Clément describes as women's anomalous position in the eyes of anthropology. Marcel Mauss, she says, classes women with madmen, shamans, and fairground acrobats as being double: on the side of the Rule, as wives and mothers; on the side of rules, i.e. *natural* periodicity, as something that disturbs the symbolic. Marie's doubleness is of a different kind. She is what has to be ruled (preserved from adultery) but also what has the power to generate the Rule: she has access to the symbolic. As a character, she defeats the patriarchal assumptions.

What makes all this so monumentally complicated is that the Rule keeps being altered by changing class assumptions. The nascent capitalistic ethos to which the coarser spirits in the novel subscribe wants Marie to circulate in a different way yet again. There is something about the processing of that exquisite idle product, the lady, that is seen to make her into an object of consumption for the lover, not the husband. After Nathan has first dazzled Marie, he goes out on a *souper fin* with bachelor cynics. Journalist Blondet spells things out for him:

> Blondet congratulated Nathan on having met a woman who was only guilty of bad drawings in red pencil, lean water-colour landscapes, slippers embroidered for her husband, sonatas executed with the chastest of intentions, who had been stitched for eighteen years to the maternal skirt, crystallized like sugar by religious practices, educated by Vandenesse and done to a turn by marriage to be savoured by love. (308)

PROJECTIONS AND SUB-TEXTS

Surely, Balzac does not agree with Blondet?

Well . . . I go on saying Balzac, as if Balzac was one, not many, and as if the man and the author and the narrator were all rolled into one. Perhaps I need this one name to make it all cohere. For the contradictions that can be openly detected are compounded by those which the sub-texts create.

Blondet may be a rake, but he has a point. Nathan has much more than a point. In many ways, Balzac has more in common with Nathan than with Vandenesse.

Socially, Raoul is closer to Balzac than Félix. Like Balzac he is an ambitious writer, hard up, hounded by creditors and bailiffs, a phenomenal worker, an outsider who wants to make it up to the upper classes and to use an upper-class woman to help him. Balzac had been helped by Madame de Berny, and it was another mistress, Madame de Castries, who had introduced him to the salons of the Fitz-Jameses and Madame Récamier – as Nathan is introduced by Blondet to Madame de Montcornet and Lady Dudley. Nathan, transformed from a *Bohême* into a dandy, following Marie in the Bois de Boulogne, is like Balzac courting the marquise de Castries. Nathan writes for the theatre; Balzac had just completed his play *L'Ecole des ménages*. Nathan had left-wing opinions in his youth as Balzac did; he is veering towards 'juste milieu' as Balzac had to Carlism. Like Balzac he is a brilliant talker. Balzac the narrator says ironically that Raoul's speeches could go straight to his publishers, but that is presumably what his own did. Pointing out the similarities, the Balzacian critic Pierre Citron has called Nathan one of the 'affreux du miroir', one of the 'mirror horrors', Balzac projecting sometimes embellished, sometimes uglified, pictures of himself on to his characters. Nathan is also a compendium of contemporaries from the Bohemian milieu. His Jewishness and the assonance in the name Nath*an* recall Leon Gozl*an*, a writer and journalist. His physique, tall, powerful, almost gangling, bearded, long-haired, is that of Laurent Jan (note the assonance again), his unkempt, dirty looks before love has made him smart are those of Gustave Planche, a journalist friend of George Sand. His eventual support for whichever party is uppermost recalls Hugo's evolution from the Restoration to the July monarchy. His boisterous-ness and success as a playwright are modelled on Alexandre Dumas, who had a liaison with an actress, Mademoiselle Ida, whom he eventually married, as Nathan does Florine. From his friend and fellow writer Théophile Gautier Balzac borrows Nathan's waistcoat and extensive passages of writing. The two writers spent much time together in those years, influencing each other. Gautier corrected Balzac's scripts and made suggestions; Balzac quotes Gautier, or rather has Nathan ironically misquote a passage from *Mademoiselle de*

Maupin about the 'blue flower' of the Ideal, after his love for Marie has come to nothing.

That Gautier, whom Balzac much admired, should be so pervasive, scattered throughout the text, and that Nathan should be drawn both from Balzac himself and from so many of his peers from the Bohemian milieu, changes the weighting of the novel. Certainly, Balzac reverses the roles. He, as narrator, chooses to make you, as reader, side with the husband rather than the Bohemian. But that, in the text, pulls against an undercurrent of sympathy for the lover. Nathan leads an exhausting life, sleeping four hours a night, writing, directing plays, editing his journal, supporting sundry enterprises, dealing in politics, *and* has to keep up with the social charade that allows him to see Marie. The contrast between the heroic exertions and financial acrobatics of the parvenu and the leisurely, despotic rituals of the rich is much to Nathan's advantage. There is also a moment in which Nathan is genuinely in love with Marie, in which the amount of labour Marie is costing him and the contagion of her own genuine passion are communicated to him. 'Besides', Balzac explains, 'there is in any writer a feeling which is difficult to stifle, and which is the admiration for what is morally beautiful' (341).

Yet another sub-text informs Nathan's love. A seemingly unrelated and far-fetched epigraph to the Italian Countess Bolognini recalls happy days spent in Milan. The author cherishes them, he says, with 'truly Italian' constancy. Countess Bolognini was just a friend; her lover was Prince Porcia. The only visible link is that the countess's daughter was called Eugénie, and that initially Balzac had called his heroine Marie-Eugénie, not Marie-Angélique (he changed the names round); the countess will be a better mother to her Eugénie than the stern mother in Balzac's tale is to hers, the dedication says. Another, less visible, link is that Countess Bolognini and Prince Porcia were waiting for the death of the elderly husband of the countess, as Balzac and Madame Hanska were waiting for the death of Madame Hanska's husband before they could marry. The countess and her Prince were luckier than Balzac and his Eve (Hanska), since they saw each other daily (Eve Hanska was in Poland). Thus, covertly, Balzac declares himself to be on the side of the lover. Thanks to Pierre Citron, we know who he was.

When in Milan, Balzac had also been made welcome by Countess Clara Maffei. It is said that upon meeting him she knelt at his feet, saying, 'I adore genius.' She was 23, dark, small, slender, pretty, fond of music: Marie de Vandenesse is the exact replica of Clara Maffei. The situation of the two women, the real and the fictitious, is also similar. Clara was married, when very young, to an older, distinguished man, Cavaliere Maffei, who neglected her. She and Balzac met five years into that marriage; Marie has been married for five years when she meets Nathan. Like Nathan, to whom he gives his own age, Balzac had a mistress, Madame Hanska, whom he neglected while seeing Clara (as Nathan forgets Florine, who is touring *abroad*, at the height of his passion for Marie). Cavaliere Maffei got wind of the mutual infatuation, and wrote his wife a wise, affectionate letter. She should listen to him, he wrote, as if to *her own mother* (Félix likewise looks after Marie more like a protective mother than a traditional husband). Clara should beware of Monsieur de Balzac, who, though ugly (as Nathan is unkempt), has powerful charm, an extraordinary way with women, and the prestige of fame. He has the reputation of 'a libertine and an immoralist'. Clara is 'the love of Milan'. Were she to yield she would forfeit that love, be left a prey to 'grief and remorse'. Clara, it seems, heeded the letter – an effective piece of writing from the Cavaliere, which had removed his wife from circulation. Balzac returned to Paris. The 'truly Italian' constancy of memory he evokes, the proffered wish that his book could jump 'over the Alps', are not for Countess Bolognini but for Clara Maffei, or rather have been transferred from the one to the other. Writing *A Daughter of Eve*, Balzac was fictionalizing and disguising his own abortive love-affair. Three years later he dedicated *La Fausse Maîtresse* (what a telling title!) to Clara.

Before he desired Clara, he desired Eve Hanska. Nathan desires Marie . . . The narrator cannot always control his own desire for Marie. The wish for seduction at times runs away with the wish for protection. Only thus can some of the more bizarre contradictions be explained. Commenting on the cynical way in which rakes such as Blondet talk about Marie, speculate about her, the narrator says that women would think twice if they could hear men's talk. 'Fresh, gracious, and modest creature that she was, how their jokes and buffoonery were undressing her and appraising her!' They're stripping her, he's indignant . . . but he adds in the same sentence: 'but also what a triumph! The more veils she lost, the more beauties she revealed.' It is as if he wished her to be stripped. Her beauty is such, and so indestructible, that she'll be the more beautiful as she becomes the more exposed.

THE MADONNA AND THE COURTESAN

> Bisexuality is not a fantasy of complete being, but the location
> within oneself of the presence of both sexes, evident and insistent in
> different ways according to the individual.[31]
>
> (Hélène Cixous)

The narrative passes on, and with it the narratorial sympathies, from
one character to another. Yet, as the title indicates, the centre is
Marie. This is the story of a woman's temptation and her salvation
from the Fall.

But that places her in a double situation. As the tempted, she is an
active conciousness, she is fully human, she feels and acts: she does,
after all, save Nathan from suicide and from bankruptcy. But, as Eve,
to be saved from the serpent, i.e. adultery, i.e. knowledge of good and
evil through love, she is passive. She is also the object of a struggle
between husband and lover: she is the odds, the prize to be won. In
short, she is, at one and the same time, someone who can and does
know, and someone who is not allowed to know. The novel is indeed
on a border, in the realm of the anomalous. Knowledge, for a woman,
means both the opposite of ignorance and the opposite of innocence.
Marie's education has aimed at making her innocent by making her
ignorant. The novelist has – ambiguously – protested against this. Yet
his narrative makes it clear that for Marie to help him achieve his
dream of a good marriage (the reconciliation of woman's happiness
with the sacrifice of her full human potential to society) she must
remain ignorant: ignorant of the full depth of life. That is supposed to
be innocence.

Marie must be seen as one who is ignorant of life, and the better for
being ignorant. She is a child, who must learn to trust the husband
Félix. She comes to know the extremes of heat and cold within the
confines of her home, as once she had soared to creation on the wings
of music, but within the *enceinte* of her chaste heart. Shame overtakes
Marie when Félix reveals Nathan's affair with Florine: 'Fire was no
redder than the cheeks of the countess.' When he asks her where her
letters to Nathan are, and she realizes what this means, she suddenly
feels cold. It is not passion as an adventure that makes her know
extremes of feeling, this suggests, but the protected paradise of the rue
du Rocher, the little rocky island where Félix has perched her. How
narrow and *vertical* this makes woman's world! Yet, prior to this scene,

Balzac has given her full stature as a heroine, he has entered her consciousness, made her encounter real life, struggle against the threat of death and ruin to the man she loves. He has invalidated his own thesis even before proving its validity.

This is not only because Balzac is so given over to his imaginary projections, so protean, that he records all that there is, including, again and again, the self-contradictory status of women in society, and the impossibility of solving that contradiction. It is also because of what has often been described as his own dual, or 'bisexual', nature. His own painfully repressed education at the hand of a cold mother equipped him with a ready sympathy for the fate of repressed girls. The heroine of his first novel, *Wann-Chlore*, is just such a girl, modelled on Balzac's sister Laurence – and she is called Eugénie ...

But there is more to it than this. The Introduction to *A Daughter of Eve* has a strange comparison in it. It describes the novelist as Scheherazade, condemned to telling a thousand and one stories (the almost infinite task of *The Human Comedy*). The public is the Sultan, always liable to have him executed if he ceases to please. The novelist has to pull himself back from the threshold of perdition. He is like Marie, whose secret text (the love letters, Balzac's own love for Clara Maffei?) has to be retrieved through a masquerade, a novel that can be exchanged for money (the *lettres de change*), that will sell and that in its turn will keep the audience in a state of suspense, will make them want to hear more, to read the next novel. The novelist is in the position of the woman as well as in the position of the man. He is writing something much more complicated than a patriarchal text, despite his title. He is both Félix and Marie. He is also Nathan, who needs Marie to save him. As the saviour, Marie is active, a tutelary figure, an end-point. If Nathan fails to make Marie his Beatrix, she has done better than that for him: she has almost been his Christ. (She has laid her reputation on the line to save him.) And perhaps Clara Maffei, as the true inspirer of the story, told by a writer who, unlike Nathan, was not a failure, has been Balzac's Beatrix.

It may be that Balzac was debating with George Sand and seeing her when he was writing this novel.[32] George Sand's own androgyny – if that's the right word – caused Balzac to perceive and accept that he himself, as writer, was both male and female, diving in and out of femininity. *A Daughter of Eve* at any rate acutely registers the fact that economic, social, and political circumstances continually place men in feminine positions – if, by 'feminine', we mean passive and the object of exchange. Nathan, virile as he may be in so many ways and in contrast with Félix, who is as small, elegant, and graceful as Nathan is tall, powerful, and eloquent, is repeatedly 'feminized'. He is dependent upon patronage, a social outsider; he is kept to a certain extent by Florine, and Marie too has to find money for him; he signs *lettres de change* that circulate and put him in the power of lenders and bankers. Furthermore, he is Jewish, his father a bankrupt. Race as well as class are at work here. The bitchy Mesdames d'Espard and de Manerville complain of having to receive Nathan: it's all for the sake of the sweet revenge against Félix, but vengeance is dear.

Socially and financially vulnerable men, in Balzac, are often placed next to women. In *La Cousine Bette*, written a few years later, Balzac lodges his immigrant sculptor, the impoverished Polish Count Steinbock, in the same submerged, under-privileged quarter of Paris as the peasant spinster Bette and the illegitimate daughter/courtesan Valérie Marneffe. For a man to be dependent upon the wealthy and institutionally powerful is almost tantamount to being a woman. Signing the *lettres de change* that can lead to his being expelled, the German music master Schmucke is being interchangeable not only with Nathan (who can go to gaol) but with Marie, who could be socially ostracized.

Schmucke is almost a possibility of *being* for her. For he is a true *innocent*, and his innocence is positive, not negative. He is drawn after an ideal model of the German man, all gentleness and naturalness, that several French writers of the period (Stendhal, Nerval) derived from their admiration for German Romanticism and German music. The figures of Bach and Hoffmann float around the eccentric chapel master. He has such purity, generosity, and faith in his former pupils and present benefactresses that it doesn't seem to occur to him that by signing bills for such – to him – fantastic sums of money he is putting his life at risk. But he intimates that *if* he realized it he would do it with the same promptness. He is the real knight of the story. He is also someone whose gaiety and love of music elevate him above his dingy material circumstances: verticality is relevant to him too.

Marie's gradual involvement with Nathan literally acquaints her with dirt. When she gets the letter intimating he's committed suicide, she rushes out into the street in her nightdress, wrapped in a shawl, and gets a cab. Finding the squalid newspaper office and squalid stove at whose fumes Nathan is asphyxiating, she revives him, and drives him to a little hotel where the bailiffs will not find him. The compromising consequences of going to such a hotel with a man are obvious. She then sets about redeeming the *lettres de change*, and this eventually takes her to Schmucke's rooms. They are incredibly, fantastically dirty. There is dust everywhere, shaving implements, leftover food, and dirty crockery, and the whole thing is suffused with the yellow hue of pipe-smoke. To get to the house, Marie only just manages to step over the mud in the street.

Mud is loaded in Balzac with metaphoric and metonymic implications. It signifies the poor, the downtrodden, the socially low. In a real way it *is* the mud of the streets of Paris: it was not until the Second Empire that the Prefect of Paris, Poubelle (who gave his name to dustbins), invented a systematic way of collecting refuse. Till then, mud, rubbish disgorged by houses, markets, shops, restaurants, mixed with the droppings of horses, made a walk through the often narrow streets impossible if you were not prepared thoroughly to dirty your clothes. Hence the enormous importance of arriving at a smart house with impeccable boots and trousers for a young man on the make, for it signified that he was sufficiently well-off to ride in a carriage or keep his own horse. Rastignac, the hero of *Old Goriot*, cringes when his spattered boots are shown up by Dandy Maxime de Trailles's own dazzling boots and spotless trousers at the house of an elegant lady whose patronage he desires: the poor student that he is has had a lot of trouble getting the gear together, but he has not been able to afford a carriage. Ladies would not have dreamt of going on foot. Being seen walking in a dirty Paris street meant you were lost: you could only have been on an amorous appointment. Characters who are socially low in Balzac's Paris (like the trio Steinbock–Bette–Marneffe) live next to, and in, dirt.

You could almost argue that Nathan's dirty looks are left-wing, a declaration of sympathy for the lower classes. Bohemian artists liked to live on the margins of society; some of them wanted to be close to the People. Hugo meditated endlessly on the equation People = dirt, elevating dirt to a mythic status. *Les Misérables* contains an extraordinary exordium on the sewers of Paris, the 'intestine of Leviathan'. The refuse they carry could become manure, could become gold. As she stretches her hand towards the apple of knowledge, Marie descends from her rock into the muddy street, the dingy office, the louche hotel, Schmucke's filthy flat. She descends from her class to a lower one. So doing, she begins truly to learn something about life – becomes dimly aware of how, not the other half, but the other 90 per cent live. Pain and trouble energize her, develop her capacities:

> The countess . . . spent the night inventing stratagems to get the forty thousand francs. In such crises, women are sublime. Driven by feeling, they arrive at designs that would surprise thieves, businessmen, and usurers, the three classes of industrials. . . . She went over the emotions [she had felt on saving Nathan] and felt herself more in love with the miseries than with the greatness. . . . The countess had wished for emotions; they were welling up in her, awesome, but beloved. She was living more intensely through pain than through pleasure. (359–60)

Balzac in the period was writing a sequel to *Lost Illusions* called 'What Love Costs Old Men'. The old man in question is the banker Nucingen. He falls in love with a beautiful courtesan called Esther, who, under the masterly supervision of the convict Vautrin, pumps a million francs out of the banker. You could say that the countess has done as well as the courtesan. You say it even louder if you reflect that Nathan[33] has previously been kept afloat by Florine's generosity: she has sold her elegant furniture, the gift of wealthy lovers, to get the 50,000 francs he needed to start his journal, and she goes touring the provinces to earn him some more. Marie gets perilously close to being Nathan's whore, Nathan to being the pimp of the angel as well as the actress. Close: not there. Marie's love is 'sublime', 'charity' its basis. Schmucke is a 'Sainte Cécile' (bisexual too); Marie appeals to his disinterested love, which is religious, like his love of music. Marie does *not quite* touch the mud in the street.

The narrative has said earlier that Marie felt in her love the selflessness of the courtesan. The courtesan in Balzac is the double, but not the alienated double, of the good woman. How does it appear that Marie calls up Mary Magdalene? Well, there is Florine, to start with. At one point the narrator hints that, as Nathan has Florine to make love to, he does not press his suit quite so ardently as a less satisfied man might have done. Marie's virtue is partly saved by Florine. And, on a more metaphoric level, there is . . . mud again, and its ability (as in Hugo) to turn into gold.

A cat inhabits Schmucke's apartment:

> The continuous use of a good old German pipe had suffused the ceiling, the wretched wallpaper scratched in a thousand places by

the cat, with a blond hue that gave all things the appearance of Ceres' golden harvests. The cat, robed in magnificent dishevelled silk that would have made a concierge envious, was like the mistress of the house, free from care, grave under its beard. From the top of an excellent Vienna piano where it sat in judiciary splendour, it cast on the incoming countess the honeyed and cold look with which any woman struck by her beauty would have eyed her. It did not disturb itself, it simply waved the two silver bristles of its moustache and went on staring at Schmucke with its golden eyes. (363)

The cat is female: it is Schmucke's companion, the mistress of the house, jealous of Schmucke's affection, queenly, it wears a splendid dress, it is a concierge, it regards the countess as a possible rival, and does whatever dusting takes place with its 'splendid tail'. It is also male, bearded and mustachioed, magisterial, the 'son' in the 'living trinity' composed of Schmucke, the cat, and the pipe, a trinity in which the holy spirit, the pipe, suffuses everything with a golden haze, making it into a place of pagan and Christian splendour all at once: blond like Ceres' harvest, suffused with 'celestial rays' by Schmucke's smile, his 'sun'-like soul (364–5). Schmucke calls the cat 'Meinherr Mirr', Mirr, a name, he tells Marie, which he has borrowed from one of the fantastical tales of his great compatriot Hoffmann.[34] The whole scene makes you feel that Marie is being confronted by a world of magic, in which all dichotomies are transcended: all genders, all modes of being, the material and the spiritual, the materialistic, the surreal and the metaphoric, the pagan and the Christian. The power of transmutation which is there *can* make gold out of mud. 'This smoky bedroom, filled with litter, was a temple inhabited by two divinities': art and religion. But the countess remains on the threshold. Alice does not go through the looking-glass. There is not enough of the artist, nor perhaps of the human being yet, in Marie for her to be able to *read* the reality that is being presented to her. She cannot interpret rubbish: in the 'heap of things' that are 'somewhere between manure and rags', Marie's eye is not 'exercised enough to find information about Schmucke's life': in the 'chestnut skins, apple peels, the shells of red eggs', the broken dishes 'crottés de *sauer-craut*', 'muddied with sauerkraut'. Balzac is challenging his reader to go through the looking-glass, to dare to step into the mud. He is inviting his female reader to be a courtesan.

In the Introduction to *A Daughter of Eve*, Balzac talks of the pains he takes to write, the nights of effort some paragraphs cost him. Through what seems an irrelevant and accidental choice, he quotes, as an instance of his most painstaking prose, a piece from 'What Love Costs Old Men'. It is the description of Esther's eyes – Esther the courtesan who pumps a million francs out of Nucingen. There are creatures in whose eyes the fascination of the deserts remains, for they are descended from races which have had a long intercourse with the vast spaces of deserts. Esther is such a creature. She is Jewish.[35] Her eyes are golden, like the eyes of another courtesan, the girl with the golden eyes.

The exotic courtesan is like gold, a currency that circulates. She is the locus of the dream of absolute pleasure, the dream of the Oriental woman, almost, you could say, the gold standard of pleasure. She is 'an allegory of the "mystery" of bourgeois society', Marc Angenot states.[36] More and more, as the century progresses, French literature will use the figure of the prostitute to create mystery, justify its fascination for refuse by making it exalting, use the prostitute as the 'synecdoche of modern society', the 'allegory of exchange-value'. In Baudelaire, Zola, and many others, the dichotomy whore/madonna will be elaborated. In Balzac, it is not a dichotomy. An earlier passage, describing Marie's gaze at Nathan, a gaze that is so unguarded that she risks compromising herself, says that it is 'violent and fixed', one of those gazes in which 'the will springs from the eyes, as luminous waves spring from the sun, and which hypnotists say penetrates the person at whom it is directed' (362). Marie in love has the power and vulnerability of the courtesan. And in Balzac the courtesan is more than exploitable allegory. She can be golden in her own right. She can love. She never ceases to be human. In her passion she is self-forgetful and sublime. With all her vulgarity, jealous Florine is magnificent. The joke may be at the expense of Félix, ready to produce Florine's jealousy as a 'spectacle' for his wife.

And so, if we notice the parallels between the two visits, the visit to Schmucke and his cat, the visit to the flat shared by Florine and Nathan, as untidy in its way as Schmucke's flat if less dirty; and if we perceive the figure of Esther, the most sublime of courtesans, behind Florine and the cat – Esther whose eyes can fascinate because she is equal to anything, because she is descended from a race that has a millenary intercourse with the absolute – we have to ask where this leaves Marie's 'innocence'. In Schmucke's flat, she is poised on the verge of a world that is dirty but also heavenly, inhabited by true innocence, a religious artist. She is on the verge of Hoffmann's fantastic world. When Félix has withdrawn her from the brink, is redeeming her letters from the soiled bedroom shared by Nathan and Florine, it is Florine, a vulgar and worldly yet passionate version of Esther, who remains in the world where transmutations can occur, where power is wielded. It is the world of ordinary material life, the narrative makes clear.

When Florine wants to rip open Nathan's secret portfolio with the letters of her rival in it, Florine first calls for a kitchen knife. 'C'est avec ça qu'on égorge les poulets', 'That is what you slit the throats of chickens with', she explains. 'Poulet', chicken, is also slang for a love letter. She then uses Nathan's razor to open the bag. A crude Freudian might say that Florine is the one who remains wielding the phallic tools, slitting open the 'female' bag. You could say, more to the point, I think, that if the voice of passion speaks plainly in her (she wants to cut her rival's throat) she is also the one who, through slang, remains mistress of metaphor. Knowledge, in its fullness, its ability to function on several levels at once, pertains to the fallen woman, who lives in dirt. Marie is left without true innocence (that remains with Schmucke) and without knowledge (that remains with Florine). It is difficult to know what to conclude: what to make of the haunting and ironic figure of the courtesan in a novel that has set out to prove that women would be well advised to remain perched on their paradise of a rock.

It is all the more difficult as Marie, the central protagonist, has been made to remain 'angélique', and as such could not *read* a text whose depth remains in excess of her. What does that make of a female reader such as myself who has endeavoured to decipher it? Woman's anomalous position in culture has been verified: her kinship is to other eccentric figures such as the Jewish poet and the immigrant Bohemian musician. What distinguishes her from these two, however, is that she is *split*. Knowledge and art are not taboo for them. Sex goes through Marie like a dividing line. Let us not forget that she is also *two*; there are two Maries, loving sisters so close to each other they are compared to Siamese twins at the beginning of the novel: marriage has parted them. Marie-Angélique, alias a daughter of Eve must fall either on the side of innocence (be a Marie, a wife and mother) or on the side of knowledge (be Eve, or Florine). It is a mark of Balzac's bisexuality, the genuine ambivalence of the text, that he lets you see how phantomatic the dividing line is, how one sentence must contradict the other: how impossible the prevailing rule makes it to *think* that constructed chimera, woman.

NOTES

1   Honoré de Balzac, *Mémoires de deux jeunes mariées*, in *The Human Comedy*, Paris, Gallimard, Bibliothèque de la Pléiade, 1966, Vol. 1, 201 (my translation). All translations from the French are mine.

2   Hélène Cixous and Catherine Clément, *The Newly Born Woman*, tr. Betsy Wing, Manchester, Manchester University Press, 1987, 78 and 79.

3   Balzac, 'Avant-Propos', *The Human Comedy*, vol. 1, 4–5.

4   'Introduction' to *A Daughter of Eve*, in the new Bibliothèque de la Pléiade edition of Balzac's *Œuvres complètes*, vol. 2, 263. References to this appear subsequently in parentheses in the text. I am much indebted to the excellent preface and notes by Roger Pierrot, especially for what concerns the 'sub-texts' of the novel.

5   In this he is closer to the English novelists of the nineteenth century than to Stendhal: to Jane Austen or Mrs Gaskell, even to Charlotte Brontë or George Eliot.

6   Madame de Staël, *Corinne ou l'Italie*, Paris, Editions des Femmes, 1979, and Balzac, *Mémoires de deux jeunes mariées*, 208.

7   The description of the upper-class young women is from Balzac *La Physiologie du mariage*, *Œuvres complètes*, vol. 1, 694–5. On the debates of the period and generally speaking on the whole question, see Arlette Michel, *Le Mariage chez Honoré de Balzac: amour et féminisme*, Paris, Société d'Edition 'Les Belles Lettres', 1978.

8   Michel, op. cit., 66, and Balzac, *La Physiologie du mariage*, 646.

9   Molière was much discussed at the time. Théophile de Ferrière, in *Les Romans et le mariage*, Paris, H. Fournier Jeune, a novel published in 1837 (the year of *A Daughter of Eve*, indeed a novel which Balzac was answering in writing *A Daughter of Eve*), quotes both from *Les Femmes savantes* and *The School for Husbands* in his preface. Balzac himself directly referred to Molière's title in his play *The School for Married Couples* (1842).

10   See Isabelle Bricard, *Saintes ou pouliches: l'éducation des jeunes filles au XIXe siècle*, Paris, Albin Michel, 1985. Only 'liberated women' like George Sand and Clémence Badère, she says, dared speak of how they were 'brutalized' by their husbands; and she quotes Marie Capelle's account of her resistance to hers. Marie Capelle became Madame Lafarge, celebrated for having poisoned her husband with arsenic. Sentenced to life imprisonment, she wrote bolder memoirs than most of her women contemporaries. It is now thought that she was wrongfully accused and condemned (ibid., 271–3).

11   Michel, op. cit., 68–9.

12   Balzac, *La Physiologie du mariage*, 661–3.

13   See *Modeste Mignon* and *Ursule Mirouët*.

14   Balzac, *Mémoires de deux jeunes mariées*, 209, 279.

15 See Michel, op. cit., 197. and 188: 'Bonald connaît sous Juillet un regain d'actualité'.
16 Hélène Cixous, 'Sorties', in Cixous and Clément, op. cit., 84ff.
17 See the first three chapters of Bricard, op. cit.
18 Bricard's own term.
19 Jules Barbey d'Aurevilly, *Les Bas-bleus*, 1st edn, 1877, Geneva, Slatkine Reprints 1968, p. xxii.
20 Joseph de Maistre, *Lettres et opuscules inédits*, Paris, 1851, vol. 1, 148.
21 Dr Fonssagrives, *L'Education physique des jeunes filles*, Paris, 1869, 50.
22 Bricard's account of school curricula in France in the period could be a demonstration of Balzac's accuracy. See Bricard, op. cit., 104–5, in particular.
23 The lot had to be learned by heart, even if your heart was not in it, which it could hardly be, if you were a girl and could inherit neither power nor title. There is much irony in another Balzac novel, *Albert Savarus*, in which the clever but ignorant heroine, Rosalie de Watteville, is an expert at genealogy, one of the few things she has been allowed to learn.
24 The abbé de Montmignon is inflicted upon other Balzac heroines, Rosalie (above) and Véronique Graslin in *Le Curé de village*.
25 Music was taught extensively at home and in schools. It was all piano. The convent of the 'Augustines Anglaises' had thirty and Saint-Denis had fifty in *one* room (Bricard, op. cit., 59)! It was thought, however, that music could have a dangerous erotic influence, as was said to have been demonstrated through experiments on animals. Music might hasten the 'oncoming of nubile desires' in girls. 'There is in melody something sympathetic which makes the heart melancholy and incites it to open up': a nice transference from the cunt to the heart! (*Dictionnaire des sciences médicales*; see Bricard, op. cit., 112–13.)
26 An 'explosion' is what happens to Rosalie de Watteville in *Albert Savarus*, *The Human Comedy*, vol. 1, 770.
27 George Sand in *Mauprat* (1837) (also the year of *A Daughter of Eve*), then in *Consuelo* and *La Comtesse de Rudolstadt* (1842 and 1844), argues that love alone, which makes man and woman into equals, will give back to marriage its sacred character. Only when this has come to pass will people be allowed to exclaim 'how beautiful humankind is!', 'Que l'humanité est belle!' (See Michel, op. cit., 120).
28 Michel, op. cit., 195.
29 Balzac, *La Physiologie du mariage*, 69.
30 See Claude Lévi-Strauss, *Les Structures élémentaires de la parenté*, Paris/La Haye: Mouton, 1971, 73: 'The exchange of women has preserved its fundamental function. On the one hand, because women constitute the essence of property [*le bien par excellence*], but above all because women are not, to start with, the sign of social value, but a natural stimulant; and the stimulant of the only instinct the satisfaction of which can be put off ('différé, deferred'): the only one, consequently, through which, in the act of exchanging and perceiving reciprocity, a transformation can be effected from the stimulant to the sign, and thus defining the passage from nature to culture, blossom into an institution.' (My translation.)

31 Cixous, 'Sorties', in Cixous and Clément, op. cit., 84–5.

32 On George Sand, see *Romantisme*, 13–14, 1976: *Mythes et représentations de la femme*.

33 The name Nathan in Hebrew means 'the one who gives'. Bizarrely, Nathan is the prophet who is sent to David to reproach him for his seduction of Bathsheba. My thanks to Marcelle Sanders for pointing this out to me.

34 The name 'Mürr' suggests *mürren*, to grumble, or *mürrisch*, surly or morose. The only readily available pun in German is *mir*, me (dative); so on the level of devious pun the cat may be Schmucke or Hoffmann, or of course Balzac. My thanks to Bob Jones for his help with this.

35 Esther is the (unknown) daughter of Gobseck, the Jewish usurer, one of the few truly wise men of *The Human Comedy*. Needless to say, it would be interesting to try for a 'Jewish' reading of *A Daughter of Eve*, with, as the title already suggests, its manifold biblical references.

36 See Marc Angenot, *Le Cru et le faisandé: sexe, discours et littérature à la Belle Epoque*, Montréal, Editions Labor, 1986, 189–91.

Chapter Two

THE LADY OF SHALOTT IN ART AND LITERATURE

KAREN HODDER

The impulse to look more closely at Tennyson's poem *The Lady of Shalott* came when I noticed how frequently references to it seem to recur, together with remarks about its variant, Tennyson's *Idyll*, 'Lancelot and Elaine', during the course of critical discussions, not only of the symbolic function of women in medieval romance and its descendants, but also in studies of the significance of Tennyson's poems in general, and of Pre-Raphaelite paintings connected with them.[1] What is more, the names of the two Tennysonian heroines have appeared conspicuously in recent feminist writing about the Victorian period by provocative authors such as Sandra Gilbert and Susan Gubar,[2] and Jan Marsh (in her general study of the female associates of Rossetti and his circle[3]).

Next, I began to feel that there had been incomplete reflection about the exact nature of Tennyson's adaptation of the Lady/Elaine figures from medieval sources, or about the differences between the 'Arthurian' poems in which they feature, as well as a lack of recognition that Tennyson's *Lady of Shalott*, in particular, has generated its own complex tradition. It is, in fact, typical of the tendency of nineteenth-century writers and painters to use the Middle Ages in order to create their own myths, rather than merely absorbing and reissuing medieval myths. The ambiguity and complexity of Tennyson's own response to one story was recognized by nineteenth-century painters and inspired an extraordinary number of them to elaborate this particular myth in a manner which is a tribute to its creative potential and its power as a feminine image.

I shall be returning, during the course of my discussion of later interpretations of Tennyson's *Lady of Shalott*, to particular examples of what I consider to be their strengths and limitations; but, at the outset, I should like to suggest that before we even begin to use *The Lady of Shalott* to support any theory of Victorian image-making in relation to gender stereotypes, we might start by examining the possible benefits of a historicist approach to such literary material. We should, for instance, be sure that we have disentangled the poem *The Lady of Shalott* and its sources from the visual renderings of the story, especially those which were produced after Holman Hunt's highly interpretative drawings and paintings and accompanying explanatory essay (see below, p. 76). We need to take into account too the critical hindsight afforded by knowledge of Tennyson's socially and morally less ambiguous recasting of 'The Lady' as

> Elaine the Fair, Elaine the loveable,
> Elaine, the lily maid of Astolat,
>> ('Lancelot and Elaine', *Idylls of the King)*

These considerations are necessary, if only to make it clear that, as feminist critics, we are aware of an ideological bias. This last point of view has coincidentally been articulated of late by one of the leading writers about women's literature, Elaine Showalter, in an essay entitled 'Representing Ophelia: women, madness and the responsibilities of feminist criticism'. Her essay concludes:

> There is no 'true' Ophelia for whom feminist criticism must unambiguously speak, but perhaps only a Cubist Ophelia of multiple perspectives, more than the sum of all her parts, . . . in exposing the ideology of representation, feminist critics have also the responsibility to acknowledge and to examine the boundaries of our own ideological positions as products of our gender and our time. A degree of humility in an age of critical hubris can be our greatest strength, for it is by occupying this position of historical self-consciousness in both feminism and criticism that we maintain our credibility in representing Ophelia.[4]

Or, indeed, the Lady of Shalott. A necessary accompaniment to exposing 'the ideology of representation' in the case of my own subject seemed to be via the examination of the meaning of Tennyson's poem in comparison with its main medieval analogues and sources, as well as through considering the commentaries afforded by some of his contemporary critics and visual artists, particularly the Pre-Raphaelites. Not least important, it appears to me, are certain recoverable data about Tennyson's own conception of his poem. The results of such a study, I think, are the kind of 'multiple perspectives' envisaged by Showalter, so that this essay's concerns, like those of others in this collection, are with many-layered and complex relationships between the female myth and its usually male creators, rather than with a single stereotype.

Tennyson was only 23 when he wrote his first version of *The Lady of Shalott* in 1832. His medieval scholarship was not yet as extensive as it would become by the time he completed even the first four of his Arthurian *Idylls*, by which time it is thought that he knew Nennius, *Mabinogion*, and Layamon's *Brut* as well as the medieval English stanzaic *Morte Arthur* and Malory's romance.[5] In his maturity, Tennyson became something of an Arthurian scholar; not merely a typical Victorian enthusiast for famous medieval chivalric romances, but also a serious researcher of the historical Arthur.[6] However, we should not read this scholarship, or the moral attitudes towards Arthurian material which increasing age and study fostered in Tennyson, retrospectively into *The Lady of Shalott*. It was a poem which he was able to write with an imagination unhampered by too much learning.

There is, however, a curious conflict in the evidence we have about Tennyson's reading of medieval sources at the time he composed *The Lady of Shalott*, in either its 1832 or its 1842 version. The conflict is between, on the one hand, external evidence together with the nature of the text itself, and, on the other, Tennyson's own testimony concerning his sources. Tennyson was emphatic that he did *not* owe his inspiration for the poem to Malory. F.J. Furnivall quotes the poet in January 1868 as saying:

> I met the story first in some Italian *novelle* . . . the Lady Of Shalott is evidently the Elaine of the *Morte D'Arthur*, but I do not think I had ever heard of the latter when I wrote the former. . . . I doubt whether I should ever have put it in that shape if I had been then aware of the Maid of Astolat.[7]

Yet, as Mark Girouard has pointed out, one of the 1816 editions of Malory was in Tennyson's father's library at Somersby Rectory, and it seems extremely probable that Tennyson would have read it there as a boy during the 1820s,[8] if not earlier, since he was already regaling his little sister and baby brothers with 'legends of knights' and 'distressed damsels' at a precociously early age.[9] Tennyson's denial of early contact with Malory is therefore surprising from the poet, with a lifelong interest in stories of Arthur, who himself re-enthused a new generation of Malory-lovers. But its unlikeliness has not very convincingly been commented on by Tennyson editors (such as Christopher Ricks), biographers, or critics, nor reconciled with the information about the Somersby library. A strong reason for disbelieving Tennyson's statement about Malory's story – or at least for not taking it entirely at face value – is the ending of the 1842 text of *The Lady of Shalott*. In this version of the poem, Tennyson introduced a final rich dramatic irony into the last stanza through the confrontation between the dead body of the Lady and the unwitting cause of her death, Sir Lancelot. In *all* other versions of the legend, except Malory's, the Lady's boat is met by King Arthur and the court, and Lancelot is conspicuous by his absence. Tennyson's denial of his most probable source (at a date long after the poem's composition) seems to me akin to Elizabeth Barrett Browning's 'forgetfulness' about the similarities between the ending of *Aurora Leigh* and Charlotte Brontë's *Jane Eyre*[10]: both seem to relate to the impugning of a poet's originality. Tennyson's comment seems quite consistent with other glimpses we have of the poet under pressure to discuss the sources of his inspiration. There is, for example, the recorded altercation with Holman Hunt about the number of steps there should have been in the artist's illustration of *King Cophetua*, when Tennyson remarked: 'I never said that there were a lot of steps, I only meant one or two.' To which Hunt replied: 'But the old Ballad says there was a flight of them', to which Tennyson retorts: 'I daresay it does, but I never said I got it from the old ballad.'[11]

Similarly, in the reminiscence about *The Lady of Shalott*, the vagueness of Tennyson's remark about 'some Italian *novelle*', the 'I do not think', and the conditional tenses imply a reluctance to be seen as too thoroughly under the influence of a source. Such reactions certainly suggest that he did not work on his poems with other texts directly in front of him. Such an attitude is a bid, too, for the autonomy and flexibility of a poet's imagination. William Boyd-Carpenter (Bishop of Ripon from 1884) recorded talking to the elderly Tennyson about religion:

> I once asked him whether they were right who interpreted the three ladies who accompanied King Arthur on his last voyage as Faith, Hope and Charity. He replied with a touch of (shall I call it?) intellectual impatience: 'they do and they do not. They *are* those

graces, but they are much more than the definition suggested or any specific interpretation advanced.'[12]

Intriguing though it might be, therefore, to speculate about just what 'shape' Tennyson's Lady would have had if he had been more aware of the Maid of Astolat, or to examine all the narrative variants between his retelling of her story and all the medieval versions, I am more immediately concerned with the growth of the legend as traceable through the relationship between Tennyson's two versions of *The Lady of Shalott*, published in 1832 and 1842, and their *admitted* source, the text of which was identified by L. S. Potwin in 1902.[13]

The Lady of Shalott was the only Arthurian poem which was ready for publication in Tennyson's 1832 volume of poems, but 'Sir Lancelot and Queen Guinevere', *Morte D'Arthur*, and 'Sir Galahad' were also in the process of composition, and appeared in print, together with the revised version of *The Lady of Shalott*, in *Poems* of 1842, as well as the non-Arthurian 'medieval' 'Godiva'. These poems were issued at a time when medieval romance had not yet become highly fashionable again with the reading public, and they were not enthusiastically reviewed.[14] Girouard suggests that the youthful Tennyson, like many other Victorians, was excited and attracted by romantic and passionate aspects of the Arthurian story, including its erotic potential, and quotes a suppressed verse from 'Sir Lancelot and Queen Guinevere' –

> Bathe with me in the fiery flood
> And mingle kisses, tears and sighs,
> Life of the Life within my blood,
> Light of the Light within my eyes

– to demonstrate that Tennyson was not, in his youth at any rate, averse to the sensual overtones of some of the romances.[15] As he grew older, Tennyson's attitudes moved in the direction of that other, 'moral', polarity which Girouard identifies as one of the Victorian responses to the past.[16] For the moment, I wish to return to Tennyson's sources for *The Lady of Shalott*, beginning with the most widespread redaction of the story which is also the source of all the other medieval analogues, including the thirteenth-century Italian tale which Tennyson admitted as the basis of his poem.

This, most ancient, version is contained within the French prose cycle, compiled *c*.1230–5, which is usually called (because of its popularity) the 'Vulgate cycle'. It occurs in the portion of that romance compilation known as *La Mort le Roi Artu*. Besides the Italian novella, it also inspired the fourteenth-century English stanzaic poem, the *Morte Arthur*, and Malory's tale of Elaine of Astolat in his *Morte Darthur*, which in turn borrowed details from the stanzaic *Morte*. Both these later English medieval romances affected Tennyson's own rewriting of the story in his *Idyll*, 'Lancelot and Elaine', and contribute to his modification of the legend in that longer poem. The two very early French and Italian stories, however, already contain a wealth of evocative detail which suggests why the story of the girl who dies for love of Lancelot was apparently such a compelling one for later writers and painters. In the French romance, the character known simply as 'la demoisele d'Escalot' (the girl from Escalot) or 'la Pucele' (the Maid) occurs in the interwoven stories which tell of the revelation of Lancelot's love affair with Queen Guinevere and the conflict which this creates in the Round Table fellowship, leading to its eventual downfall and dissolution. The 'demoisele's' role is, therefore, a very significant one in a complex network of intrigue, albeit not the central one. That she is not individualized by name among so many other important Arthurian characters who are named draws attention to her nature as a typical unmarried female. There are other aspects of her characterization which are similarly traditional and suggestive in terms of what they imply about the possibilities for free development of the narrative. For instance, she is said to be the daughter of a 'vavasour', one of those conventional romance figures who offer hospitality to questing knights and invariably have a beautiful daughter who in some way provides recreation and light relief for heroes. Not infrequently, these girls' desires, or their father's aspirations, complicate the knight's single-minded pursuit of honour. Often this is because of their hopeless love for the hero. In his study of *La Mort le Roi Artu*, Jean Frappier points out the analogues for the girl from Escalot abound in twelfth-and thirteenth-century fiction.[17] Their function in literature appears to be that of enhancing the hero's reputation, both by showing that he can inspire great devotion and by creating pressures which demonstrate his superior powers of concentration on the task appointed. In the case of the *Mort Artu*, the aim appears to be to emphasize the single-minded devotion of Lancelot to Guinevere, although the girl's infatuation and others' misinterpretation of her relationship with Lancelot set the Queen and her lover at cross-purposes.

The sorrows of such susceptible maidens are seldom a matter for much real regret in the medieval romances. Indeed, their chagrin is sometimes even an occasion for comedy. The special distinction of the girl from Escalot, however, is that she is one of those relatively rare women who dies for love, thus associating herself with a tragic heroine such as Dido (whose fate was so celebrated in the Middle Ages) or with the pious virgin martyrs of a type of medieval fiction often scarcely distinguishable from the genre of romance.[18]

The *Mort Artu* stresses the hopelessness of the 'demoisele's' passion, not merely because of the pre-existence of Lancelot's affair with Guinevere, but because of the 'demoisele's' relative social insignificance compared with a knight whose reputation is that of the undisputed leader of his profession.[19] When the girl first meets Lancelot at her father's castle, she does not know his name, since he is incognito, only that he 'is the finest knight in the world'.[20] Only after he has worn her favour in the lists, under the duress of a rash promise, and has been wounded and nursed by the girl, does Lancelot's cousin Bors reveal the knight's true identity to her and we are told then that 'the girl loved Lancelot as strongly as was humanly possible'.[21] She then proposes to him, confessing her love. The proposal is hopeless because she knows that he has already set his heart in 'a higher place'.[22] Lancelot reacts by describing her declaration as 'madness' and 'was most upset and angry'.[23] The girl then 'takes to her bed', and a rational explanation is suggested for her subsequent decline and death by her words 'I have not been able to eat or drink, rest or sleep'.[24] After her death, 'a rich and beautiful boat', 'covered like a vault', floats down beneath the towers of Camelot, and the king and 'a great company of knights' assemble round it. A bed is discovered within, and Sir Gawain identifies the corpse on it as the girl from Escalot. Lancelot is not present. Gawain finds a purse hanging from the girl's belt, from which he takes a letter. This is what it says:

> To all the knights of the Round Table, greetings from the girl from Escalot. I will address my complaint to all of you, not because you could ever put it right, but because I know you to be the noblest [*la plus preude*] and most joyous [*la plus envoisiée*] people in the world. I am telling you quite plainly that I come to my end through loving faithfully. If you ask for whom I suffered the pains of death, I shall reply that I died for the noblest man in the world, and also the wickedest [*por le plus preudome del monde et por le plus vilain*], Lancelot du Lac. he is the wickedest as far as I know because however much

I begged him with tears and weeping, he refused to have mercy on me, and I took it so much to heart as a result I died from loving faithfully.[25]

The outcome of this 'aventure' is that it is commemorated (and celebrated) by burying the girl in the cathedral at Camelot, with an inscription on her tomb 'which tells the truth about her death, so that our descendants may remember her.'[26] Death is her achievement and apotheosis in a manner, and with accessories, curiously reminiscent of Arthur's own eventual fate. The Italian story, indeed, concentrates on this climatic death, compressing much of the remainder of the narrative:

The daughter of a great vavasour loved Lancelot du Lac out of measure. But he did not wish to return her love, since he had given it to Queen Guinevere. But the damsel loved Lancelot so much that she was brought near to death. And she gave orders that when her soul parted from her body there should be prepared a rich boat covered with red samite, with a rich bed put into it, with a rich and noble coverlet of silk, ornamented with rich and precious stones, and with a rich girdle and purse. And in the purse was to be a letter, which was worded as set out below. But first I shall tell of her who bore the letter.

The damsel died of the pangs of love, and all was done according to what has been said. The boat, without a sail, was put into the sea with the lady [in it]. The sea bore it to Camelot. And it stayed on the shore. There it was seen by the people of the court. Knights and barons came down from the palace. And the noble King Arthur came, and marvelled greatly that it could have come without a steersman.

The king went into the vessel, gazed at the damsel and the accoutrements. He had the purse opened. The letter was discovered. He had it read. And it said as follows: 'To all the knights of the Round Table, greetings from the maiden of Scalott, as to the best noblemen of the world, and if you wish to know why I have met my end, it is through the best knight in the world, and the worst, that is, my Lord Lancelot du Lac who, however much I besought his love, would not have mercy on me. And so alas! I am dead of loving faithfully as you can see.'[27]

As might be expected, this version reads very much like a synopsis of the longer French prose story, with slight variations, such as the unusual reference to Camelot's being on the sea-coast, rejected by Tennyson in favour of the more customary river referred to by all the other romances. The salient features of both early narratives are the hopelessness of the girl's passion for Lancelot (he was impossible to dissociate from Guinevere by the twelfth century at least);[28] her location away from court; her namelessness; her special reclothing; and her death voyage; and the letter. Tennyson reworks all of these motifs most imaginatively.

His poem is so well known that it might seem excessive to summarize it; but to do so emphasizes how much he has improvised on the medieval narrative, as well as how eclectic is that improvisation. The summary relates to the popular, 1842, poem.[29]

Part I sets up a contrast between Camelot and Shalott ('a softer sound than Scalott', said Tennyson[30]), where the mysterious Lady dwells invisibly within 'four gray walls' on an island in the river, and is occasionally heard singing by reapers in the fields. In part II we are told that she is the victim of an unspecified curse and, not knowing what it is, spends her time weaving, and watching the events of the world of Camelot without, through 'a mirror clear'. These sights, described in an ascending order of interest to the Lady, cause her to feel restless about her fate: 'I am half sick of shadows', she says, in one of the lines which Hallam Tennyson claimed held 'the key to this tale of magic symbolism'.[31] In part III, the sight of the glamorous and colourful Lancelot reflected in her mirror causes the Lady to leave her loom and look directly out of the window:

> Out flew the web and floated wide;
> The mirror crack'd from side to side;
> 'The curse is come upon me,' cried
> The Lady of Shalott.

In part IV, we reach at last the principal matter of the novella as the Lady floats singing her death-song, 'robed in snowy white', down the river to Camelot, where her corpse is greeted by wondering citizens and courtiers, including Lancelot, who (in the 1842 version) is given the last word:

> She has a lovely face;
> God in his mercy lend her grace,
> The lady of Shalott.

As Tennyson himself said, 'the web, mirror, island etc. were my own'.[32] Among the details also included in the 'etc.' were the curse, the Lady's song, her white dress, and the substitution of the river for the novella's 'sea'.

The 1832 version had also included a letter to the court, as in the medieval romance, and its final stanza had the 'well-fed wits at Camelot' reading the Lady's cryptic words:

> The web was woven curiously
> The charm is broken utterly
> Draw near and fear not – This is I
> The Lady of Shalott.

The change in 1842 was probably made in response to the criticism of J.S. Mill, who had castigated the earlier ending as 'weak' in his review of the 1832 *Poems*.[33]

The second version is certainly an artistic improvement, providing, as it does, a counterpoise to that other semi-encounter between the oblivious Lancelot and the fatally attracted Lady, as he 'flash'd into the crystal mirror'. Tennyson, with sound dramatic instinct, has highlighted the poignance of her death for both parties, so strongly emphasized by the medieval romancers, including Malory. In 'Lancelot and Elaine', the ironies of the situation, in a passage verbosely adapted from Malory, are heavy-handedly expressed by King Arthur:

> Now I would to God
> Seeing the homeless trouble in thine eyes,
> Thou couldst have loved this maiden, shaped it seems,
> By God for Thee alone, and from her face,
> If one may judge the living by the dead,
> Delicately pure and marvellously fair,
> Who might have brought thee, now a lonely man
> Wifeless and heirless, noble issue, sons
> Born to the glory of thy name and fame.

In the 1842 version of *The Lady of Shalott*, Lancelot's simple final apostrophe to God aligns him with the 'red-cross knight' on the shield that, in the first stanza of part III, forms part of the first impression his image makes on the Lady:

> A red-cross knight for ever kneel'd
> To a lady in his shield.

Her ignorance about his true status as the lover of Guinevere, the actual 'lady' alluded to, and the illusion on which the Lady of Shalott's passion is therefore founded, so explicitly articulated by the medieval romancers, are economically and delicately hinted at by Tennyson in this detail of the shield's blazon. This is his own invention (though fictional medieval knights are often assigned coats of arms and it is reminiscent of Malory's description of Lancelot's shield). The ambiguity of the word 'field' in the next line, 'That sparkled on the yellow field', merges the literal barley-fields around Shalott with an anticipated continuation of the description of the shield via the relative conjunction 'that' and the heraldic significance of 'field', reinforcing the blend of fantasy and reality.

Lionel Stevenson has suggested convincingly that Tennyson borrowed the weaving, solitude and supernatural qualities of the Lady from Shelley's *Witch of Atlas*.[34] The mirror is attributed to Spenser's *Faerie Queene*, book III, canto ii – that is Britomart's 'wondrous myrrhour, by which she in love with him did fall'.[35] Since the 'him' in these lines is the good knight, Sir Artegall, their association with Tennyson's poem is one of honourable passion. In other words, like so many other pieces of nineteenth-century 'medievalism', *The Lady of Shalott* is somewhat eclectic in its gathering of images and relies at times more on the creation of what its contemporary audience might have felt to be the appropriate 'atmosphere' than on authentic medieval scholarship. As in the Pre-Raphaelite paintings on medieval topics by Rossetti, 'red' is a colour used to create this archaic feeling in 'the red cloaks of market girls' and the 'long-haired page in crimson clad', as are flowing locks, shining armour, and gemstones.

Speaking generally, the revisions made between Tennyson's 1832 version of *The Lady of Shalott* and the more popular one which was published in the considerably more successful *Poems* (1842) were extensive. Comparison between the two texts is interesting chiefly in terms of the poet's response to early criticism of his art, and Tennyson scholars seem to agree that the differences represent an overall improvement on the first poem.

The majority of the changes occur in the first and final sections of the poem and relate to five of those six 'salient features' of the medieval narratives which I defined above, namely, the Lady's relationship with Lancelot, her location, her special clothing, her letter, and her death voyage. I have already noted some modifications relating to Lancelot, the voyage, and the letter. Concerning Tennyson's treatment of the matter of her namelessness, I shall have more to say separately presently. First, I should like to note his adaptation of the location and clothing of the Lady. In both versions of his poem, he considerably expands the description of the location, Shalott. He created a lonely, rural isle, on which stand 'four gray walls and four gray towers'. In the 1842 version he removed from this expanded description some colourful detail such as 'yellow-leaved waterlily', 'green-sheathed daffodily', 'sun beam showers', and 'green Shalott', leaving the later Shalott more monochrome, 'silent', 'remote', and mysterious than before. Similarly, the richness of the 1832 Lady's funeral attire, including its 'cloud white crown of pearl' and her 'zone . . . / Clasped with one blinding diamond bright', elaborated from the authentic medieval source, is simplified to a loose-flowing white garment alone. Such emendations seem potentially more suggestive than some of the more publicized ones, such as the famous response to Croker's ridicule of the name written 'Below the carven stern', which Tennyson changed to 'round about the prow'.[36]

Given the emphasis which has been placed by many of the painters and some of the critics on the *virginal* nature of the Lady of Shalott – her affinity with Ophelia, for example[37] – it is worth noting that her maidenhood and the expression of it in her white garment appear to be a natural attribute of her solitude and isolation, and her affinity for the similarly pale or ghostly accessories of Shalott (where Tennyson deprives her even of the relatives of the French and Italian stories), rather than an aspect of her depiction as an innocent, passive prisoner of the domestic mores and taboos of Victorian middle-class life which it seems some commentators would like us to make of her. Philip Henderson, for example, who in his biography of Tennyson calls the poem *The Lady of Shalott* 'this cry of crucified sex',[38] offers the following trivializing and withal slightly inaccurate account of the poet's two retellings of the legend:

> The Victorian public dearly loved a pathetic story of pining
> maids, the most spectacular being Elaine, who pined and died of
> love for Sir Lancelot and had herself laid out on a bier in her
> wedding-dress and went floating down the river to Camelot with a
> note to Lancelot in her dead hand. Like Elaine, the unfortunate
> Lady of Shalott also floated down to Camelot in a barge, singing till
> she died. But doubtless this reflected the feelings, in an idealised
> form, of many unwed middle-class maids in the nineteenth
> century.[39]

2.1 John William Waterhouse. Waterhouse painted the Lady three times. This from 1888, is his earliest image of the legend. The Tate Gallery.

A less literal-minded and facetious response to Victorian represen-ation of maidenhood is possible, and it is one which the poem's own language of etherealness urges upon the reader, prompting, rather, a symbolic interpretation of the central figure, particularly in her 1832 manifestation, where what impresses is the aura of sumptuousness and radiance and the quasi-religious connotations of the Lady's white attire, her pearl and diamond, and the reference to her singing, first 'Like an angel',[40] and later 'a ... carol, mournful, holy', as in the 1842 version. But the lady is not only angel-like; she is also a 'fairy lady', an enchantress weaving 'a magic web', ideas which belie in another way the image of forlorn frustration. Such language, based as it is on the complexities of poetic response, seems more satisfactorily to impel readers towards a metaphoric interpretation of the Lady than to invite them to recognize the stereotype of a Victorian spinster aunt or unmarried sister. Her potential as the representation of a spiritual state or social ideal has been attractively explored by critics such as Lionel Stevenson[41] and John Killham.[42] Stevenson, most pertinently in the context of this study, suggests plausibly, and with some foundation in Tennyson's own recorded comments about his poem, that the persona of the Lady allegorizes Tennyson's own existence as an artist. I shall return later to this traversing of the gender boundary.

The virginal aspect of the Lady's white clothing is, of course, one of its obvious attributes, and one which some Victorian painters, such as John William Waterhouse, chose to emphasize (see figure 2.1). Tennyson can preserve the delicacy and mystery of the Lady's identity in poetry:

> But who hath seen her wave her hand
> Or at the casement seen her stand?

This lack of explicitness in the poem left the painter free to interpret, but, of course, visualization has to suggest a specific personality in a way that a poem does not. So here, Waterhouse has given the Lady a number of additional attributes of maidenhood: long, flowing hair, a simple white garment, and pearls, which together with the foreground waterlilies, are highly suggestive. He has also added an anguished, rather than mournful, expression and posture, and has placed a crucifix in the bow of the boat. Evidently he did not recall, or chose to disregard, the 1832 text's line describing the Lady in her deathbed as lying 'with folded arms serenely', or both texts' reference to her 'glassy countenance'. Nor has the painter been attentive to the poet's statement, in both versions, that it is 'raining' 'heavily' as she embarks, since, as Rossetti did in his illustration to the 1857 edition of Tennyson's poems published by Moxon (see figure 2.2), Waterhouse has included lighted candles at the front of the boat, which increase the religious atmosphere generated by the crucifix. The general effect of Waterhouse's earliest depiction is reminiscent in some ways of the passage in Mrs Gaskell's novel *Ruth*, where the beauty and innocence of the doomed 'fallen' heroine is stressed in a tableau beside another lily-strewn stretch of water:

> She stood in her white dress against the trees which grew around; her face was flushed into a brilliancy of colour which resembled that of a rose in June; the great heavy white flowers drooped on either side of her beautiful head, and if her brown hair was a little disordered, the very disorder only seemed to add a grace.[43]

Waterhouse's third and final image of the Lady of Shalott illustrates the same moment in the story, and in a very similar manner, as

2.2 Dante Gabriel Rossetti. From Moxon's edition of Tennyson's Poems, 1857, p. 75. *La Mort du Roi Artu* mentions a boat like this one 'covered like a vault' (see above, p. 66)

Meteyard's picture discussed below (p. 77), which depicts a more fleshly and mature Lady.[44]

Victorian visual interpreters of *The Lady of Shalott* seemed to appreciate the medieval distinction between a 'donna', 'dame', or 'lady' and a 'damigella', 'demoiselle', 'pucelle', or 'maid'. Even the 'Lady' epithet links her with the first two figures, rather than with the 'Lily Maid of Astolat' in the second group. Once again, though, it is necessary to stress the relative reticence of Tennyson's *Lady of Shalott* compared with some of the vivid, sensational visualizations of scenes from it. It is the namelessness of the girl who dwells at Escalot, Scalot, or Shalott which, of course, inevitably draws attention to her symbolic feminine status, just as the naming of 'Elaine of Astolat' is symptomatic of the more realistic tone and treatment which Malory's story and Tennyson's *Idyll* accord this legend. The distinction between the unnamed 'demoisele' and the 'dame' is preserved in the iconography of womanhood in the nineteenth-century paintings.

Pictures of *The Lady of Shalott* tend to concentrate on just two scenes from her story: the breaking of the web and mirror, or the death-scene. The cover of our book includes the final version of the picture which William Holman Hunt made of the first scene. He depicted this several times, beginning with a drawing in 1850. In the final version there is a heavily symbolic representation of the Madonna and Child which the Lady, in her moment of crisis, turns her back on. In Hunt's second version of this drawing, made in 1857, she bows her head as she faces an even less ambiguous crucifix (see figure 2.3).

Holman Hunt is one of those chiefly responsible for moralizing the 'Shalott' story, which he interpreted as a 'parable' illustrating 'the failure of a human soul towards its accepted responsibility', casting 'aside duty to her spiritual self' and bringing 'her artistic life to an end' for the sake of the momentary fascination of the superficial worldly values represented by Lancelot.[45] It was characteristic of Hunt to discover a moralistic reading of the poem; but, in addition to his pious tendencies, it is worth noting that by the 1850s Tennyson's own moralized version of the same narrative, 'Lancelot and Elaine', had superseded *The Lady of Shalott* in the public's imagination, so that a *moral* rather than a romantic interpretation was more likely to be taken up and elaborated by subsequent Victorian painters. This development, I would suggest, together with the fame of Hunt's image, may be responsible for confusing many later critics about *The Lady of Shalott*.[46]

Tennyson objected to the floating hair in Hunt's picture: 'My dear Hunt, I never said the young woman's hair was flying all over the shop.' 'No, but you never said it wasn't,' replied Hunt.[47] In fact, Tennyson's poem does not describe the Lady's hair at all. This added visual detail, together with Hunt's Lady's exotic costume, associates her with a class of enchantresses and sorceresses like Sir Frederick Sandys's 'petrified spasm', Morgan le Fay (*c*.1862–4), with its

2.3   William Holman Hunt. From Moxon's edition of Tennyson's poems, 1857, p. 67. The costume of the Lady in this drawing, as well as her hair, are closer to the final painting of this scene than to Hunt's first sketch in 1850.

'disturbing emotional intensity and an underlying mood of mania and violence',[48] or Frank Cadogan Cowper's *La Belle Dame Sans Merci* (1926) (see figure 2.4). The 'fairy' Lady of Tennyson's poem has, perhaps, more affinity with a dreamy, hesitant enchantress like Burne-Jones's Vivien than with such pictures, just as Burne-Jones's Vivien herself seems to resemble the Lady more than her own poetic counterpart, corrupt, sensual, and shrill.

Sidney Harold Meteyard's late painting (1913) of the 'web' scene

2.4 Frank Cadogan Cowper, *La Belle Dame Sans Merci.* This picture was painted in 1926 and Christopher Wood describes Cowper as 'The very last of the Pre-Raphaelites' (*The Pre-Raphaelites*, p. 155). The painting is reproduced from *The Pre-Raphaelites* (London, Weidenfeld & Nicolson, 1981, p. 154).

perhaps represents the ultimate visual realization of the latent sensual potential in *The Lady of Shalott*'s poetic imagery. Titled '*I am half sick of shadows*', *said the Lady of Shalott*, it shows the moment where the Lady sees the 'two young lovers, lately wed' in her mirror, while she weaves the image of a knight ('She hath no loyal knight and true') on a tapestry frame reduced to somewhat amateur proportions.[50] This picture could not conceivably be mistaken for one of a 'demoiselle'; it plays too strongly upon the note of sexual languor, with its voluptuous central figure with her coiled hair, her pose reminiscent of Botticelli's

2.5 Julia Margaret Cameron, *Elaine* (1874–5).

Venus or an odalisque, and her clinging, vivid gentian-blue dress, all suggestive of a sexually mature woman.

Just as inconceivably could the photograph by Julia Margaret Cameron created to illustrate the *Idyll* of 'Lancelot and Elaine' be of the seductive type of enchantress (see figure 2.5). The marked similarity of the composition between this and Meteyard's painting make one wonder whether he knew the 1874 Cabinet edition of

Tennyson's works or the 6-guinea illustrated edition of *Idylls of the King and Other Poems* (1875) and was transposing and subverting the innocence of Mrs Cameron's vision into blatant sexuality. In his painting the demure posture and white shift of the Cameron Elaine are subtly modified. A mirror hangs in place of Lancelot's very un-Malorian round shield, and the tapestry echoes one which, in the photograph, is part of the domestic furnishings, though no doubt meant to remind us of Elaine's tragic associations with the Lady of Shalott.

Such contrasts of innocence versus experience were juxtaposed in the murals which the Pre-Raphaelites painted on the walls of the Oxford Union, for instance, in Lancelot's vision of the Holy Grail as depicted by Rossetti. The Grail, denied to Lancelot because of his adultery with Guinevere, is held in the hands of a serene, angelic figure, while between her and the slumbering Lancelot stands the sinuous figure of his lover, the queen, in a pose travestying the crucifix.[51] As Girouard notes, the contrast between her and Elaine, in the first four *Idylls* which were published in 1859, is aptly summed up by the title it was first intended to publish them under, 'The False and the True'.[52]

In 'Lancelot and Elaine', the girl who first became the 'Lady of Shalott' in Tennyson's imagination has been transformed into a 'wild flower' with 'blue eyes', 'bright hair', and 'serious face', who, like Gaskell's Ruth, feels the lack of her dead mother and is described as a child in relation to both her father and Lancelot, sitting on the knee of one, and distracting the other from weightier cares like some domestic pet.[53] Quite apart from its sentimentality and unabashed conformity to an approved stereotype of domesticated Victorian femininity, the specific detail in Tennyson's portrait is very different from the absence of concrete description of his Lady of Shalott, particularly as manifested in the 1842 version of the poem. 'Fairy' is the only adjective directly applied to her, and this explains much of the dramatic impact of Lancelot's final 'She has a lovely face' – a fact we suddenly realized we have been assuming until that moment.

Tennyson was opposed to illustrated editions on principle, as an inadequate representation of his ideas, though he was not entirely uninterested in painting,[54] so that when Moxon's 1857 illustrated edition of his poems was in preparation, while Moxon chose most of the artists, Tennyson personally recommended the Pre-Raphaelite group, while his wife influenced him to recommend Lizzie Siddall,

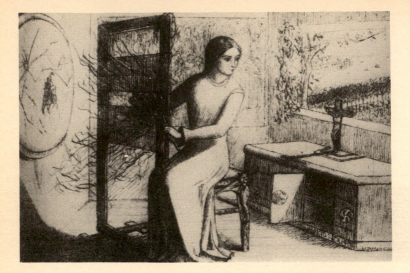

2.6   Elizabeth Eleanor Siddall (1853). The Tate Gallery.

Rossetti's companion and, later, wife, as an illustrator.[55] However, Moxon rejected her. Figure 2.6 shows the sketch made by Siddall in 1853, in pen-and-ink and pencil, of the scene also depicted by Hunt, whose 1850 drawing may show its influence in the form of the mirror, while the bird and furniture appear to be her own additions, and she seems to have anticipated Hunt's 1857 drawing by introducing the crucifix into the scene. Hunt's conception of the scene is also radically rearranged in Siddall's sketch. The Lady is seated, calmly, in a realistic, airy workspace. The crucifix placed as it is in front of the window (whereas Hunt put it next to the mirror), seems to compel her gaze towards the outside world, upsetting the 'dereliction of duty' message. A great deal has been made recently of this drawing in terms of 'the construction of gender differences'; but this question is complicated by uncertainty about the extent of Rossetti's interference in Siddall's art, and by the slight nature of the drawing itself.[56] Nevertheless, this does not invalidate the sketch's significance as a differently conceived interpretation of Tennyson's poem, less threatening than Hunt's, which simultaneously condemns the Lady and seems to revel in the voluptuousness of her form, emphasized in his painting by the constricting threads of the broken web.[57] I have subsequently discovered another calm and demure Lady of Shalott in a neat workroom, similar to Siddall's, in the 1907 edition of selected Tennyson poems edited by H. J. C. Grierson.[58] The illustrator in this case is Gilbert James. His Lady also has her hair plaited and bound, is seated, and glances up, almost in surprise, at the sight of Lancelot in her everpresent round mirror. James's precise, sedate illustrations to Tennyson's poems contrast with J. L. Byam Shaw's more mysterious and magical evocations of Arthurian legend in the same volume, such as that of Guinevere.[59]

Referring to even such a brief selection of visual interpretations of *The Lady of Shalott* gives some sense of the diversity of creative impulses which the poem inspired, and the diverse images of woman which it could evoke. We know already that Tennyson was critical of Hunt's visualization, nor did he like Rossetti's (see figure 2.2), though there is a case that could be made for admiring the artist's unusual dramatic choice of Lancelot as the main subject of his picture, and his focus on the intent gaze of this figure, with the crowding onlookers of Camelot pushed to the edges of the small picture. Tennyson himself, however, preferred the photographic images of Julia Margaret Cameron.[60] Yet, for posterity, it is probably Waterhouse's 'wonderful Lady of Shalott', 'painted in an exceptionally broad and strong realistic style',[61] or even the moralizing Holman Hunt's images, which come nearer to recording a sense of wonder in response to the poem which, itself, as John Killham has suggested, perhaps operates 'to produce rare effects of feeling or mood rather than any detachable meaning'.[62] Killham himself, however, tentatively explores some of the deeper significance of *The Lady of Shalott* in an introductory review of the potential effect of the poem on its modern readers, for example:

> Although it may show in allegory the possible fate of the artist who cannot bear too much reality [it] lavishes so much artistry on the pathetic figure of the Lady that one may connect it with the impulse to compose lyrics.[63]

Elsewhere, the same critic also connects the intensity in presenting such images of women, with its concomitant tendency toward idealization, with the workings of Tennyson's social conscience.[64] Such a reading of *The Lady of Shalott* would attach its concerns to those of other important Tennyson poems: the Lady as projection of the poetic 'persona' rejecting the 'shadows' of Shalott, for example, might be associated with more personal Tennysonian statements of positive humane concern, such as the passage in *In Memoriam* (1850) to which Edgar Shannon draws our attention,[65] as articulating Tennyson's need for human association and sympathy:

> I will not shut me from my kind,
> And, lest I stiffen into stone,
> I will not eat my heart alone,
> Nor feed with sighs a passing wind....
>
> I'll rather take what fruit may be
> Of sorrow under human skies.

Mark Girouard has convincingly described the way in which the pervasive medieval fantasies of Victorian fiction, painting, architecture, and so on reflect a need for nineteenth-century men to express emotions as various as eroticism and patriotic fervour, and shows how chivalric novels such as Charlotte Yonge's *The Heir of Redclyffe* (1853) gave respectability to 'feminine' impulses in the Victorian male: impulses such as gentleness, self-repression, self-sacrifice, and the surrender of self to another through love, even if such surrender means self-destruction.[66] Tennyson's fascination with the figure of the Lady, viewed from this perspective, is not incompatible with his platonic reflections on gender in *The Princess* (1848).

> either sex alone
> Is half itself, and in true marriage lies
> Nor equal, nor unequal: each fulfils
> Defect in each, and always thought in thought,
> Purpose in purpose, will in will, they grow,
> The single pure and perfect animal,
> The two-celled heart beating, with one full stroke,
> Life ...

Marion Shaw has recently suggested that many of Tennyson's poems are concerned with reconciling Victorian society's demands on the male psyche, which was expected to be 'manly' and restrained, with admiration for the 'feminine' ideal of 'nervous susceptibility', which is actually closer to the poet's nature. She has described Tennyson's adopting of female personae, which she calls 'poetic transvestism', as one means of escape from this dilemma, and has spoken of his 'obsession with female figures in, for instance, his early, so-called

"Lady poems" '(that is, 'Claribel', 'Lilian', and so on), as a guise for the exploration of psychological states.[67]

It is now something of a critical commonplace to say that the masculine creation of images of femininity is associated with psychological need.[68] According to Jung, such images represent the suppressed feminine part of the male, and are given release in dreams, or in artistic creation, in order to retain personal equilibrium. Such feminine manifestations are given the name of the 'anima' (in Latin, literally, 'the soul'). The equivalent feminine psyche is also present, exemplified perhaps by a creation such as Jane Eyre's portrait, from memory, of Rochester, in Charlotte Brontë's novel of 1847; and Christina Rossetti's poem 'In the Artist's Studio' (1856) seems to describe her recognition of the existence of such psychological projections. Reference to such theories may help to explain why most sensitive interpreters of literary and visual images of femininity have a sense that they are often not simply created out of repressed physical attraction to the female, or a desire to fix her (as did Browning's mad Duke of Ferrara in 'My last Duchess' in a subdued and idealized form, but that they have a non-material significance which is reinforced by their very repetitiveness in Victorian paintings and literature. One might also add that such images were likely to answer a very special psychological need in a society which overtly tended to define its gender roles very strictly, and that this may help to account for their appearance in Victorian art as various as, for example, Pre-Raphaelite painting,[69] the poetry of Browning[70] and Hopkins,[71] the novels of Dickens,[72] and the works of Lewis Carroll.[73] The presence of such images in the works of male artists of such great diversity of temperament and conviction invites us to explore their works anew via the concept of gender.

I would, however, renew the plea for caution and open-mindedness with which I began this paper, which might be summarized as receptiveness to the idea that art actively defies formulation. This is the essential uniqueness of each individual work of art, and in my view art is served less well by disambiguating imagery than it is by re-creating 'multiple perspectives'. I feel, for instance, with Phyllis Rose, that 'By sexualizing experience, popular Freudianism had the moralistic result of limiting possibilities';[74] and that I prefer the multiple associations of the description of Lancelot with his 'mighty silver bugle' with the sound, martial action, colour, and 'medieval' glamour which Camelot, as opposed to soundless, colourless Shalott, exert upon the Lady, to the specific sexual connotation put upon it by Jan Marsh, since the former reading also permits simultaneous response to the Lady and Lancelot as woman and man and as representatives of different psychological reactions to the ordeal of living in Victorian society.[75] The legend of the Lady of Shalott, as inherited by Tennyson from the medieval romances, projects a potent image of woman destroyed by misplaced love – love which brings to the surface the dilemmas of the man who is the object of that love, and of the society that surrounds them both. Tennyson responded to this story in a complex way which inspired a succession of painters to use his re-creation of a medieval tale to explore their own responses to a powerful poetic image of woman. All these works of art need to be scrutinized individually before we can make glib generalizations about what 'the Victorians' thought of *The Lady of Shalott*. We do not necessarily have to prefer Tennyson's own mystification of the story to any other particular interpretation which has been placed on his poem. But I do feel that at least we should have some sense of the complexity and richness of the options opened to us by reading an extraordinary work of art which motivated subsequent verbal criticism and pictorial imagery to the equivalent of a cult, and through which Tennyson was responsible for the regeneration of a myth.

NOTES

1 See, for example, Christopher Wood, *The Pre-Raphaelites*, London, Weidenfeld & Nicolson, 1981, 139: '*The Lady of Shalott* was almost a cult subject among the later Pre-Raphaelites.' See also *Ladies of Shalott: A Victorian Masterpiece and its context*, Exhibition Catalogue of Brown University, 1985; Jennifer Gribble, *The Lady of Shalott in the Victorian Novel*, London, Macmillan, 1984.

2 Sandra M. Gilbert and Susan Gubar, *The Madwoman in the Attic*, New Haven, Conn., and London, Yale University Press, 1979, 617–20.

3 Jan Marsh, *Pre-Raphaelite Sisterhood*, London, Quartet Books, 1985, 7–8, and *Pre-Raphaelite Women*, London, Weidenfeld & Nicolson, 1987, 142–52.

4 Elaine Showalter, 'Representing Ophelia: women, madness and the responsibilities of feminist criticism', in Patricia Parker and Geoffrey Hartman (eds), *Shakespeare and the Question of Theory*, London, Methuen, 1986, 90.

5 Elizabeth Jenkins, *The Mystery of King Arthur*, London, Michael Joseph, 1975.

6 Dr Faith Lyons recently demonstrated the seriousness and attentiveness

of Tennyson's reading on a variety of Arthurian themes in an unpublished paper delivered to the British Branch of the International Arthurian Society at St Andrew's University, September 1986, entitled 'Tennyson's King Arthur and British Antiquities'.

7 Quoted in Tennyson, *Poems of 1842*, ed. Christopher Ricks, Plymouth, Macdonald & Evans, 1981, 288.

8 Mark Girouard, *The Return to Camelot*, New Haven, Conn., and London, Yale University Press, 1981, 178. 'Almost certainly', says Girouard.

9 Norman Page (ed.), *Tennyson: Interviews and Recollections*, London, Macmillan, 1983, 1.

10 See Elizabeth Barrett Browning, *Aurora Leigh with Other Poems*, ed. Cora Kaplan, London, The Women's Press, 1982, 23–4.

11 George Somes Layard, *Tennyson and his Pre-Raphaelite Illustrators*, London, 1894, 40–1.

12 Page (ed.), op. cit., 187.

13 L. S. Potwin, 'The source of Tennyson's "The Lady of Shalott"', *Modern Language Notes*, 17 December 1902, 237–9.

14 Girouard, op. cit., 179.

15 ibid., 180–1.

16 ibid., 180.

17 Jean Frappier, *Etude sur la Mort le Roi Artu*, Paris, Droz, 1936, 267–730.

18 Dido's love was, of course, consummated, perhaps rendering the 'demoisele's' fate even more like that of the saints who died virgin for love of Christ. The Vulgate account of the death of the Lady of Beloë, slain by her husband for her devotion to Gawain, has little in common with the tale of the 'demoisele d'Escalot'. (*La Mort le Roi Artu*, ed. Jean Frappier, Paris, Droz, 1964, 223.) See also *The Death of King Arthur*, tr. James Cable, Harmondsworth, Penguin, 1971, 202.

19 *The Death of King Arthur*, tr. Cable, 51, 55–6, 94.

20 ibid., 30.

21 It might be noted that this ordering of the narrative makes the girl's love for Lancelot seem to be an endorsement of his worth: as in Malory's version, there is a kind of logic in her choice of the best Arthurian knight. As Mark Lambert has remarked, 'The heart has its reasons which reason understands very well': *Style and Vision in 'Morte d'Arthur'*, New Haven, Conn., and London, Yale University Press, 1975, 104.

22 *The Death of King Arthur*, tr. Cable, 56.

23 ibid., 76.

24 ibid., 75

25 ibid., 94.

26 ibid.

27 My translation from the text in C. Segre and M. Marti (eds), *La Prosa del Duecento*, Milan and Naples, Ricciardi, 1959, no. 82, 42-3.

28 Their affair is dealt with at length by Chrétien de Troyes (*c.*1165),for example.

29 Tennyson, *Poems of 1842*, ed. Ricks, 57-63.

30 ibid., 288.

31 ibid.

32 ibid.

33 Edgar Finley Shannon, Jr, *Tennyson and the Reviewers*, Hamden, Conn., Archon Books, 1967, 42.

34 Lionel Stevenson, 'The high born maiden symbol in Tennyson', in J. Killham (ed.), *Critical Essays on the Poetry of Tennyson*, London, Routledge & Kegan Paul, 1960, 129–30.

35 *Poems of 1842*, ed. Ricks, 290.

36 Shannon, op. cit., 41.

37 Gilbert and Gubar, op. cit., 618. Their reading of 'the Victorian iconography of female whiteness' (615) does not, however, take into account the richness of the Lady's apparel or her status as a 'Lady'; and the association which is made between her and mad Victorian ladies in white, culminating in Tennyson's heroine being described as actually sharing 'the madness of fictional characters like Anne Catherick [and] Miss Havisham' (620), lacks proper textual support. As Jan Marsh points out, it is Elaine of the later *Idyll* who might more justifiably be perceived as having become less than sane (*Pre-Raphaelite Women*, 146).

38 Philip Henderson, *Tennyson, Poet and Prophet*, London, Routledge & Kegan Paul, 1978, 56.

39 ibid., 116.

40 *Poems of 1842*, ed. Ricks, 289.

41 Stevenson, op. cit.

42 John Killham, 'Tennyson and Victorian social values', in D. J. Palmer (ed.), *Writers and their Background: Tennyson*, London, G. Bell & Sons, 1974, 147–79.

43 Elizabeth Gaskell, *Ruth*, ed. Alan Shelton, Worlds Classics, London, OUP, 1985, 74–5.

44 It is perhaps significant in this respect that Tennyson's vague reminiscences of his Italian source, perhaps under the influence of Thomas Roscoe's 1825 translation, transform its 'damigella' into a 'donna', just as he transformed her person into a 'lady' in his poem (cit. Ricks, *Poems of 1842*, 288).

45 W. Holman Hunt, *The Lady of Shalott by W. Holman Hunt at Arthur Tooth & Sons' Galleries, 155 New Bond Street, 1909*, 7–14.

46 Cf. Elaine Showalter's comments on the influence of Millais's painting of Ophelia on interpretation of the role in Shakespeare's *Hamlet* (op. cit., 83).

47 Layárd, op. cit., 41. Apparently, Tennyson later became reconciled to this aspect of Hunt's depiction (ibid.).

48 Joanna Banham and Jennifer Harris (eds), *William Morris and the Middle Ages*, Manchester, Manchester University Press, 1984, 170.

49   Then crying 'I have made his glory mine',
            And shrieking out 'O fool!' the harlot leapt
            Adown the forest, and the thicket closed
            Behind her, and the forest echoed 'fool'.
    'Merlin and Vivien', ll. 969–72, *Idylls of the King*, in *The Poems of Tennyson*, ed. Christopher Ricks, London, Longman, 1969, 1,620. Burne-Jones's picture *The Beguiling of Merlin* alludes to the equivalent scene in the

medieval French romance, *Merlin*.

50   Reproduced in Wood, op. cit., 140. In this picture certain symbolic elements are retained from earlier versions of the legend, such as pearls and diamonds among the Lady's adornments, white flowers (though, in this case, peonies), as well as the tapestry, mirror, and other details already mentioned.

51   The watercolour which formed a study for this mural is reproduced in Banham and Harris (eds), op. cit., 161.

52   Girouard, op. cit., 182.

53   when he fell
From talk of war to traits of pleasantry –
Being mirthful he, but in a stately kind –
She still took note that when the living smile
Died from his lips, across him came a cloud
Of melancholy severe, from which again,
Whenever her hovering to and fro
The lily maid had striven to make him cheer
There brake a sudden beaming tenderness
Of manners and of nature.

'Lancelot and Elaine', ll. 318–27, in *The Poems of Tennyson*, ed. Ricks, 1,630.

54   June Steffensen Hagen, *Tennyson and his Publishers*, London, Macmillan, 1979, 101.

55   Emily wrote to Moxon that 'she had rather pay for Miss S's designs herself than not have them in the book': ibid., 103.

56   See *The Pre-Raphaelites*, Catalogue of the Tate Gallery Exhibition 7 March to 28 May 1984, London, Tate Gallery Publications, 1984, Introduction and notes by Alan Bowness *et al.*, 266–7. The catalogue note is an exceptionally full and interesting one for such a small drawing.

57   Many of Holman Hunt's other moralistic paintings, such as *The Awakening Conscience*, and including the other reproduced on our cover, have this tendency to evoke simultaneously sensual attraction and a stance of moral superiority in the onlooker.

58   H. J. C. Grierson *Poems of Tennyson*, Golden Poets, 1907, opposite 21.

59   ibid., opposite 254.

60   Hagen, op. cit., 138.

61   Wood, op. cit., 144. Wood remarks that 'Hunt's reputation can rest securely on his last great work, the *Lady of Shalott*. In this wonderful picture, Hunt's elaborate symbolism, decorative richness, and the swirling Art Nouveau figure of the red-haired model are successfully combined to produce a powerful and effective composition. One wishes that Hunt could have painted more pictures like this' (ibid., 106).

62   John Killham, 'Tennyson and Fitzgerald', in Arthur Pollard (ed.), *The Victorians*, Sphere History of Literature in the English Language, 6, London, Sphere Books, 1969, 269.

63   ibid. Cf. Stevenson, op. cit.

64   Killham, 'Tennyson and Victorian social values'.

65   Shannon, op. cit., 160.

66 Girouard, op. cit., 147–8.
67 Marion Shaw, 'Tennyson's masculinity', lecture delivered at the University of York, June 1986.
68 See, for example, J. D. Hunt, *The Pre-Raphaelite Inspiration 1848–1900*, London, Routledge & Kegan Paul, 1968, 177–8, and J. Stern 'Lewis Carroll the Pre-Raphaelite', in Edward Guiliano (ed.), *Lewis Carroll Observed*, New York, Clarkson N. Potter Inc., 1976, 162–5.
69 See J. D. Hunt, op. cit. One might note that Holman Hunt called his painting of the Lady of Shalott the parable of 'a human soul' (Holman Hunt, op. cit.).
70 See, for example, 'Evelyn Hope'.
71 For example, 'Spring and Fall'.
72 For example, Little Nell, Little Dorrit.
73 See Stern, op. cit.
74 Phyllis Rose, *Parallel Lives*, Harmondsworth, Penguin, 1985, 20.
75 Marsh, op. cit., 8. For example, on the lines

> Out upon the wharfs they came,
> Knight and burgher, lord and dame;
> And round the prow they read her name
>   'The Lady of Shalott'.

Marsh comments: 'The missing, but half-heard rhyme "shame" hints at the mysterious nature of the Lady's crime. As I read it, she is punished for taking action . . . for initiating sexual encounter.' But why not 'fame'? Cf. 'Let us pay her the great honour of burying her in the Cathedral of Camelot, and put on her tomb an inscription which tells the truth about her death, so that our descendants may remember her' (*The Death of King Arthur* tr. Cable, 94).

Chapter Three

'SEX' AND 'RACE': THE CONSTRUCTION OF LANGUAGE AND IMAGE IN THE NINETEENTH CENTURY

JOANNA DE GROOT

They cannot represent themselves; they must *be* represented.
(Karl Marx, *The Eighteenth Brumaire of Louis Bonaparte*)

Both racism and sexism belong to the same discursive universe.
(A. Brittan and M. Maynard, *Sexism, Racism and Oppression*)

Sexuality is recognized as a crucial issue in the history of western societies in the nineteenth century, just as it is recognized that subordination is a central theme in the history of women during that period; yet there remain substantial gaps in analysis and areas of confusion in the historical work which deals with these questions. As the Introduction to this volume observes, it is no longer adequate to treat the history of sexuality in nineteenth-century Europe solely in terms of control, hypocrisy, and repression; similarly, the framework of women's history has extended beyond exclusive concern with female subordination to explore the many and diverse forms of subversion, accommodation, and resistance which women developed in order to deal with their situation. This contribution to our examination of themes of sexuality and subordination will seek both to clarify some confusions and to illuminate new areas of discussion opened up in the historiography of the last decade. It will argue that nineteenth-century representations and discourses of sexual identity and difference drew upon and contributed to comparable discourses and representations of ethnic, 'racial', and cultural identity and difference.

This 'cultural' approach is offered not as an alternative to material analysis but rather as an essential component of the history of a social whole within which both elements interact. It takes the view that perceptions and definitions of women's identities and roles emerged from and in turn influenced the material circumstances of their lives. These circumstances underwent radical change during the nine-teenth century with the growth of new forms of production, of family life and residence, and of new forces of market relations and international interconnections. Such changes were experienced by women of all kinds, from wage-workers in northern English textile districts to Egyptian peasant women, and from Afro-American slave women to housewives in the residential suburbs of Birmingham. Their experiences can be analysed from a materialistic and structural perspective through the study of paid employment, childrearing, and consumption, or of urban development and household organization, as well as the shifting forms of legal and political authority. However, both productive and reproductive relations, like political systems, have a social and personal character which requires the historian to give attention to the language, feelings, values, and meanings which are part of such systems and relations. It is within this framework that an analysis of the construction of 'sex' and 'race' in which experience, image, and discourse interact is now offered.

I should like to clarify the treatment of the history of 'sex' and 'race' adopted in this essay by making some general points about how women's experience will be observed and analysed. First, it can be observed that women's situation as women, and the rules or values applied to that situation, evolved not in isolation but as part of the material and cultural history both of feminine and masculine genders, and the development of boundaries and/or interactions between them. While in no way questioning the central importance of studying women's histories in their own right, I would argue that such histories need to be situated in relation to the history of gender relations and masculine histories. Second, one notes that, just as women's experi-ence develops in relation to the other side of the gender divide, so on that female side of the divide there are important distinctions of class and culture which interact with gender-specific aspects of women's lives. Thus, while I would argue that ethnic or class divisions should undoubtedly be approached from a gendered point of view, so too gender questions and female specificity need to be seen in relation to these other divisions, and to the interactions of gender, class, and ethnic aspects of women's experience.

Studies of how gender boundaries were drawn in Europe during the nineteenth century have frequently discussed possible connections between the differences and power relations between men and women and those based on class.[1] There have also been numerous studies of the ways in which westerners (actually western men of the dominant classes) redrew the social, cultural, and political boundaries between themselves and people in other societies, although interaction of this process with the evolution of class and gender divisions is less often explored. This essay seeks to make connections between the expression of gender and of cultural/ethnic difference (both verbal and visual) which may complement the more extensive existing treatment of gender–class questions. It will argue that there are not only similarities but structural connections between the treatment of women and of non-Europeans in the language, experience, and imaginations of western men. The structural link is constructed around the theme of domination/subordination central both to nineteenth-century masculine identity and to the western sense of superiority. It will be explored through *cultural* forms – art, travel literature, media imagery – but linked to the *material* aspects of male–female relations and European hegemony in the world at large in the post-Napoleonic era.

In western Europe during the nineteenth century one can observe the reshaping and intensifying of a range of social boundaries and differences. On the one hand this process involved the emergence of clearer distinctions between female and male, worker and employer, and between different ethnic or cultural groups; on the other hand it required closer, more compelling interactions and interdependence between 'sexes', 'classes', or 'races'. In gender terms this meant sharper male/female distinctions within families but also close mutual economic and personal reliance, a paradox manifest in struggles around the 'family wage', women's rights, and the cult of domesticity. In class terms it involved growing divisions and commercialization in production, and conflicts over the control and exploitation of workers, but also new forms of involvement and interdependence at work which sustained the system. In international terms the growth of a world system based on European economic, political, and cultural dominance generated increased involvement of westerners with non-westerners alongside greater stress on western superiority, success, and self-confidence as opposed to difficulties, defeats, and doubts in other societies.

The emergence of new relations and perceptions of class, race, and gender was a matter not so much of total change as of the development of new additions, forms, and directions for existing beliefs and practices. Established political patterns, religious traditions, or social customs and values interacted with new scientific ideas, divisions of labour and status, or forms of political action, as is evident in the history of class conflicts, of feminist or anti-feminist movements, and of controversies over race and empire during the period. Moreover, we may note that sharpening theories of gender, race, and class distinction were not merely accidental or academic developments, but rather clear political, pragmatic, and personal responses to attacks on those distinctions by those who found them injurious. 'Class' protest over economic and political subjection, feminist opposition to subordination and to the gender-blindness of both liberal individualism and radical collectivism and populism, and challenges to slavery and imperialism all produced increasingly developed responses both of actual discrimination and of intellectual justifications for discrimination, whether on grounds of race, gender, or class.[2]

The political and cultural activity of the period provides evidence not only of how various groups *responded* to difference or functionally defended sex, race, and class interests, but also of how they *constructed* themselves within and against such differences. The concepts of 'Self' and 'Other' or of 'us' and 'them' which are frequently invoked to explain the *separation* of masculine and feminine, or civilized and savage, or occidental and oriental in nineteenth-century perceptions of the world need also to include the sense of the symbiotic *connections* joining each apparently opposed pair. Such connections did not, of course, belie the fundamental *inequalities* embedded in the developing characteristics and relations of gender, race, and class. The discussion which follows will explore all three of these aspects of the experience, perception, and representation of gender and ethnic difference; I shall consider how concepts of 'sex' and 'race' were founded on increasingly strongly drawn distinctions; I shall discuss the ways in which these concepts also involved interaction, reciprocity, and mutual need; finally I shall see how these apparently contradictory elements existed within a framework of relations of domination and subordination.

Whereas the theories and practices related to 'class' distinctions and relationships were founded on the new 'sciences' of political economy and social investigation, theories and practices related to 'race' and 'sex' drew on biological, anthropological, and medical scholarship, often grounding themselves in part on observable and 'inescapable' physical aspects of difference. The inequalities inherent in male–female relationships and western hegemony in the world in the nineteenth century involved elements of personal intimacy and cultural encounter very different from the experiences and perceptions which constructed the history of 'class' in that period. For these reasons, and others that will emerge in the course of discussion, it is the parallels and interactions between the images and languages of 'sex' and 'race' that evolved during the nineteenth century which will be the focus of this essay. The material upon which the discussion will be based is drawn from verbal and visual depictions of societies in the Middle East,* and in particular of women in those societies. Such material was initially offered to elites in England and France in the form of highly successful 'orientalist' genres of literature, painting, and travel writing, but reached a wider audience through reproduction in popular and accessible media forms (journals, cartoons, novels, lithographic reproduction). It finally entered twentieth-century 'mass culture' via photographic and cinema versions of themes and images originally elaborated in the early nineteenth century.

It was during this period that the development of increasingly explicit and elaborated arguments for the crucial importance of gender and ethnic differences took place. Religious and moral arguments for the distinctive roles of women as mothers and helpmates, and of men as providers and heads of households, and opinions about the moral, intellectual, and psychological differences between the sexes, were extended and reinforced in new ways. As shown elsewhere in this volume, medical 'science' was invoked to reconstruct concepts of female identity around women's biological cycles and reproductive functions, 'proving' their inadequacy and categorizing any who would not accept biology as destiny as 'diseased' or 'abnormal'[3] This scientific addition to conventional wisdom about women converged with middle-class concern to distinguish the female/domestic sphere from the male/public sphere, and to argue that separation of these spheres was essential to the maintenance of virtue, progress, and stability. It also converged with

---

*This misleading term is retained without comment, since it is a familiar, though ethnocentric, name applied to societies around the eastern Mediterranean and coast of North Africa by western commentators.

93

lower-class concerns about deskilling and competition in the labour market, and about the material and personal insecurity of families experiencing changes in production, urban and demographic growth and mobility, and sharp fluctuations in incomes and employment. For (male) middle-class opinion-makers or entrepreneurs, as for (male) working-class critics of the new political economy and 'old corruption', the family was reified as a guarantee of moral and material progress and order, but simultaneously defined in terms of sexual division and subordination.[4]

Such views were not, of course, unchallenged, and indeed, as has been mentioned, they developed in part through engagement with opposed opinions and arguments. There was debate and disagreement among workers and political activists, as among middle-class intellectuals and reformers, as to women's fitness for or rights to education, political involvement, paid employment, or citizenship; there were similar disagreements over the respective roles of biological and social influences on women's abilities, over the significance of domesticity, and over marriage and the nuclear family.[5] It was the process of confrontation with critiques of women's subordination, and establishment of a hegemonic view of gender roles, relations, and boundaries, which gave force and shape to evolving concepts of femininity in which morality, science, and convention intertwined.

Significant parallels to the emergence of this gender discourse can be found in the changing views of cultural and physical differences between human groups during the same period. Here too there were by the late eighteenth century established opinions on these matters, combining religious traditions and philosophical ideas on the 'chain of being', human nature, and history, with new theories and techniques of classification in natural and social science. In our period this was expanded, altered, and elaborated by the use of a rapidly growing body of empirical and descriptive material produced by European visitors to non-European societies, but also by the development of the 'scientific' disciplines of biology, ethnology, and anthropology. These were based on measurement and classification but equally importantly on the construction of systematic theories about the differences and inequalities between various types of humans. Increasing stress on physical characteristics (skull or brain size, bodily form and structure) and on biological heredity, itself a 'scientific' recasting of older ideas on the importance of blood descent, redirected and reinforced social and cultural arguments about non-

94

European societies expressed by writers like James Mill on India and Volney on the Middle East.[6] What became a widely accepted picture of the 'savage', 'decadent', 'uncivilized', i.e. *inferior*, character of African, Indian, Aboriginal, or Middle Eastern societies was based not just on prejudice or convention but on systematic comparisons, empirical detail, and developed theoretical argument.

Thus the images, values, and stereotypes used to define both femininity and non-European cultures and people, combined the newly prestigious insights and techniques of science with older cultural myths and traditions. Just as the skull and brain size of Negroes or Eskimos was part of the evidence for their cultural and social inferiority, so the size of women's brains was brought into the argument about their capacity for education. When James Macgrigor Allen lectured on female invalidism and its link to menstruation, he did so at the Anthropological Society of London, and the lecture was published in the *Anthropological Review* of 1865.[7] Science and expertise seem to converge on both women and non-European here, and indeed this is merely one example of a whole new set of structures within which 'knowledge' and 'understanding' of these groups were established by European males. The founding of learned societies, journals, and academic institutions for medicine, anthropology, geography, and linguistic studies brought the study of human characteristics, differences, or cultures firmly into the sphere of science, rationality, and professional expertise. As will be shown, this is by no means the only or even the most powerful source of images of 'sex' or 'race', but it certainly constituted *one* of the most authoritative and influential ways of grounding the 'Otherness' of femininity or ethnic identity in 'real' knowledge wielded by prestigious professionals (doctors, academics, 'experts').

Not only did the power of definition and prescription in matters of gender and race come into the hands of similar 'experts' in each case, but also the arguments which constructed and justified the subordination of female or non-European persons in both cases followed comparable lines. Three prominent elements are worth noting. First, differences between women and men, or between one 'race' and another, were considered to be *essential*, that is to say differences of 'nature' (a significant term) or kind, not of specific or transient detail. Basic biology, whether in the form of reproductive functions, intelligence, physical attributes, or genetic heritage, was made central to definitions of gender or ethnic identity, using the powerful language and 'evidence' of science as described above. 'Femininity' or 'negritude' or 'oriental' characteristics were conceived of as inborn or given features with which 'nature' endowed people – 'nature' now carrying a new forceful meaning of the (scientifically understood) 'real' world, as well as the older meaning of someone's true and proper place or role in the world.[8] This, of course, allowed any woman or 'race' who resisted conformity to the norms thus established to be defined as *not* normal or natural, while also allowing the argument that if 'natives' or women were not fitted *by nature* for civic rights or education there was little point in offering such benefits to them. If gender and race were conceived as *essential*, 'naturally' fixed categories, then they could not be affected by *contingent* factors, whether history, social change, or demands for reform.

Second, the fixed 'natural' and essentialist definitions of gender and race were also based on an assumption of inequality between genders and races. The physical and cultural differences between women and men, or between different groups of humans, which had been observed by linguists, anthropologists, historians, or medical and social investigators, were placed along a spectrum, one end of which was more highly valued than the other. Not for nothing was the Comte de Gobineau's famous study of racial issues entitled *Essay on the Inequality of Human Races*. Discussions on femininity or ethnic character were frequently presented in terms of the ways in which women or particular ethnic groups deviated from, or lacked, or failed to achieve the qualities, attainments, or indeed the potential considered 'normal' for European males of the dominant classes. Here is the philosopher and philologist Ernest Renan comparing 'Semitic' with 'Indo-European'* characteristics:

> in all things the Semitic race appears . . . *an incomplete race* by virtue
> of its simplicity. The race – if I dare use the analogy – is to the Indo-
> European family what a pencil sketch is to painting; it *lacks* that
> variety, that amplitude, that abundance of life which is the
> condition of perfectibility. Like those individuals who possess so
> little fecundity that, after a gracious childhood they *attain only the
> most mediocre virility*, the Semitic nations . . *have never been able to
> achieve true maturity*. (my italics)[9]

*The categories 'Semitic' and 'Indo-European' originally described groupings of related languages but by the mid-nineteenth century had also become accepted terms for the people (= races?) who spoke them.

It is interesting to note the intertwining of gender metaphors (fecundity, virility) with the assertions of the inequality of Semite and Indo-European, an inequality founded on the inability of the former to improve or mature as the latter can. Similar perceptions of the inadequacy, inequality, and incapacity of women as compared to men can be seen in the comments of a pseudonymous writer of the 1860s:

> The reasoning powers are more perfect in [man] than in [woman]. The creative powers belong almost exclusively to him. . . . it was impossible for her ever completely to know or to realize the tempest of passions which sway the souls of an Othello or a Faust.[10]

As will be seen, there were also perceptions of gender or race difference which stressed complementarity if not equality, but it is hard to ignore the force of the conviction that by their very nature women and non-Europeans could not or would not attain the cultural, political, or social achievements of white males.

Two images of inferiority evolved to evoke both that conviction and the intimacy of gender relations and race relations in the family in colonial systems and in sexual encounters. Powerful and old-established images of the parent–child relationship on the one hand, and the master–servant relationship on the other, provided models and metaphors blending the unquestioned subordination, physical closeness, and servicing of personal needs involved in the role both of women towards men and of 'natives' to imperial superiors. In both cases men valued natives or women according to their obedience, devotion and ability to serve and nurture. In her study of the relationship between Hannah Cullwick and Arthur Munby, Davidoff has shown that a powerful combination of male/female, master/servant, and even black slave/white owner images drew on common elements of loyalty, intimacy, and hard physical work which contributed both to their everyday activity and to highly charged erotic fantasy.[11] Similarly, among the most positive depictions of non-Europeans in the travel books, social comment, and fiction of empire and exploration were the 'loyal servants' (or soldiers) – Arab, African, Indian – who were shown as simultaneously personally close and properly obedient to dominant European males. In such depictions, service and devotion might even extend to a willingness to sacrifice life for their imperial superiors (Gunga Din), or of women to do the same in bearing or protecting children, favourite themes in popular art and literature.[12]

Women and natives might also be portrayed and treated as children in need of the protection and care of male/imperial authority by virtue of their weaknesses, innocence, and inadequacy. The use of a parental concept of authority combined a sense of care and involvement with the subordinate sex or race as well as power and control over them, and as such was equally appropriate for the definition of the power of men over women or of dominant over subordinate races. 'Treat them as children; make them do what we know is for their benefit', robustly advised one 'China hand' in 1860 as British entrepreneurial and strategic interests tried to push into Chinese markets; he was echoed in numerous other uses of the 'child' metaphor for Africans, Tibetans, Tahitians, or the Indians of Kipling's work, uses which can also be paralleled by comparable images of femininity ranging from Dickens's child-women to Burke's ideal of 'infantine' female beauty and Carlyle's addressing a girl child as 'little woman'[13] Indeed, Davidoff and Hall comment that the 'young, dependent, almost child-like wife was portrayed as the ideal in fiction, etchings, songs and poetry'.[14]

The third stage in the argument developed precisely the points about *power* which begin to emerge in the images described above. It can be seen that these analyses and images of 'difference' and 'inequality' of sexes and races contributed to the view that it was necessary, justifiable, and proper that the superior sex/race control the inferior, that the weaker sex/race accept the authority of the stronger. It was frequently argued that, since Indian or African societies could be shown ('scientifically'!) to be unable to produce acceptable forms of government, religion, or law, it was appropriate (and beneficial) for Europeans to provide what they lacked and could never achieve for themselves. Scholarly and popular histories of British rule in India depicted it as an act of salvage from the violence, corruption, and instability of the regimes that preceded it, which were vividly described. A Frenchman like Lamartine could characterize the people he saw on his visit to the provinces of the Ottoman Empire as 'nations without territory, *patrie*, rights, laws or security . . . waiting anxiously for the shelter' of European occupation.[15] Such themes were taken up by western missionaries wishing to rescue the benighted heathen, by political economists and reformers planning the 'improvement' of backward economic and social systems, and by entrepreneurs anxious to open up the world to modern, progressive, commercial market forces.

In a similar way, men argued that women's nurturing, domestic, spiritual talents, their mental and physical frailty, and their inability to act successfully in the public spheres of economic life, politics or high culture, should be protected by male political, legal, and social authority. Since, because of their physical and mental nature, women lacked the stability or assertiveness to compete effectively or take responsibility without damaging their 'essential' femininity, they needed men to play the role of 'sturdy tree' to which their 'vine' could cling (a metaphor found not only in Charlotte Brontë's *Jane Eyre* but in popular sermons and poems collected in middle-class families[16]). Trade-unionists like Broadhurst, advocating the exclusion of women from competition in the labour market, and writers like Ruskin, defining men as 'givers of laws' protecting women from temptation and danger, contributed to the arguments against female access to higher education, paid work, and political or trade-union rights. Others contributed to similar controversies over the rights of 'natives' and colonial subjects, and in each case examples of 'naturally'/ 'normally' unreliable or irrational behaviour were given as evidence that women or 'natives' were by nature unfit for public life and achievement in work, politics, or creative activity. Moreover, it could be argued that the 'natural' virtues and qualities which western males 'discovered' and valued in women were best protected from damage by excluding them from those public spheres. Thus the circle was closed, as dominant males, having constructed definitions and descriptions of the female or non-western 'Other', could resist challenges or alternatives to their views, not in the interests of male power, but in defence of the 'true' identity and needs of those Others whom western men had discovered and needed.

This account of new perceptions of ethnic and gender identity developing in nineteenth-century Europe has by no means dealt with all the facets, complexities, and contradictions within such a major area of European culture. While not fully discussed here, other historical work has shown how the role of religion in both idealizing and restricting the 'female sphere', the ambiguities in male attitudes to the very western 'civilization' of which they were the makers and bearers at home and abroad, and the conflicting views of 'nature', 'culture', 'reason', or 'emotion' were all significant for the history of sexuality and ethnicity.[17] Two important points emerge from the discussion so far and and now need to be emphasized: first, in examining concepts of 'sex' and 'race' we are dealing with the terrain of male power; second, such power should be understood not just as a practical function but also as a process of defining the self and others. Explanations and justifications of male advantage and authority over women, or of western superiority to non-westerners, were deployed quite specifically against feminists and anti-imperialists, but to argue that this was the purpose of the images and arguments involved would be a mistake. We shall need to go beyond any merely functionalist account of them as tools for the creation and maintenance of western male power over or against women and non-Europeans.

The images of Otherness and subordination which will now be examined further in the particular setting of 'orientalism' need to be understood as ways for men to explore and deal with *their own* identity and place in the world as sexual beings, as artists and intellectuals, as imperial rulers, and as wielders of knowledge, skill, and power. The concepts of 'sex' and 'race' which came into use in European culture, elite and popular, did not just make the control of women or natives easier, but also expressed the conflicts, desires, and anxieties which were part of the lived relationships between sexes and races, the *realities* of sexuality and imperial power. The fact that these areas of experience were dealt with through fiction, through artistic fantasy and imaginative constructions of the female and non-western Other in travel literature, popular journals, and high theory, should not mislead us about the sharp personal and practical importance of the images concerned. This point will be pursued and amplified in the discussion of orientalist art and writing, which will also stress that this material illustrates not merely similarity but actual symbiotic intermingling of the racial and sexual themes which concerned its creators. As male writers, artists, and journalists in England and France constructed their versions of gender difference, they drew on a repertoire of images, ideas, and information about alien societies and cultures. As they constructed their concepts of societies and cultures in the Middle East and North Africa, they drew on a body of language and opinion about sexuality and sexual difference. The outcome, it will be argued, was a sexualization of western definitions of these non-western societies, and an exoticization of definitions of sexuality in European culture.

First, however, it will be useful to establish the circumstances in which orientalist art and literature developed. From the later eighteenth century, growing British and French commercial and strategic interests in the Middle East led to diplomatic, commercial, and military intervention in Egypt, Algeria, and Syria/Lebanon as well as the Ottoman court, while trade and communication with the eastern Mediterranean and North Africa increased similarly. Politically, European powers confronted the issues posed for them by movements for 'national' autonomy and for government reform and centralization in the Ottoman Empire.[18] Economically, new opportunities for Europeans were provided by the demand for their manufactures and technology in the Middle East, the emergence of cotton production in Egypt for the western market, and the interest of Middle Eastern rulers in attracting European financial support and investment.[19] This expansion of material involvements was paralleled by growing cultural and intellectual interest on the part of the British and French (and German) writers, artists, travellers, and scholars. Some took practical advantage of improved opportunities to visit the Middle East, collect linguistic, historical, ethnographic, and archaeological evidence for study, or to depict their experiences in books or pictures. The publication of the work of the scholars who accompanied Napoleon's expedition to Egypt began an era of European investigation, accumulation, and transmission of material about the Middle East, and of extensive use of Middle Eastern themes by artists and writers. Observations, translations, and interpretations of author/travellers like Edward Lane or Richard Burton, and imaginative flights by Goethe, Hugo, or Byron and other Romantics, added new dimensions to the established conventions (reaching back to the Crusades) about what now became known as the Orient.[20]

Perhaps one of the most important features to note in the orientalist art and writing of our period was the absence of clear distinctions or boundaries between observed and imagined reality. Travellers to the Middle East drew not just on their actual observations, but on concepts, images, and quotations taken from fellow French or British writers, to describe and explain their experiences. Artists repeatedly reworked sketches and rearranged artefacts brought back from North Africa, Turkey, or Egypt to create their own pictures of 'oriental' scenes and people in French or British studios, or drew on European literary sources to inspire such pictures. Thus Gérard de Nerval's *Journey to the Orient* incorporated unacknowledged material from Lane's *Manners and Customs of the Modern Egyptians*, while Gautier and

101

Lamartine, arriving in Smyrna or Istanbul or Cairo, drew on phrases or images from Chateaubriand or Victor Hugo to convey their reactions.[21] Painters like Ingres could construct pictures of odalisques and 'Turkish baths' from Lady Mary Wortley Montague's travel letters, and it was Byron's work that inspired the 'oriental' picture of *The Death of Sardanapalus* produced by Delacroix before ever he visited the Middle East.[22] Others like Jean-Léon Gérôme and John Frederick Lewis did indeed make use of objects and sketches from life acquired during extended stays in Egypt and Turkey, blending them with Parisian model girls and judicious rearrangements to produce their personal versions of harem or street scenes. While it is to some extent true that between the 1820s and 1870s there was a shift from depictions of a romantically imagined Orient by Hugo or Ingres, to a realistically detailed Orient as portrayed by Gérôme or Doughty, it is the *interweaving* of imagination and observation to create complex images and explanations which was more characteristic of orientalism.[23]

When Lamartine described his 1833 journey to the Orient as 'a great episode in my interior life', as much the product of his reading and theorizing as of actual travel, he conveyed exactly the blend of observed and constructed experience so important to travellers and writers.[24] Similar features emerge from the debate over the accuracy of accounts of the Arabian explorer Palgrave, Nerval's use of a friend's experience with a slave girl as part of his own experience of life in Egypt, and indeed the whole structure of his *Journey to the Orient*, with its combination of storytelling à la *Arabian Nights* and autobiographical travel narrative.[25] A similar synthesis can be seen in the presence of western female models in orientalist settings, posed among 'genuine' details of architecture, décor, and objects from the Middle East. Sometimes the tensions and disappointments arising from the encounter between orientalist imaginings and actual experience were themselves an important theme, a source of romantic sadness such as Nerval described, regretting that Egypt was 'driven out of my imagination, now that I have sadly placed it in my memory.'[26] Flaubert too found that observing realities in Egypt produced a sense of barrenness and loss:

> what we lack is the intrinsic principle, the soul of the thing, the very idea of the subject. We take notes, we make journeys: emptiness! emptiness! We became scholars, archaeologists, historians,

doctors, cobblers, people of taste. What is the good of all that? Where is the heart, the verve, the sap?[27]

However, his Egyptian experience and his orientalist imaginings also came together in a complex whole, as he explained in a letter to his mother:

You ask me whether the Orient is up to what I imagined it to be. Yes, it is; and more than that, it extends far beyond the narrow idea I had of it. I have found, clearly delineated, everything that was hazy in my mind. Facts have taken the place of suppositions – so excellently so that it is often as though I were suddenly coming upon old forgotten dreams.[28]

However, there is another significance in Lamartine's comment on oriental travel as an episode in *interior* life. If on the one hand the emergence of orientalist writing and art in the nineteenth century was the product of external circumstances favouring contact with and interest in the Middle East, on the other hand the work that came out of the encounter of westerners with the Middle East contributed to their *self-development*. The depiction of the Orient involved the self-discovery of the writer or artist as well as voyages of discovery to the Orient, and the construction of this Orient through fiction, art, and scholarship involved also the construction of the identities and careers of those who produced such work. At a mundane level the production of orientalist material could be the key to success and reputation; John Frederick Lewis's achievement as president of the Watercolour Society and Royal Academy exhibitor was founded on orientalist work; the fame of Richard Burton began with his adventures on the pilgrimage to Mecca and was later consolidated by his version of *The Thousand and One Nights*; many more writers and artists earned a living from orientalist material, whether it was the salon success of Gérôme or the anonymous illustrators of periodicals, travel books, or Jules Verne novels. In a more complex and personal sense the experience of oriental travel and the encounter with orientalist ideas might be part of the emergence of creative talent, as Steegmuller argues was the case for Flaubert.[29] The Orient, said Lamartine, is the 'fatherland of my imagination', expressing both the sense in which it is something which he invents, but also the sense in which it provided a creative personal opportunity for him as a writer and theorist.[30]

In general, scholars have discussed the contribution of orientalist

103

experience and work to the self-development and self-discovery of writers and artists primarily in just those terms. However, this approach is less than adequate if it ignores the fact that these writers, travellers, and artists were defined by their masculinity, their class, and their European culture. They dealt with Middle Eastern societies as males from professional, gentry, or middle-class backgrounds in Britain or France, formed by and connected to the gender, class, and cultural structures of their own societies, and influenced by the emerging views of race, gender, and class already examined. The 'Otherness' which was central to westerners' concepts of the Orient – it was what they were not – is expressed in terms which are both racial/cultural and profoundly sexual, both elements combining to define a terrain – the Orient – for control, power, and domination. It is therefore worth exploring the verbal and visual terms in which the Orient was presented in order to reveal features already identified as being characteristic of gender and race discourses generally.

Perhaps the more obvious approach focuses on the use of women and of gender and sexual themes and concepts to depict and define 'the Orient'. Oriental societies were frequently characterized by reference to the way in which women were treated, by descriptions of the laws and customs affecting women, by references to polygamy, veiling, and the seclusion of women, or by fascinated anecdotes of harems, dancing-girls, and sexual encounters. All these provided powerful evidence for the 'Otherness' of the Orient, whether it took the form of Edward Lane's self-consciously learned ethnographic descriptions, or the famous encounters of Flaubert and Nerval with prostitutes and slave girls, which became powerful literary *tours de force*.[31] Moreover, whether the treatment of these subjects was voyeuristic and indulgent, or judgemental and moralizing, it also contributed to the emergence of the most widely accepted stereotypes of the Orient as corrupt and decadent, uniting sexual licence with violent cruelty. Victor Hugo's poetic cycle *Les Orientales* (1829) and Delacroix's *Death of Sardanapalus* (1827) portrayed luxury, cruelty, and sexuality in ways which allowed the audience both to enjoy and to judge the oriental images before them. Pierre Jourda sums up the exotic Orient of the 1820s and 1830s as 'blood, voluptuousness, and death', themes which were alive and well a century later in films like *The Sheik* and *Lawrence of Arabia*, and in a product as recent as a television film of 1987 entitled – *Harem* (!).[32]

However, the sexualizing of race, culture, and society in the Orient was a matter not just of colourful reportage of exotic stereotypes, but of persuasive definitions and symbols. Since European commentators endowed the Orient they had created with qualities with which men of the period also endowed females, they came on occasion to characterize the Orient as essentially or generally 'feminine'. The use of the phrase 'mysterious Orient', like 'mysterious female', indicated that both were seen as hard for western men to understand; references to the irrationality and emotional extremes to which 'orientals' were inclined carried the implied comparison with similar tendencies attributed to women. More generally the Orient, like women, is discussed by western men in terms of its actual or potential susceptibility and need for their control and authority, whether that was Lamartine's vision of the 'European right to power' in the east, or Burton's bold assertion that 'Egypt is a treasure to be won ... the most tempting prize that the East holds out'. Feminine images of nature and landscape, common in a European context, also appear in oriental travel literature, as when Flaubert describes the pleasure of swimming in the Red Sea 'as though I were lying on a thousand liquid breasts', or when Thomas Moore talks of the 'light of Eve' over 'Syria's land of roses'.[33] Above all, women were presented as the *means* for imagining or finding out about the Orient. In the romantic travel literature it is the sight of veiled women which tells the voyager that he is in the Orient, just as their presence on the eastward voyage poses the first challenge to understanding.[34] They are the image of what the 'Other' actually *is*, their veils and harems the symbol of that 'Other', just as in visual terms they are one of the commonest subjects of orientalist painting, both exotic and 'realist'.

The fact that the 'Otherness' and subordination of the Orient was reinforced through the use of the gender connection and female subject matter itself requires discussion, and its implications further examination. In particular we should look at how women represented an Other which was not merely different and subordinate, but also desirable, intimate, and necessary to men. It follows that to introduce a feminine element into the construction of the 'oriental' was therefore to introduce notions of the *attraction* and *close connection* of the oriental for the western male. Indeed, the encounters and representations by travellers and artists with oriental women did precisely suggest that desire and personal contact were part and parcel of their reaction to the oriental experience as a whole. More than many alien cultures, those in the Middle East were seen by westerners as part of Europe's

past and heritage, and both radical Saint-Simonians and conservative Catholics like Chateaubriand imagined it in that way, using
feminized language and images to reinforce that sense of familial
intimacy. A highly sexual version of male–female intimacy was
provided by the prostitute episodes in Flaubert, the story of Nerval's
'Zeynab', and the numerous women displayed in harem, bath, or
bedroom settings who populate so much orientalist art.

By producing such material, ranging from the explicit reminiscent
writings of Flaubert to the parade of sexological scholarship in
Burton's *Thousand and One Nights*, or the popularized semi-pornogra-
phic products of the period, several messages are conveyed. These
products not only made the 'oriental' into the sexually desirable, but
also made the desirable Other more so precisely because She was
oriental (as no doubt Rider Haggard realized!). European men could
not only revel in the (real or imagined) purchase or possession of
Egyptian or Algerian women as sexual partners, as models for their
paintings, even as slaves, but could also have their enjoyment
reinforced by the 'alien' character of the women concerned. The
cultural gaps, the limited ability to communicate, the 'exotic' dress,
or undress, or squalor that are evoked in these situations actually
helped Europeans to construct the experience itself in their writing,
pictures, and theories. In doing so they not only gratified male power
and male desire but had also to confront that desire, and even give
voice to the ambiguities and anxieties involved in the erotic and the
intimate, and in male need itself. If it was shown that the female/
oriental was desired as well as dominated or despised, if need was
admitted as well as superiority, then the nature of male power and
desire becomes very complex. That complexity is expressed in the
multiple voices and images of orientalist writing and painting, as has
been shown by Harper in the case of Nerval and of Lane.[35]

From this it follows that, while the Orient came to be explored and
characterized through images of gender and sexuality, it is equally
important that the 'oriental' became an image through which gender
and sexuality in turn could be defined within European culture. The
popularity of terms like 'seraglio figure', 'Turkish beauties' (meaning
female buttocks), and 'Asiatic ideas' (meaning sexual desire) in the
discourse of male British writers on sex and male responses to
femininity brings the oriental theme back to Europe, giving a
significant new dimension to discourses of sexuality there.[36] The very
market for orientalizing erotica and sexual imagery suggests that both

masculinity and femininity were constructed by such means. Princess
Pauline Bonaparte's refusal to hang Ingres's painting *The Turkish Bath*
in her rooms can be seen not as prudery but as rejection of the male
fantasies of desire and domination which the painting represents and
gratifies, and which degrade, subordinate, and exploit women. The
picture offers the viewer a room full of nude females displayed in a
variety of attitudes expressing sensual abandon and availability in an
'oriental' setting. It invites a *male* gaze to enjoy the stimulus of their
sexualized nudity, the voyeuristic thrill of observing a private female
scene (and even some suggested lesbian loveplay), and the vicarious
pleasure of identification with the Turkish delights of the harem.
Princess Pauline's refusal of such an invitation should not be
dismissively categorized as prudish.[37] There is an echo of her problem
in Louise Colet's attempt to come to terms with her lover Flaubert's
involvement (personal and literary) with the Egyptian woman Kucuk
Hanem, an involvement recounted by him with sexually explicit and
intellectually imaginative detail.[38] While Flaubert dismissed both
Louise and Kucuk Hanem with male artistic confidence, it is clear
that this episode in his Egyptian voyage was both an exercise in male
sexual gratification and also the occasion for a complex and confused
encounter with his own sexuality and his ambitions as a writer within
the oriental setting.

For these endlessly reproduced male fantasies of harems and
dancing-girls, of gratification through domination, and of intimacy
with subordinates, represented not only the indulgence of male desire
and power, but also one of the few means of dealing with the
contradictions of masculinity and male needs as they developed at
this period. The very existence of needs (personal, sexual, emotional)
in men for which they sought satisfaction from women itself raised
questions about the nature and limits of male domination. Male
power, enshrined in law and custom, gave men sexual advantages
over women, but it did not eliminate the reality of desire, attraction,
and bonding between men and women. To this contradiction should
be added others posed by the separation of spheres and different
gender identities in this period. While masculinity was becoming
based on the distinctions between the male sphere of power,
authority, reason, and public activity and the female sphere of
nurture, service, emotion, and domestic activity, it also involved not
only the right but the desire for access by men to the 'female' sphere.
New forms of male socialization, whether through the working-class

107

discipline of the labour process, or the middle-class discipline of schooling, sought to get young males to restrain or control emotion, weakness, and self-indulgence in order to earn a living, rule the empire, or gain authority in home, business, or state.[39] Hard work, (mental or physical), and self-discipline, involved a control of the self which in turn allowed men to control others (their women and children, their subjects, their employees).

However, in the process of attaining such control, men did not so much eliminate emotional and personal needs as transfer responsibility for them to women, whose caring, nurturing, feeling role was to satisfy them. The paradox was that this transfer embodied both the male power which made it happen, and the *loss* of power to understand and deal with the world of emotion, personal expression, and intimacy. It was this world which could be repossessed through male fantasies of the female, who stood not only for the Other which they had created, but for aspects of their selves which they did not wish to lose.

As has been often observed, it was the Romantic vision and its products which helped the European middle classes of the period to deal with the contradictions inherent in the change and disruption caused by the very economic processes of which their own progress was a part, but which also entailed squalor, loss, and insecurity. This vision might draw on images of the rural and the natural, on the idealization of domesticity as the haven 'where Womanhood waited and from which Manhood ventured abroad to work, to war, *and to the Empire*' (my italics), and on constructions of the medieval and the exotic as imaginary spheres where the conflicts of reason and emotion, of desire and duty, and of competition and harmony could be resolved.[40] In this context the feminized image of the sensual oriental (like those of natural/primitive Africans, spiritual Indians, or chivalrous medieval knights) enabled European men to handle the ambiguities in their situation. It was, of course, a function of their power that they could make, use and impose such images to protect sexual and racial privileges, manage their contradictions, and consolidate their dominance.

It is not surprising, therefore, that images of oriental sexuality were a feature not only of western relations with the Middle East but also of discussions of male – female relationships in Europe. When Charlotte Brontë's heroine Jane Eyre is sparring over her relationship with her lover, the harem metaphor appears to illustrate the problems of women's autonomy and equality in love. He claims to value her more than a 'whole seraglio'; she refuses her allotted role in the fantasy, but pursues it by sketching out how she will enter his harem to subvert it. She has already seen his 'sultan's' smile and earlier watched him dress up convincingly as 'the model of an Eastern emir' since he has 'Paynim features'.[41] What at one level is play-acting at another raises questions of male despotism and sexual licence which are in fact central problems in Jane's relationship to Mr Rochester. Nor was this the only occasion when Brontë used oriental motifs to illuminate contradictions in westerners' sexuality. In *Villette* her use of episodes concerning a portrait of Cleopatra (clearly drawn from orientalist art of the period), and a stage performance about the eastern queen Vashti, to develop the internal struggles of her heroine over emotional/sexual need and female autonomy, is equally striking.[42] The fact that these are all situations involving make-believe, performance, disguise, and artistic invention heighten rather than weaken their role as conscious dramatizations of problems that cannot easily be presented at the level of 'realism'.

One could multiply examples of both casual and extended use of oriental references, images, and motifs as part of the 'common wisdom' as to what (western) male sexuality and female identity are actually about. In Tennyson's *Princess* and *Fatima*, in Byron's Haidee in *Don Juan*, in Trollope's *Unprotected Female at the Pyramids*, such usages give an exotic, sometimes superior and critical, sometimes fascinated and yearning, dimension to love stories, to explorations of gender in male artists and female heroes, and to public interest in poetic/fictional resolutions to their own anxieties on those questions. Flaubert returned repeatedly to his oriental material to provide a source of fantasy (and comment) for the sexuality of Emma Bovary or Frédéric Moreau, as well as for full-scale orientalist fictions in *Salammbô* and *Hérodias*. Another tourist in Cairo, Thackeray, fleshed out the picture of aristocratic decadence in *Vanity Fair* with a staged harem charade at Lord Steyne's house. Thus the fantasy that 'appealed to an instinct of possession and domination as well as of mere pleasure' in European males also entered the mainstream of middle-class culture, becoming an accepted part of the discussion of sexuality, as influential when trivialized as when elaborately presented.[43] By the 1880s, not only could a major literary figure like Flaubert benefit from access to orientalist material, but the material had also inspired a whole range of popular genre writing of which the novels of Pierre Loti are still remembered, not to mention providing a stock of metaphors, clichés, and references casually and frequently used in western art and writings to this day.

Of course, the power of orientalist imaginings was available for audiences as well as authors. Through writing and painting, others could share in the harem femininity created by Gérôme or Lewis, or the sexual explorations of the Orient undertaken by Flaubert or Nerval, and extensive reproduction and imitation of their works widened the audience, and hence the participation in these imaginings. Their power rested on the combination of 'realistic' detail and 'Romantic' invention of which orientalist work was composed. It is the sweat and smell of Kucuk Hanem as well as Flaubert's 'story' about her which make our encounter with her memorable; it is the vivid portrayal of Egyptian architecture, Turkish carpets, Syrian tilework as well as of the delights of imaginary female availability and desirability which makes Gérôme's odalisques so attractive. Through these safely seductive and exotic scenarios, western middle-class men could recover enjoyment of a sexuality which had become problematic in their own homes, just as some did through involvement with working-class women, a parallel which Flaubert realized when commenting on his recollections of Parisian brothels while in bed with Kucuk Hanem.[44] Through the familiar form of (commercialized) sexual contact, such men could deal with the demands posed by their encounters with other societies, just as they used the equally familiar structures of military hierarchy and domestic service for similar purposes. Personal and sexual contact mediated cultural Otherness, just as culturally exotic formats mediated sexual Otherness. The conflicts, desires, and anxieties within the sexual or cultural involvements between western males and the subordinate Other could be expressed and perhaps contained, however precariously, within oriental images, stories, or travels. Nature and feeling, both now controlled in a very real sense by science and reason to an extent hitherto unknown in human history, could be allowed back into men's lives in forms and conditions established by them.

It is not surprising, therefore, that sexual and ethnic relations were often expressed in terms of power and domination. The term 'penetrate', used by explorers travelling in unfamiliar territory, by imperialists describing conquests, or by voyeurs speculating on what lay behind veils and harem doors, is, of course, a forcefully male sexual metaphor as well. When Lamartine and other travel writers

110

speak of penetrating the seraglio, or the orientalist Hogarth (who combined archaeology with intelligence work for the British government) entitled his history of western exploration *The Penetration of Arabia*, they evoked an image of male aggression both sexual and imperial.[45] The depiction of women in harem or bath scenes accompanied by guards, or Negro attendants, or even on occasion their male masters, ties their sexual attraction closely to possession, control, and subordination. In fact the apparent parallel between the submission of Middle Eastern societies to western economic, cultural, and political influence, and the subordination of women to male needs and authority, actually converges in a single image of sexualized imperial power or imperial masculine power.

The blending of conquest and enjoyment, of power and pleasure, of desire and domination, became part both of the lived experience of travel, conquest, and authority, and of the imaginative world of writing and painting of the western men who created the Orient as well as ruling and exploiting it. These complex themes have been analysed through the written record of explorers, novelists, imperial officials, and scholars, notably by Said, but some of the most powerful depictions of sex/race images were contributed by the visual arts. It is to these that I shall now turn as the final stage in my exploration of the history of 'sex' and 'race'.

3.1 John Frederick Lewis, *The Hhareem* (1849). Victoria and Albert Museum

111

The two scenarios most expressive of the combined image which, in Kiernan's phrase, 'appealed to an instinct of possession and domination as well as ... pleasure', and were repeatedly used as topics in painting, were those of the harem and the bath. Here, then, is J. F. Lewis's 1849 evocation of the former and J.–L. Gérôme's depiction from around 1870 of the latter. Both Lewis and Gérôme spent long periods in Egypt as well as travelling to Turkey and the Levant, and both depended considerably on their orientalist work for their professional standing and success (in contrast to, say, Ingres or Leighton, whose oriental paintings were only one element in their classical or classicizing and academic work).[46] Lewis's painting *The Hhareem* [*sic*] (figure 3.1) caused a sensation when first exhibited, and is an illuminating version of a topic whose treatment ranged from the vividly physical *Women of Algiers* (Delacroix, 1824) to the picture-book fantasies of *The White Peacocks* (Clairin, 1890) or *Harem Women* (Constant, 1880s).[47] The elaborate rendering of the carved wooden window screens and patterned fabric of the sofa, and of the light effects at top left and far right of the picture, contrast with the total lack of character or even modelling in the faces of the women who lounge among the draperies. The former asserts the painter's expert 'knowledge' of ethnic detail, the latter the unimportance of the figures as people. Indeed, they seem to dissolve into the fabric, and this, along with the drooping wrists and collapsed poses, conveys passivity and languor. The turban- and beard-framed face of the harem 'owner' seated among them and profiled against the light makes him a focus of attention, the 'hard' shape of his dagger counterposed to the drooping peacock fan of the standing female. Here is the exotic, luxurious, and male-centred world of women evoked in light and pattern, staged among 'genuine' props for the viewer.

Gérôme's *The Turkish (or Moorish) Bath* (figure 3.2) deploys a similar use of light-effects and architectural décor to frame a display of available femininity, in this case nude. The obviously European model who is the centrepiece is placed in a bath-house setting drawn (despite the title) from Turkish and Egyptian sources, to judge by the roof lighting and the tilework, and the 'Sudanese' attendant.[48] The reddish hair and creamy skin of the white woman contrast with the highlighted turban and dark skin of the attendant, whose arm points us towards the central nude, portraying an aesthetic, racial, and sexual hierarchy. The voyeuristic pleasure in our invasion of this female privacy is established by the pointing corner of the pool, and

3.2   Jean-Léon Gérôme, *The Turkish (or Moorish) Bath* (1870). Courtesy,
Museum of Fine Arts, Boston. Gift of Robert Jordan from the collection of
Eben D. Jordan.

the women's arms inviting the gaze inward to the white nude, whose
three-quarter back view with shoulder and breast in profile suggests
an erotic vulnerability and modesty waiting to be appropriated. Her
unadorned nakedness contrasts with the emphasis on the turban and
jewellery of the black woman, and the sense of space and quiet around
the two figures reinforces the sense of privileged intrusion into

113

3.3 Jean Auguste Ingres, *Odalisque and Slave* (1842). The Walters Art Gallery, Baltimore.

secluded space and private activity which is being offered for the enjoyment of the viewer.

That the seclusion of women in the harem as invented by Europeans involved the control or possession of prized objects rather than a sphere of personal privacy is made clear in Ingres's *Odalisque and Slave* of 1842 (figure 3.3), just one striking example of his treatments of oriental women extending over four or five decades.[49] Here we have a nude very obviously put on display, portraying both the languor and availability which westerners associated with oriental female sexuality. She waits and offers herself to the viewer as she does to her absent male possessor. Her status as an imprisoned, owned creature is stated through the presence of the black guard, and the treatment of the balustrade and walls enclosing the luscious nude and the sorrowful musician beside her. The highly coloured (literally as well as figuratively) portrayal of exotic femininity draws on prestigious western artistic conventions for portraying the female body, on the orientalist fantasies of the French intelligentsia of the period, and on Ingres's own close personal concern with the depiction of female nudes over a long career. The arms-over-head pose of this nude and her flowing hair offer a potent blend of passivity and abandon, while the luxury of fan and fabric and the exotic touches of water-pipe, archway, and turban give the viewer permission to indulge in appreciation of this female sexuality, by constructing it within the oriental setting.

The theme of ownership and unfettered power is seen at its most explicit in the depiction of slavery, a recurrent theme in the western art of our period. It combined both racial and sexual features (*female* slaves predominate in the paintings on this topic), and aroused ambivalent responses among westerners, who on the one hand came to condemn it as an institution for exploiting non-Europeans, but who on the other hand (as feminists of the period were quick to note) denied western women legal identity and autonomy just as slave owners did to slaves. In Gérôme's *Slave Market* (figure 3.4) we see the charged presentation of a pale, nude, female slave framed in the robes of men whose draperies highlight her nakedness. Slave-market scenes, with central female nudes, were a regular subject for Gérôme, who made use of classical Roman as well as oriental settings for his depiction of this ultimate form of subordination.[50] This woman (like the others he painted) is displayed for the benefit of the viewer as much as for prospective buyers in the picture, while the size of the male hand probing her mouth and her drooped, passive pose convey as much about the power of male over female as about slavery. Of course, the ethnic 'authenticity' of the dress of the men involved allows the western audience to disapprove of the continued practice of this institution and of the society which practises it, while simultaneously enjoying the aesthetic and sexual pleasures which the picture also offers.

The accurate and realistic details which sustained orientalist visions should not obscure the fact that the exoticizing and sexualizing of non-western cultures was becoming quite generalized, and involved the arrogant assumption of the right to collapse cultural differences if it contributed to the creation of an effective image of Otherness. Thus Gautier referred to the Lewis picture as a display of 'Chinese patience and Persian delicacy'. A favourite reaction to any or all Middle Eastern and North African societies was to refer to them as living embodiments of society and culture in biblical times, as though the history of 5,000 years, geographical distance, and cultural variety within the Middle East just did not exist. Artists made as much use of this concept as writers, as the comments of Delacroix on Morocco and Algeria alongside those of Chateaubriand, Lamartine,

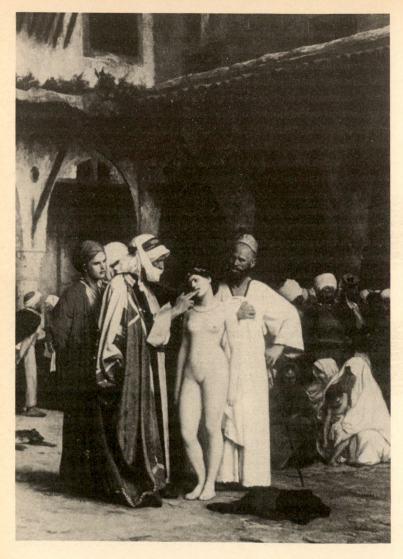

3.5 Horace Emile-Jean Vernet, *Judah and Tamar* (1840). The Wallace Collection.

116

3.6 Henri Regnault, *Salome* (1870). Metropolitan Museum of Art, New York.

Guillaumet, and Holman Hunt made clear.[51] Horace Vernet's *Judah and Tamar* of 1840 (figure 3.5) offers a vivid pictorial example of how this worked. In this depiction of the legend recounted in Genesis 38, Judah is portrayed as a nineteenth-century Arab chief complete with 'authentic' robes, camel saddle and bridle, worry beads, and riding crop – doubtless all observed or acquired by Vernet during his visits to Algeria with the conquering French armies in the 1830s.[52] By contrast, the provocatively semi-undressed figure of Tamar, with distinctly *un*-oriental (or indeed *un-biblical*) drapery and the hairstyle of a Balzac heroine, is an erotic fantasy, although it also illustrates the moment when Judah mistakes her for a harlot 'because she had covered her face'. The gesture with which she veils her face may evoke the Orient but also draws attention to her naked breast. What Vernet is depicting is a 'timeless' (and sexual) Orient alongside a femininity which is neither biblical nor contemporary but the creation of his artistic will and western conceptions of women and orientals.

An equally clear illustration of how the oriental and the feminine could be subsumed into a more universalized image of exotic femininity is Henri Regnault's *Salome* (figure 3.6). This picture of a young woman seated, knees apart, with a bowl in her lap, legs and breasts titillatingly displayed through a gauzy skirt and a blouse falling open almost to her waist, began as a study of a girl from the Roman Campagna while Regnault was in Rome, was continued during visits to Spain and Morocco, and was completed in Tangier in 1869. What is particularly interesting is the variety of titles used for the picture, which have included *African Woman, Herodias, Poetess of Cordoba,* and *Favourite Slave.*[53] Clearly the viewer is being presented not with a portrait of a person (real or fictional) – note how the facial expression is half hidden – but an *image* to which the label 'oriental', 'gypsy', or 'African' can equally easily and validly be attached. The portrait of femininity with exotic touches (the brooch on the girl's shoulder, the oriental style of the stool and the metal bowl) 'places' that femininity in a setting capable of any ethnic definition that artist or viewer chooses, belonging to any culture and therefore to none. It becomes a decorative generality, ancestor of a thousand chocolate-box illustrations and line-ups of Hollywood starlets in ethnic costume. One could hardly ask for a clearer demonstration of male artistic power to define and redefine femininity through ethnic identity, and hence of male control and possession of both concepts.

These, then, are some of the influential and recurring images (and

118

3.4 Jean-Léon Gérôme, *The Slave Market* (1866), Sterling and Francine
Clark Art Institute, Williamstown, Massachusetts.

there are many other examples of work evoking each theme illustrated here) portraying a sexualized Orient and/or orientalized sexuality for a receptive audience. The discussion of these images has offered neither a full analysis of all the aspects of the pictures in question nor a comprehensive account of the whole range of subjects treated by orientalist painters. None the less these visualizations of 'sex' and 'race' are a central feature of the developing European consciousness of those matters during the nineteenth century. The salon art which developed in Paris from the 1840s onward was paralleled in the work of British, Italian, central European, and Spanish orientalist artists from the era of Romanticism to that of post-impressionism. Lithographs and etchings spread the images beyond the limited audience of collectors, dealers, and patrons to a larger public who could see them in illustrated travel books, in periodicals like the *Magasin Pittoresque* and *Le Tour du Monde* and their British and German counterparts, and in orientalizing illustrations of fiction like Jules Verne's *Michel Strogoff*, let alone the *Arabian Nights*.[54]

Equally striking is the demonstration of the actual material power of artists to control and indeed manufacture the images which they offered to the public. Fantasy pictures of harems and dancing-girls were composed from objects *purchased* by the artists for their studies, from sketches *taken home* from travel and regularly reworked, and from female models *paid for* and arranged in the settings chosen by the artists. These might be European women earning a living by working as models in the studios of Paris, London, Rome, or Vienna, or they might be Turkish, North African, or Egyptian women from lower classes or religious minorities more willing to allow themselves to be portrayed by western artists. In either case they were socially marginal, sexually powerless, and vulnerable, and regarded by westerners and Middle Eastern societies as inferior, morally suspect, even virtual prostitutes. Their faces and bodies were labelled Circassian or Greek (supposedly light-skinned groups), their naked pallor contrasted with the skin colour of other Negro or Indian models posing as slaves or attendants, or with the richly robed guards and masters of the harem; *they* remain anonymous (unlike portraits of their sisters in the privileged classes), transformed into the 'odalisque' or 'the *almeh*' (dancer), or into Cleopatras, Scheherazades, or a dozen other heroines of western imaginings, from the 'Zuleika', 'Leila', and 'Haidee' of Byron, to Nerval's 'Queen of Sheba' or Oscar Wilde's 'Salome'. They 'become' whoever artists want them to be, yet they were actually flesh-and-blood women whose lives were no less real for being hidden from history. It was the social, gender, and colonial power of western men which made such subordination and conceal-ment possible.

As can be seen, there were close links between the visual and the verbal forms of the sexual-exotic images under discussion. At one level it was a case of literature and painting inspiring one another: the poetic Orient of Byron stimulated Delacroix, Corot, and others; Hugo's *Orientales* and the exotic travel literature of the mid-century did as much to shape the orientalist art of Ingres, Lewis, and Gérôme as did their own studies of female models and Middle Eastern scenes; publication of western versions of the *'Arabian' Nights* provided opportunities for orientalist illustration, as did the proliferation of travel books; the celebrated artist Eugène Fromentin produced major travel books about North Africa as well as influential paintings of its scenery and people; Lane's descriptions and drawings of Cairo reappear in the paintings of Gérôme and Deutsch, and in turn Gérôme's 1861 work *The Prisoner* (set on the Nile) inspired one of José-Maria de Heredia's sonnets; similarly, some 1830s rendering of an oriental female provided material for Brontë's 'Cleopatra' in *Villette*, while travellers to Egypt, Morocco, or Turkey took with them recollections of orientalist pictures which shaped their written accounts of their travels as much as the actual experience.[55] Whether one considers the 'literary' quality of orientalist painting, linked as it was to orientalist poetry, travel writing, and fiction, or the strong 'visual' elements in the literary depiction of harems, odalisques, etc., it is clear that the sexual and exotic elements in the western concept of the Orient rested on both, and the language of glamour, power, and desire is manifest in either form.

Thus, when Harriet Martineau satirized Bulwer-Lytton 'on a sofa, sparkling and languishing, among a set of female votaries – he and they dizened out, perfumed and presenting *the nearest picture to a seraglio* to be seen on British ground – only the indifference or hauteur of the *lord of the harem* being absent' (my italics), or when J. S. Mill noted that 'men desire to have, in the woman most nearly connected with them, not a forced slave, but a willing one, not a slave merely, but a favourite', they were using images which readers could both visualize and understand.[56] That such images were used by liberal 'pro-woman' writers like Martineau and Mill testifies to the depth of their absorption into the consciousness of the dominant culture, shaping

even 'enlightened' critiques of that culture. Mill's clear perception of
the ambiguous nature of male power – 'men do not want solely the
obedience of women, they want their sentiments' – does not belie the
fact that he uses an accepted discourse of gender and domination with
its exotic and colonial overtones.[57] Like Jane Eyre dealing with
Rochester's 'seraglio' discourse, Martineau and Mill may dislike or
challenge the oriental image, but they do not deny it.

Such cultural observations would have little more than curiosity
value, were they not bound up with real material, legal, and political
subordination and discrimination which gave western men power
over gender, class, and ethnic 'inferiors'. Slavery, sexual discrimination, and imperialism did actually exist in the nineteenth century, so
that references to 'votaries' or 'favourite slaves' cannot be set aside as
mere colourful language, but rather should be seen as comments on
the *real* subordination of women and non-Westerners, made sharper
by the introduction of the 'exotic' motif into the Victorian milieu.

Jane Eyre ends not with the 'happy ever after' of the marriage
celebrated at the opening of the final chapter, but with an account of
the missionary St John Rivers 'labouring for his race' in India,
glorified as a stern 'warrior' and 'indefatigable pioneer', with the
'ambition of a *master* spirit'.[58] It would seem that the affirmation of
male achievement (and sacrifice) is given pride of place over the
'feminine' goals of marital and domestic happiness. Perhaps this
authorial choice tells us something about the world as perceived and
experienced by Charlotte Brontë in the 1840s; it certainly provides
readers with a poignant picture of the imperial male/male imperialist.
Forty years later Kipling's *The Man Who Would Be King* similarly
makes male sacrifice (of women and drink) central to the realization
of the ambition to rule expressed in the 'contract' drawn up by the two
would-be kingdom winners and to their downfall.[59] Self-control, sexuality, imperial power, and male integrity are evoked in two otherwise very different fictions. Manliness and empire confirmed one
another, guaranteed one another, enhanced one another, whether in
the practical disciplines of commerce and government or in the escape
zones of writing, travel, and art. It is for this reason that the history of
orientalism and its contribution to new perceptions and practices of
'race' and 'sex' relations is worth the attention which it has been given
here. On the principle of 'knowing the enemy', let Kipling have the
last word: he was the author of the famous cliché 'East is East and
West is West and never the twain shall meet' – a classic formulation of

Otherness; however, the end of the verse which opens with that line and stands at both the beginning and the end of one of his 'ballads' merits fuller attention as a far more revealing evocation of the deep mutuality of sex/race images and consciousness:

> There is neither East nor West, nor Border nor breed nor birth
> When two strong men stand face to face, tho' they come from
> the ends of the earth.[60]

NOTES

1 See L. Davidoff, 'Class and gender in Victorian England: the diaries of Arthur J. Munby and Hannah Cullwick', *Feminist Studies*, 5, 1979, repr. in J. Newton, M. Ryan, and J. Walkowitz (eds), *Sex and Class in Women's History*, London, Routledge & Kegan Paul, 1983, from which subsequent references are taken; see also S. Alexander, 'Women, class and sexual difference in the 1830s and 1840s: some reflections on the writing of feminist history', *History Workshop Journal*, 17, 1984.

2 This and some of the subsequent discussion are drawn from a variety of sources, the most relevant of which are J. Rendall, *The Origins of Modern Feminism: Women in Britain, France and the USA 1780–1860*, London, Macmillan, 1985; L. Davidoff and C. Hall, *Family Fortunes: Men and Women of the English Middle Class 1780–1850*, London, Hutchinson, 1987; N. Stepan, *The Idea of Race in Science: Great Britain 1800–60*, London, Macmillan, 1982; C. Bolt, *Victorian Attitudes to Race*, London, Routledge & Kegan Paul, 1971; E. Said, *Orientalism*, London, Routledge & Kegan Paul, 1978; V. Kiernan, *The Lords of Human Kind*, Harmondsworth, Penguin, 1972; R. Meek, *Social Science and the Ignoble Savage*, Cambridge, CUP, 1976. For the development of dominant ideas in response to challenge, see J. Swindells, *Victorian Writing and Working Women*, Cambridge, Polity, 1985; J. Burstyn, *Victorian Education and the Ideal of Womanhood*, London, Croom Helm, 1978; F. Hutchins, *The Illusion of Permanence*, Princeton NJ, Princeton Univesity Press, 1967 (chs 4, 7–9); R. Austin and W. Smith, 'Images of Africa and slave trade abolition: the transition to an imperialist ideology', *African Historical Studies*, 1969; Said op. cit., 31–49, 195–7, 220–5.

3 See Anne Digby's contribution to this volume; Burstyn, op. cit., chs 4, 5; L. Duffin, 'Prisoners of progress; women and evolution', in S. Delamont and L. Duffin (eds), *The Nineteenth Century Woman: Her Cultural and Physical World*, London, Croom Helm, 1978; C. Dyhouse, 'Social Darwinist ideas and the development of women's education in England 1800–1929', *History of Education*, 3, 1977.

4 See B. Taylor, ' "The men are as bad as their masters": socialism, feminism and sexual antagonism in the London tailoring trade', *Feminist Studies*, 5, 1979; Alexander, op. cit., S. Lewenhak, *Women and Trades Unions*, London, Benn, 1977, chs 2–4; C. Cockburn, *Brothers: Male Dominance and Technological Change*, London, Pluto, 1983, ch. 1.

5 See Taylor, op. cit., and Lewenhak, op. cit., 39–40, 73, 88–91, for
evidence of trade-union support for women, more fully analysed in S.
Boston, *Women Workers and the Trade Union Movement*, London, Lawrence
& Wishart, 1987, chs 1,2. Other debates can be followed in K. Millet,
'The debate over women: Ruskin *vs* Mill', in M. Vicinus (ed.), *Suffer and
Be Still: Women in the Victorian Age*, London, Methuen, 1980; Rendall, op.
cit., 74–101, 208–15; C. Moses, 'Saint-Simonian men/Saint-Simonian
women: the transformation of feminist thought in 1830s France', *Journal
of Modern History*, 54, 1982; B. Taylor, *Eve and the New Jerusalem: Socialism
and Feminism in the 19th Century*, London, Virago, 1983, 32–8, 53–4, 68–70,
183–92.
6 J. Mill, *History of India*, London, 1819, book 2, 'Of the Hindus'; Comte de
Volney, *Voyage en Egypte et en Syrie*, Paris, 1787.
7 Quoted by E. Showalter, 'Victorian women and menstruation', in
Vicinus (ed.), op. cit., 40, referring to *Anthropological Review*, 7, 1869,
98–109. There are other examples of discussions on women appearing in
anthropological journals, e.g. W. Distant, 'On the mental difference
between the sexes', *Journal of the Royal Anthropological Society*, 4, 1875,
78–87, and E. Wallington, 'The physical and intellectual capacities of
Woman equal to those of Man', *Anthropologia*, 1874, 552–65.
8 The shift in the connotations of the concept 'nature' from the
philosophical to the scientific/empirical came about through the work of
Enlightenment theorists and the development of 'physical' sciences
(chemistry, geology, physics, zoology), which in turn provided models
for the 'human' sciences (anthropology, medicine, sociology).
9 Said, op. cit., 149, citing E. Renan, *Œuvres complètes*, Paris, Flammarion,
1947–61, vol. 8, 156.
10 *Christian Observer*, 64, 1865, 547 ('The education of women'), cited in
Burstyn, op. cit., 73.
11 Davidoff, op. cit., 24–7, 40–1, 46–8.
12 The poem 'Gunga Din' appeared in R. Kipling's *Barrack-Room Ballads*,
London, 1892; and Kipling's 'Her Majesty's Servants', in *The Jungle
Book*, London, 1894, is a classic depiction of the links between service,
empire, and military sacrifice, links publicly expressed in Queen/
Empress Victoria's display of her Sikh soldier-servants. The emotive
depiction of mothers dead in childbirth or sacrificing life for children was
a staple of middle-class novels and popular fiction in the nineteenth
century.
13 Captain S. Osborn, *The Past and Future of British Relations in China*,
Edinburgh, 1860, 15; on Tibet, see the comment in Kiernan, op. cit.,
180; on Africa, see J. H. Speke, *Journal of the Discovery of the Source of the
Nile*, London, 1863, 14 ('a grown child'), or David Livingstone, quoted
in J. I. McNair, *Livingstone the Liberator*, London, Collins, 1940, 99 ('they
are mere children'). Dickens's Dora and Little Dorrit are well-known
child/woman images, interestingly placed in context in P. Rose, *Parallel
Lives*, Harmondsworth, Penguin, 1985, 143–93, which also tells the story
of Carlyle and the little girl on p. 257; Burke's ideas of infantine beauty
are discussed in Davidoff and Hall, op. cit., 28. See also Ruskin's

comment on 'majestic childishness' as central to female 'loveliness' in 'Of Queen's Gardens', in *Sesame and Lilies*, London, 1865.

14 Davidoff and Hall, op. cit., 323.

15 Alphonse de Lamartine, *Voyage en Orient*, Paris, 1835–87, vol. 2, 533.

16 C. Brontë, *Jane Eyre*, London, 1847, Harmondsworth, Penguin, 1966, 469; Davidoff and Hall draw attention to the tree/vine metaphor in op. cit., 325, 397, quoting popular poems of 1828 and the 1830s.

17 A very full discussion of the role of religion in the definition of gender roles in the nineteenth century can be found in Rendall, op. cit., ch. 3, and Davidoff and Hall, op. cit., chs 2, 7–9. Ambiguities in male attitudes to femininity are examined in C. Christ, 'Victorian masculinity and the "angel in the house"', in M. Vicinus (ed.), *A Widening Sphere: Changing Roles of Victorian Women*, Bloomington, Indiana University Press, 1977; and M. Harper, 'Recovering the Other: women and the Orient in writings of early nineteenth century France', *Critical Matrix*, 1, 1985. Many studies of imperial and racial thought draw attention to the fact that the authors of such ideas were aware of both the inferiority *and* the attractions of the primitive, the wilderness, the exotic, and the natural.

18 See M. Anderson, *The Eastern Question*, London, Macmillan, 1966; or S. Shaw, *The Ottoman Empire*, 2 vols, Cambridge, CUP, 1976–7.

19 The best up-to-date survey is R. Owen, *The Middle East and the World Economy 1800–1914*, London, Macmillan, 1981.

20 The Napoleonic *Description de l'Egypte* appeared between 1809 and 1828, Edward Lane's *Account of the Manners and Customs of the Modern Egyptians* in 1836, and Richard Burton's *A Pilgrimage to al-Medinah and Mecca* in 1856. The orientalizing poetry of Goethe (*West-östlicher Diwan*) and Hugo (*Les Orientales*) appeared in 1819 and 1829 respectively. Byron's *The Giaour* and *The Bride of Abydos* appeared in 1813, *The Corsair* in 1814, *Don Juan* in 1819–24, and *Sardanapalus* in 1821. Successful translation/versions of the *Thousand and One Nights and a Night/Arabian Nights* were produced by Lane in the 1840s and Burton in the 1880s. See Said, op. cit., 116–21.

21 See Said, op. cit., 176–7, 179–81; P. Jourda, *L'Exotisme dans la littérature française depuis Chateaubriand*, 2 vols, Paris, Boivin, 1938, 1956, vol. 2, 37–47, shows how different travellers echoed one another.

22 Delacroix's painting, *The Death of Sardanapalus*, inspired by a play of Byron's on the tale of a despot defeated in war destroying his whole household prior to his own death, appeared in 1827, and he had already painted an odalisque in 1825–8; his only visit to the Orient was to Algiers and Morocco in 1832.

23 The move from 'Romanticism' to 'realism' is discussed in P. Jullian, *The Orientalists*, Oxford, Phaidon, 1977, 28, 56–74; and M. Stevens (ed.), *The Orientalists*, London, Royal Academy, 1984, 15–24. The blend of observation and imagination is discussed in Said, op. cit., ch. 1, pts II, III, ch. 2, pts I, III, IV; and also Harper, op. cit., 9–10.

24 Lamartine, op. cit., vol. 1, 10; Said, op. cit., 177–9.

25 G. de Nerval, *Journey to the Orient*, tr. N. Glass, London, M. Haag, 1984, was originally published in 1851, the journey having taken place in 1843; for the 'borrowing' from his friend's and Lane's experiences, see the

Introduction, p. 16; and Said, op. cit., 176–7, 181. For an analysis of the use of 'storytelling' in Nerval, see Harper, op. cit., 15–24.

26   On Palgrave, see P. Brent, *Far Arabia: Explorers of the Myth*, London, Quartet, 1979, 120–32; Nerval to Théophile Gautier (also a traveller to the Orient) in *Œuvres*, ed. A. Béguin and J. Richer, Paris, Gallimard, 1960, vol. 1, 933.

27   *Flaubert in Egypt*, tr. and ed. F. Steegmuller, London, M. Haag, 1983, is a selection of Flaubert's notes and correspondence during a visit to Egypt in 1849–50 with a friend, Maxime du Camp, some of whose notes and recollections are also included; the quotation is on pp. 198–9.

28   ibid., 75.

29   ibid., 11–17, 221–2.

30   Lamartine, op. cit., vol. 1, 179.

31   Nerval's fictional relationship with the slave 'Zeynab' forms 'Part One' of the *Journey*; the disturbing accounts of Flaubert's pursuit of prostitutes can be found in *Flaubert in Egypt*, 39–40, 43–50, 69–70, 76, 110–11, 113–22, 128–31, 153, 157–8, 192, 215, 219–21.

32   Jourda, op. cit., vol. 1, 184: 'voilà tout l'Orient romantique; du sang, de la volupté et de la mort'.

33   R. Burton, *A Personal Narrative of a Pilgrimage to al-Medinah and Mecca*, ed. I. Burton, London, G. Bell & Sons, 1913, vol. 1, 112, 114; T. Moore, *Lalla Rookh: An Oriental Romance*, London, numerous edns in 1820s.

34   Jourda, op. cit., vol. 2, 37–8, 42–4, drawing on Lamartine, Gautier, Flaubert, and du Camp.

35   Harper, op. cit., 13–14, 15–23.

36   P. Fryer, *Mrs Grundy: Studies in Victorian Prudery*, London, Transworld/ Corgi, 1965, 40, 273; C. Ryskamp and F. Pottle (eds), *Boswell: The Ominous Years*, London, Heinemann, 1963, 65, 293–4.

37   For a discussion of the painting (which defends Ingres's work as healthily masculine – *sic!* – and pure), see W. Pach, *Ingres*, New York, Harker Art Books, 1973, 131–6; see also N. Schlenoff, *Ingres: ses sources littéraires*, Paris, Presses Universitaires de France, 1956, 281–4.

38   *Flaubert in Egypt*, 113–19, 129–30, 219–21, where Steegmuller seems to identify with Flaubert rather than with what is pejoratively described as Colet's 'jealousy'.

39   Davidoff and Hall, op. cit., 22, 25–8; see also L. Davidoff, J. L'Esperance, and H. Newby, 'Landscape with figures', in J. Mitchell and A. Oakley (eds), *The Rights and Wrongs of Women*, Harmondsworth, Penguin, 1976; Christ, op. cit., and Harper, op. cit., 4–10, are also evocative of ambiguities in gender and male desire.

40   Davidoff and Hall, op. cit., 28; Kiernan, op. cit., 132, 136; Said, op. cit., 182–3, 184–91, 194–7; H. Ridley, *Images of Imperial Rule*, London, Croom Helm, 1983, 14–30, chs 3, 4, 6; see also Karen Hodder in this volume and M. Girouard, *The Return to Camelot: Chivalry and the English Gentleman*, New Haven, Conn., and London, Yale University Press, 1981.

41   C. Brontë, *Jane Eyre* (1847), Harmondsworth, Penguin, 1966, 297–8, 212–3.

42 C. Brontë, *Villette* (1853), Harmondsworth, Penguin, 1979, 275–7, 338–42.
43 W. Thackeray, *Vanity Fair*, ch. 51; Kiernan, op. cit., 140.
44 *Flaubert in Egypt*, 130.
45 Lamartine, op. cit., vol. 2, 159; D. Hogarth, *The Penetration of Arabia: A Record of the Development of Western Knowledge Concerning the Arabian Peninsula*, 1904.
46 Jullian, op. cit., 148; Stevens (ed.), op. cit., 194, 201; Pach, op. cit., 49, 99–100.
47 These works are reproduced in L. Thornton, *The Orientalists: Painters and Travellers 1828–1908*, Paris and New York, Universal, 164, 167; and Jullian, op. cit., 83.
48 Stevens (ed.), op. cit., 141, suggests that Gérôme drew on visits to bath-houses in Cairo, quoting his travelling companion Lenoir, and on Flaubert's literary description of the same. The title work is clearly a version of the so-called Isnik designs evolved in Turkey in the fifteenth and sixteenth centuries, and widely reproduced thereafter in the eastern Mediterranean. 'Moorish' North African tilework was very different, using highly geometric rather than plant motifs as seen in the pool here. The bath theme is repeated frequently by Gérôme – e.g. in *The Bath* (1880s) and *Moorish Bath* (1874), illustrated in G. Ackerman, *Jean-Léon Gérôme*, (catalogue), Dayton, Ohio, Dayton Art Institute, 1972, 77, 99, which entitles the work illustrated here *The Moorish Bath* (ibid., 20–1).
49 The earliest Ingres treatments of odalisque/oriental bath themes date from 1807–8 (*Bather*) and 1814 (*Recumbent Odalisque/Great Odalisque*; another version appeared in 1825). In 1828 he produced a 'harem interior', and the two versions of the *Odalisque with Slave* appeared in 1839 and 1842. His work on what became *The Turkish Bath*, discussed earlier, began in 1819 with notes on Wortley Montague's *Letters*, and over the years he developed poses and sketches for the work, but the main period of its production was in the 1850s, and it was finalized between 1859 and 1862. A last study derived from it appeared in 1864.
50 Similar poses appear in Gérôme's *Phryne before the Tribunal* (1861) and *Greek Slave* (1870), illustrated in Ackerman, op. cit., 10, 100. Other slave-market paintings of his are shown in ibid., 21, 88, 89.
51 Thornton, op. cit., 38, describes how Delacroix declared the people whom he saw in Algiers and Morocco were 'living figures from classical history', saying 'Rome is no longer in Rome'; Schlenoff, op. cit., 282–3, suggests this as a common reaction among artists of the time; Lamartine, op. cit., vol.1, 178, talks of biblical poetry engraved on the land of Lebanon and vol. 2, 92–3, deals with his pilgrimage to the Holy Sepulchre; Chateaubriand, *Œuvres romanesques et voyages*, Paris, Gallimard, 1969, vol. 2, 999, declares of Judaea, 'all the scenes from the scriptures are present here'. Holman Hunt's approach to Egypt and Palestine was powerfully focused on their biblical significance (see Stevens, op. cit., 186–94), and Guillaumet described his encounter with a caravan in Kabylia, North Africa, 'as if I were re-reading a page from

Genesis', Jullian, op. cit., 110.

52   Vernet first went to Algeria with the French army in 1833 and returned in 1837, 1839–40, and later; see Stevens, op. cit., 230; Jullian, op. cit., 122–5.

53   Thornton, op. cit., 158–60; Regnault died young (aged 28) fighting in the Franco-Prussian war. He was also the painter of one of the most forceful evocations of 'oriental' violence and cruelty, *Execution under the Moorish Kings of Granada*, 1870.

54   Mathias Sandor used orientalist subjects to illustrate Verne, according to Jullian, op. cit., 112–13, which also illustrates an 1840 *Arabian Nights* (110).

55   Jullian, op. cit., Fromentin's works are *Un Eté dans la Sahara*, Paris, 1856, and *Une Année dans le Sahel*, Paris, 1858. See note 48 above for Flaubert's influence on Gérôme; for the role of Byron, see Jullian, op. cit., 47 (*Sardanapalus*), 114 (Corot's *Haidée*); for appropriations of Lane's material, see Ackerman, op. cit., 16–17; M. Verrier (ed.), *The Orientalists*, London, Academy Edition, 1979, plates 12 (Gérôme) and 40 (Deutsch). Compare with E. Lane, *Manners and Customs of the Modern Egyptians* (1836), New York, Dover, 1973, 314, 316, 317; the titles drawn by Lane on pp. 12–13 recall those in the pool of Gérôme's *Turkish Bath* (figure 3.2).

56   H. Martineau, *Autobiography* (1877), ed. G. Weiner, London, Virago, 1973, vol. 1, 350–1; J. S. Mill, *The Subjection of Women* (1869), Everyman, London, Dent, 1970, 232.

57   J. S. Mill, op. cit., 232.

58   Brontë, *Jane Eyre*, 474–7.

59   R. Kipling, *The Man Who Would Be King*, first published in a collection of stories in the Indian Railway Library series, called *The Phantom Rickshaw*, in December 1888. It was reprinted in England in 1890 and 1892. I have used the World's Classics edition, *The Man Who Would Be King and Other Stories*, ed. L. Cornell, Oxford, OUP, 1987. The eponymous story is on pp. 244–79. The 'Contrack' is described on p. 254.

60   The lines are from 'The Ballad of East and West', dated 1889, first published in Britain in *Barrack-Room Ballads* (1892), 75–83 (also available in *Rudyard Kipling's Verse: Definitive Edition*, London, Hodder & Stoughton, 1960, 234–8). The lines used here occur in the opening and closing verses, which 'frame' the poetic tale of an encounter between an officer of the British Indian Army and a chieftain of the North-West Frontier in which manly gallantry (officer/gentleman style) transcends the confrontation of the 'native' with imperial military power.

Part II

SEXUALITY, SUBORDINATION, AND FEMINISM

INTRODUCTION

The second group of essays focuses on the politics of changing gender relationships. These essays consider the boundaries of gender in particular contexts, the rationales of authority adopted by those who claimed to define women's lives, and feminist questioning and analysis of such authority. The political arguments of the second half of the nineteenth century were rooted in, and inextricable from, the language of sexuality, of ignorance, innocence, and experience. Private and public worlds were integrally related.

Jane Rendall shows how Bessie Parkes and Barbara Leigh Smith in their early lives experienced the frustrations and the limitations of a restricted sphere of activity. Jeanne Peterson has argued in a recent article that young women in fortunate and often indulged circumstances – like the daughters of the Paget family whose lives she traced – might enjoy fruitful and often fulfilling activities, conscious of no overwhelming sense of loss or absence.[1] There are many aspects of the lives of Parkes and Leigh Smith traced here which parallel the world of the mid-nineteenth-century Pagets. Nevertheless there is also a clearly defined and increasing sense of deprivation, for their lives were at odds with the imperatives of their class: occupation, action, purpose. Individually, they could express themselves not through action, in the market-place or the political sphere, but through writing and art. They shared some unease at the values of their class – identifying both with material and economic progress, and also with the duties of philanthropy. Brought up in radical political worlds, at the heart of political dissent, they did perceive the contrast between the patriarchal authority claimed by many middle-class fathers and liberal forms of political culture. Paradoxically, the freedom to engage in close and romantic friendships with young women of their own class brought a closer understanding of the boundaries of the separate female world they inhabited together. By the mid-1850s Bessie Parkes claimed the right to the knowledge shared by men of her class: the knowledge of the relations between the sexes, and of the world of social and political economy. And Barbara Leigh Smith led a campaign to reform the law of marriage in a direction which was not incompatible with John Stuart Mill's concept of an ideal companionship, though it came out of a more personal apprehension of the subjection of women.

These two women came from a background of Unitarian culture not dissimilar to that of Harriet Taylor Mill: their own admiration for Mill's early work suggests the power of his example within such a liberal culture. Susan Mendus stresses that *The Subjection of Women* should be read not simply as a plea for legal and political equality but as a positive statement about the marriage relationship. The complementary and companionate marriage that Mill proposed rested on a common western and liberal view of the progressive development of the monogamous family, in an ordered, fulfilling, even perfectible world. But his ideal could seem far removed from the realities of nineteenth-century life. The family of Mill's dreams was one withdrawn from market imperatives, from the competitive world which set a price on women's labour. And the stress which Mill laid on the quality of complementarity as a means to moral development led him ultimately to retreat from the prospect of equality between men and women. He failed to confront the roots of masculine authority in the inequality of the home, and, most of all, his ideal relationship rested on the prospect of a perfectibility to be achieved through the suppression of sexuality, on the ultimate subjugation of matter through the marriage of minds. Mill's influence was considerable, and his arguments for the improvement of women's education, for civil equality, for marriage as cultivated companionship, appealed to liberals throughout the country, from the intellectual aristocracy to middle-class provincials. Yet, unless both private and public implications of Mill's viewpoint are absorbed, the nature of that influence cannot be fully understood.

The case for girls' education was, of course, open to attack by the defenders of such privilege, using the languages of utilitarianism and science, of biology and anthropology. Sir James Fitzjames Stephen – in a powerful attack on Mill's work as a whole, *Liberty, Equality, Fraternity* (1872) – identified Mill's standpoint on women's position as one which negated the very principle of authority. He rejected Mill's progressive view of human development, in which a civilized and liberal world had displaced the barbaric rationale of military strength. For Stephen, 'it is force in one shape or another which determines the relationship between human beings'; and the existing shape of marriage could be justified on a general and utilitarian basis as for the good of society as a whole, better than the exercise of individual force in individual relationships.[2] Liberal culture, for Stephen, assumed a consensual agreement at its heart, and took no account of the means by which the ordered worlds of the west were maintained. The realities of Stephen's world lay in the military organization which maintained the India he had just left, in that imperial bureaucracy which ruled British colonial territories. Stephen's argument was one which continued to be raised against those of Mill, in many debates on the suffrage issue, throughout the late nineteenth and well into the twentieth century.[3]

Denying political rights to women negated the liberal assumptions of the Enlightenment. Anne Digby has argued that the justification for this inegalitarian position was found in the rationale of biological hierarchy. From the late eighteenth century, doctors increasingly perceived women's health in terms of their reproductive system: their experiences were defined as distinctive and separate from those of men. Woman's sexuality became the subject of 'scientific' study, a knowledge largely though not entirely denied to women themselves – and culturally biased to maintain gender differentiation in society. A networking of assumptions between the emerging disciplines of gynaecology and psychiatry led to perceptions of mental illness to which women were peculiarly liable, and to more general conclusions on the nervous instability and irrationality of the female. As these arguments were developed, they later became a deliberate and defensive response to the encroachment of women into the territories of higher education. The kinds of ideas propagated by Mill and liberal educationalists were identified by members of the medical profession as damaging both to individual girls and to the future of the race: 'the ideas which would exalt culture above motherhood are suicidal and should be abandoned. It will not do to say that women should have a choice.' Such medical authorities, resting on supposedly scientific authority, were hard to deny; yet women doctors and educationalists, Elizabeth Garrett Anderson and Sophie Bryant, perceived and strongly opposed the social prejudices incorporated within such assertions.

Medical and biological arguments were supplemented by others, rooted in increasing knowledge of other peoples, filtered through the assumptions of western superiority. In terms of anthropology, both physical and social, the claims to white and masculine authority were to be formulated in the second half of the nineteenth century. By 1869 members of the London Anthropological Society were deliberately focusing on the question of sexual difference to demonstrate scientifically masculine and in particular white masculine superiority. Craniology – skull measurement – provided one means by which the inferiority of women as well as that of different races might be irrefutably demonstrated. Victorian social anthropologists turned to the rationale of monogamous patriarchy, in the face of their awareness of exogamy, polyandry, polygamy, matrilineality. Henry Maine's defence of the natural patriarchal order, derived from his study of India, *Ancient Law* (1861), was followed by Sir John Lubbock's *Origin of Civilization and the Primitive Condition of Man* (1870), which stressed that the patriarchal family, monogamous, unequal, rooted in patrilineal property and masculine superiority, was at the apex of historical development. Such arguments were by no means unquestioned within their respective sciences; yet they suggest the extent to which the framework of the debate had shifted, and the extent to which new ways of justifying masculine authority, in different disciplines, were evolving.[4] Still, resistance did not effectively check the expansion of women's secondary and higher education, which was (albeit slowly) growing to meet a middle-class demand. It was an education which rested on the assumptions of a liberal culture, which even within that culture perhaps looked more towards the arguments of John Stuart Mill's *Subjection of Women* than to Barbara Leigh Smith's *Women and Work*.

Feminists recognized the strength of such specific arguments for male supremacy. They still retained a sense of separateness, of a different destiny. Yet from within that they were able to meet and combat masculine reaction. Mary Maynard has identified the emergence of a critique by women – still perhaps embryonic, yet nevertheless comprehensive in its scope – of male power, as exercised by individuals, through the construction of masculinity and in institutional relationships. By the second half of the nineteenth century the contradictions inherent in the theme of separate yet unequal spheres were specifically confronted. That sense of separateness embedded in women's lives enabled them to analyse the nature of the masculine privilege of their own society in employment, in economic dependence in marriage, and in the sexual double standard, as well as in political institutions.

Yet such analysis was hard to separate from other forms of inequality. The balance between loyalty to class and gender was to continue an uneasy one. It was, of course, fundamental to the analyses of Frances Power Cobbe and Josephine Butler that masculine privilege was not confined to one class in society; nevertheless, the remedies proposed could at times appear to take the form of a repressive sexual code directed against the working-class young.[5] The contradictions between the advanced liberal case for rights for women, as individuals, and their responsibilities – philanthropic or collective – to or over other women, were apparent in late nineteenth-century feminism. Nevertheless, women such as Josephine Butler and Frances Power Cobbe had moved beyond the mystifying language surrounding Victorian womanhood, to define in a new language of feminism the economic, political, and cultural structures which drew precise boundaries to women's lives, to serve that masculine authority.

NOTES

1 M. Jeanne Peterson 'No angels in the house: the Victorian myth and the Paget women', *American Historical Review*, 89, 3, 1983, 677–708.
2 Sir James Fitzjames Stephen, *Liberty, Equality, Fraternity*, ed. R. J. White, Cambridge, CUP, 1967, 188–210.
3 See Brian Harrison, *Separate Spheres: The Opposition to Women's Suffrage in Britain*, London, Croom Helm, 1978.
4 See Janet Sayers, *Biological Politics: Feminist and Anti-Feminist Perspectives*, London, Tavistock, 1982, chs 3, 5, 6; Elizabeth Fee, 'The sexual politics of Victorian anthropology', in M. Hartman and L. W. Banner (eds), *Clio's Consciousness Raised*, New York, Harper & Row, 1974, and 'Nineteenth century craniology: the study of the female skull', *Bulletin of the History of Medicine*, 53, 1979, 415–33.
5 Judith Walkowitz, 'Male vice and feminist virtue: feminism and the politics of prostitution in nineteenth century Britain', *History Workshop Journal*, 13, 1982, 79–93; Deborah Gorham, 'The "Maiden Tribute of Modern Babylon" re-examined: child prostitution and the idea of childhood in late Victorian England', *Victorian Studies*, 21, 1978, 353–69. For a different view, see Sheila Jeffreys, *The Spinster and Her Enemies: Feminism and Sexuality, 1880–1930*, London, Pandora, 1985.

Chapter Four

FRIENDSHIP AND POLITICS: BARBARA LEIGH SMITH BODICHON (1827–91) AND BESSIE RAYNER PARKES (1829–1925)

JANE RENDALL

Dear Barbara,

> ... earth has shown
> We have some brains among our Sex, our own.
> Some kindly woman heart, some female mind
> To swell the chorus which uplifts mankind ...
> You cannot need another word to show it;
> I need but name a Martineau and Howitt.
> Nay leave the walks of Genius; look below ...
> How many a Mother labors for her son,
> His guide upon a higher path begun
> How many hovel homes behold a wife
> Shedding the hearts best sunshine over life.[1]

Bessie Parkes addressed these lines to Barbara Leigh Smith in 1847 at the age of 18, when Barbara was 20. Over the next ten years they shared their growing consciousness of the limitations of women's lives. The development of their friendship – regardless of the quality of the poetry – offers an insight into the relationship between personal and political worlds for these two exceptional young women from the Victorian middle classes. Much discussion of nineteenth-century feminism begins with the prescriptive and public literature, with the literature of women's sphere. That literature takes as its starting-point the male-defined boundaries between public and private life, boundaries which were an essential part of liberal political thinking. That perspective offers only half the answer. The politics of Bessie Parkes and Barbara Leigh Smith were related both to the committed liberalism of their family backgrounds and to their shared awareness of a world of experience, of sexuality and politics, from which they were themselves excluded, to which they were subordinate. Gradually they came to express their opinions and frustrations, to understand the nature of their subordinate status, to take political action. The relationship between the two women was critically supportive, and offers one example of the growth of a female political network which cannot be understood without the identification of personal and political themes.

Carroll Smith-Rosenberg, Lilian Faderman, and others have traced the ways in which nineteenth-century middle- and upper-class women were often likely to find their emotional support and fulfilment, before and after marriage, in others of their own sex.[2] The absence of sexual feeling ascribed to women of a certain class and status meant that such friendships, intensely and passionately expressed, were socially acceptable. Within a middle-class female world, in many ways very separate from the masculine one, it was possible to share a knowledge of frustration and confinement, and, in the right context, to take action. And at times in the lives of Bessie Parkes and Barbara Leigh Smith the choice of female friendship meant resistance to enforced social expectations, even of marriage, and could be the basis of a wider pattern of association among women with a political purpose.

The political activities of the two women are generally thought to have begun in 1854 with the campaign launched by Barbara Leigh Smith to reform the law affecting married women's property, and to have continued with the foundation in 1858 of the *English Woman's Journal* – financed by Leigh Smith (Bodichon) and edited by Parkes – which lasted till 1864. These public commitments have been studied elsewhere; but as yet the growth and nature of their friendship from 1847 remains unexplored.[3] This essay will consider its development in the years before the two women took over the *Waverley Journal*, the precursor of the *English Woman's Journal*, from 1847 to 1857. It is inevitably a partial view, dependent in particular on the viewpoint of Bessie Parkes.

The backgrounds of these two women appear very similar. They both came from families that were wealthy, Unitarian, and, in the context of their period and class, politically radical for several generations. Patterns of political and religious dissent were intrinsic to their family lives. Benjamin Leigh Smith, Barbara's father, from a mercantile and property-owning family, made a fortune in his distillery business in his own right. A leading Unitarian, he stood for rational religion, for all advances towards political and religious freedom, just as his own father had done. He was an MP from 1838 to 1847, a supporter of Robert Owen's educational programme, of the emerging Liberal Party, and of the repeal of the Corn Laws, as well as giving continued and unobtrusive backing to many hospitals, schools, and political refugees.[4]

Bessie Parkes's father and mother came from long-established Unitarian families: Bessie's maternal great-grandfather was Joseph Priestley, a pioneer of religious and political reform during the American and French revolutions. Joseph Parkes, her father, began his life as a prosperous solicitor in Birmingham, from a strict Unitarian family – though he himself retained some Anglican sympathies.[5] Politically he was rapidly drawn from the provinces to the challenge of national organization. He was in his early years associated with Jeremy Bentham and the elder Mill, and by the 1830s, as a philosophic radical, played a central organizational role in the Whig/Liberal Party in the House of Commons, though as he grew older his interest in political theory and progressive reform declined.[6] He was more likely to identify himself, especially to his daughter, as a pragmatic man of experience. By the 1840s he held a lucrative legal position in the Court of Chancery, yet still maintained political interest and influence.

Yet there were also very important differences between the two families, differences in the relationships between Barbara and Bessie and their parents, differences which may suggest the complexities of their personal and political worlds. Both were the eldest daughters in their families. But Barbara and her two brothers and two sisters were all illegitimate. Her mother, who died when Barbara was 7, had been a milliner's apprentice, with whom her father lived openly without marriage; very little is known about her, or why they did not marry. Their household was unconventional, and informal, and Benjamin Smith took some pleasure in flouting convention. He brought to London James Buchanan, from Robert Owen's New Lanark school, who taught in the infant school which he founded in Vincent Square, and acted as private tutor in the holidays to the Leigh Smith children, until 1839; at times the children took their places in the infant school, where all were treated quite alike. Buchanan's teaching was exciting, eccentric, and excluded formal discipline. Barbara recollected his reading aloud from his 'three sacred books: the Bible, the Arabian Nights, and Swedenborg'. And she continued to find his religious teaching, that of a Swedenborgian committed to the symbolism of nature, to the love of Christ, and to the tender care of children and animals, inspiring – though she recollected later also how dependent he had been on the labours of his wife and daughters.[7] Father and tutor shared in the children's activities. There were no restrictions on the children's reading, but the formal education of the Leigh Smith daughters was limited, dependent on their own individualistic choice of reading and direction.

In 1848, when Barbara was 21, her father settled upon her £300 a year and her own private invitation to philanthropy, the title deeds of an infant school in Westminster. She was to receive other resources, sufficient for her, for instance, to build her own country cottage in Sussex, at the age of 26, in 1853. Benjamin Smith respected the autonomy of his daughter – though even he ended the affair between Barbara and the publisher John Chapman, in 1856, in spite of his own history. The consequences of her unprecedented financial and social independence will be considered later.

But that independence was not shared by her friend. Joseph and Elizabeth Parkes, though Unitarians and liberals, believed in an orthodox and conventional code of behaviour for young women, one observed by her mother and by an extended family circle in Warwickshire, where Bessie spent much time. There is a suggestion in the work of Marie Belloc Lowndes, Bessie's daughter, that Joseph Parkes was not a faithful husband; no evidence has been found to support this, but it is clear that both the Parkes parents took for granted different standards of morality and propriety for young men and young women.[8] Bessie remembered, perhaps a little romantically, a lonely early childhood, cheered by extensive and imaginative reading – fairy-tales, Scott, the *Arabian Nights*. From the age of 11, she then boarded at what seems to have been a good Unitarian school for girls in Leam, Warwickshire, run by William Field, an elderly but still influential Unitarian minister, who had been a critical influence on Bessie's father. The school was small, and run on a family basis. Field, his wife, and three daughters offered an education which Bessie remembered a few years later in 1849 with some pleasure, as run 'on very different principles to those most in vogue' by 'women of high and cultivated minds'. The pupils were allowed novels which dealt with love and marriage, were encouraged in active games, and in acting, and yet were also introduced, at the least, to 'more solid branches of instruction', including Latin, geometry, and even lectures from Mr Field on optics, hydrostatics, and astronomy. Bessie's memory was partly of the pleasures of that shared female world of 'the calm sunny warmth ... our gardens with their dear flowers; the coterie of friends, the poetry writing, the theological discussions' presided over by the Field sisters. Yet the atmosphere was also that of intellectual independence, of a determined dissenting faith, of a household 'chastened by a stern, almost puritanical sense of duty such as I have seldom elsewhere beheld, infusing a whole establishment'.[9] Unitarian circles could retain an older puritan outlook, however moderated by liberal educational ideas.

Bessie was her parents' only daughter, and after the death of her brother Priestley in 1850 she was their only child. She lived at home, though with many holidays and expeditions, until her marriage in 1867, at the age of 38, two years after her father's death. She had no independent income from her parents and only £50 a year from an uncle, until the death of a elderly friend in 1859 gave her £150 a year. Her parents kept a close and continuously watchful eye on her behaviour; and friendships with young men were not permitted. Conflicts were frequently to arise.[10]

There was a deep split between Bessie's many activities – travelling, writing, philanthropy, campaigning – and the life she led as a daughter at home: she was not free to invite her friends to her home in Savile Row, which she later recalled as one of 'conventual exclusion'.[11] Her relationship with her mother, Elizabeth Parkes, whom she found often harsh and cold in her conventional expectations of her daughter, was not always easy.[12] Joseph Parkes followed the writing and political campaigns of Bessie and Barbara with an interested if unsympathetic eye. In correspondence he expressed some bitterness to Bessie that she failed to submit to him before publication of her manuscripts, whether poetry, a children's story, or more committed reflections on women's education: he saw that as the natural wish of a parent, especially of a daughter, about to commit herself in public.[13] His political contacts, as with Lord Brougham over the campaign against the law on married women's property, were often of considerable importance to Bessie and Barbara. Yet he threw against their enthusiasm the weight of his age, his experience, his masculine and paternal authority. In 1858, stung by public criticism of the *English Woman's Journal*, and of the published work of both Bessie and Barbara, he wrote to his daughter:

Young English women will not believe, till older, in the natural distinctions of the two sexes; & that the Males will never allow the Females to wear their Clothes – much less to usurp their natural sexal [*sic*] superiority. You will learn a lesson, as you grow older; & as your Grand-Mothers & Fore-Mothers learned before you were were born. Your GrandMother Priestley, & my Mother in Law before your birth, commenced life with the same aspirations; & Mrs Montagu did; but Experience told them, as I often tell you, that Society cannot be so largely or practically revolutionarised as you young inexperienced women imagine & desire.[14]

The first meeting of the two families had taken place when these two were children, on holiday in Hastings; all Bessie remembered of this was being struck by the way in which Barbara's father had himself cared for his children – for instance, putting their boots on. Such services had never been performed by Joseph Parkes.[15]

Their first meeting as young women probably took place again in Hastings in 1846, when Bessie was 17 and Barbara 19. For the next three or four years, their friendship was at its most 'romantic'. Bessie's feelings for Barbara are most fully represented in her private journal; there are many entries which express intense affection. She wrote in October 1849:

> Wrote my darling Barbara, yesterday I heard from her & she spoke of my *dear letters*, to be dear to Barbara seems wonderful to me, she seems so lofty, so magnificent, so half divine to me. That beautiful bright face, how enchanting it is.

She admired that 'fearlessness of action' which she and so many others saw in the young Barbara.[16] And she looked continually for a return of her affection. While staying with the Smiths, she noted in November 1849, 'B. was peculiarly loving to me', and again:

> Oh how dearly I do love and reverence Barbara; how I long for her to love me dearly; I wonder if she ever will; I feel when I am looking at her so utterly unworthy of her deep affection.[17]

And, when the relationship was clearly not going so well, she could fear to be 'cut' by Barbara. Though Barbara clearly returned affection, there is little to indicate her side of the correspondence; and there are some hints of a less demonstrative side to her character, as when Bessie wrote of the 'christian sorrow' felt by Barbara at her own 'utter want of sympathy with the pleasure I feel when you come into a room'.[18]

They met in Hastings and London, and corresponded regularly when apart. Bessie wrote very regularly to her 'Dearest Barbara', 'Barbarossa', 'Dearest Fellow', 'Frater'. Their friendship was rooted in a way of life fortunate and in many ways indulged. Their life was made possible by the existence of domestic servants, who in the early years of their relationship are virtually invisible in their correspondence. In these leisured lives, they painted, shared their reading, wrote poetry, took frequent holidays abroad and in this country: Bessie writes in 1849 of her journey to Hastings 'thinking of that glorious winter to come, all the books to read, all the lovely rides, all the reading & talk with Barbara, all the acting & the music', and of 'those free wild spirits the Smiths always seem to have, how glorious to feel them rush in one's own heart'.[19]

Yet their friendship was not an exclusive one. In 1849, when Bessie kept the journal in which she expresses most strongly her feelings for Barbara, she could also write of her own love and affection for an older Warwickshire friend, Emma Evers, and of Barbara's for a fellow art student, Anna-Mary Howitt, the daughter of Mary and William Howitt.[20] There are no expressions of jealousy or of rivalry in this correspondence, but rather of sympathy and identification. Barbara wrote to Bessie of the 'poetical' qualities of Anna-Mary, Bessie replying by comparing her own affection for Emma.[21] By 1852, Barbara was strongly attracted by 'Elizabeth', who has not been firmly identified but may have been Eliza Fox, the daughter of William Johnson Fox.[22] Bessie was involved in a close relationship with a former schoolmistress, Lucy Field. In a letter to Barbara in November 1851, she described an idyllic day spent in the country, driving a pony-chaise from Leam to Stratford with Lucy. But some conflict about which we know little led to Lucy Field's withdrawal from this friendship, leaving Bessie in misery and with a sense of betrayal. It was Barbara who took the initiative, and without Bessie's knowledge and against her wishes wrote a long and detailed letter to Lucy. In an attempt to achieve a reconciliation (which proved to be unsuccessful) Barbara defended the character of her friend, against what might be imputations of untruthfulness, and noted the difficulties of her life with her parents, for one of her particular 'poetic and enthusiastic temperament' – difficulties which Barbara herself did her best to smooth.[23]

Such friendships were described in terms which might also be used for heterosexual relationships. Bessie wrote to Barbara about the relationship of a man and woman, lovers in her own unpublished novel: that writing about love seemed to her a desecration of her feelings for a 'few beloved names' – the names of Emma and Barbara.[24] She complained of Anna-Mary's publication of her work *An Art Student in Munich* (1853), revealing her feelings for Barbara, under the name Justina:

> these idealisations of strong affection ought to be sacred to private life.
>
> She sees in you that strong sunny light because she loves you, and you know I see those whom I love in the same light, but I think you should remonstrate with her from telling the public about it. I could write poems and tales without end, if, as Goethe did, I used the materials of my life. How poetical our Hastings relation was: the long evenings of reading and talking, and all sorts of things I felt and never told you. Then again my friendship of years, from early youth to maturity, with Mr B— why it would be *exquisite* material.
> . . .
> But I don't like these things being cooked up for the public.[25]

There were also practical decisions about marriage to be made. To her surprise, Bessie received a proposal in 1849 from a Robert Fane, whom she knew only slightly. Rejecting him without hesitation, and with some hilarity, initially without reference to her father, she replied to him that she knew nothing of him, that before marriage she must thoroughly know her future husband and his aims. To her journal she added:

> To live with him; & give up in some measure my beloved Emmie & Barbara, to be dependant on that quiet (?) face for my intellectual nutriment, after living with BLS, with her flashing beauty. . . . A single woman is so free, so powerful; an intense love will free marriage to her but *that alone* in the present state of society.[26]

To her father she wrote of the pleasures of her daily life, and of her distaste for marriage as yet. Her initiative and also her amusement over this episode were sharply censured by her father, though he acquitted her of impropriety.[27]

A more serious suitor for Bessie was her cousin Samuel Blackwell, a widower and Dudley ironmaster, regarded by her family as unsuitable for his financial instability. He remained on the fringes of her life for seventeen years from 1847 till 1864. To him in 1854 she could write that, since they had scarcely been alone together for the last seven years, they could not gain 'that confidential knowledge of the intimacies of character which occurs with friends of the same sex'. He had never seen her free to speak and act, as she was with those friends. She wrote to him of the fear which 'cultivated women' of her generation felt in contemplating 'marriage as it now is'.[28] She suggested that he should come to know her as she really was, by meeting her friends, especially through calling at Barbara's and learning her true interests.[29] It is a relationship difficult to reconstruct; yet there are signs that Bessie may consciously or unconsciously have deployed this association, one unwelcome to her parents, to delay difficult decisions. The impenetrable, ultimately disastrous, financial situation of Samuel Blackwell, the attractions of living in London rather than in Dudley, the contrast between the London literary and political world and provincial manufacturing circles – all these factors meant that Blackwell, a widower, remained a shadowy figure in Bessie Parkes's life, neither accepted nor rejected. And Bessie continued to enjoy many developing female friendships, and to participate in literary and political circles.

Of Barbara's relationships we know much less. She clearly had a brief affection for a young tutor, Philip Kingsford, who died of consumption. In 1854 she formed a relationship which lasted a year with John Chapman, who tried to persuade her to live with him openly. Barbara, already deeply discontented with the structure of marriage, nevertheless hesitated, and, finally telling her father, was taken by him from Chapman. Later, on a long winter's holiday in Algiers, she met for the first time her future husband, Eugène Bodichon. Much correspondence between the two women on these events was destroyed, though Bessie was clearly in Barbara's confidence.[30] Barbara wrote to Bessie of the differences between them, of her own strong desire for children and a husband:

> to find someone worthy to take what is almost a necessity to me to
> give, it will be a dreadful waste of my life if I can't find anyone. You
> don't understand the feelings at all nor the desire for children,
> which is a growing passion in me. Where are the men who are good?
> I do not see them.[31]

By the early 1850s both Barbara and Bessie were expressing determined dissatisfaction with the contemporary situation of women. Their friendship continued: though earlier relationships

144

became less important, and new ones appeared, their own still continued to gather strength from their analysis of the condition of women, and self-conscious commitment to its improvement. I want to look at the early development of that analysis through their common reading, and their expressed desire for action and occupation.

There is no doubt of their discontent. In the first surviving letter between Bessie and Barbara, Bessie wrote of the lack of depth of domestic life, of the absence of anything beyond 'the surface of everyday concerns' in which 'all kinds of demands are made on time, temper & spirits in small domestic life'. Her frustrations in households where constant conformity to the desires of others was required of her were true for 'most girls & women & what makes the hindrances to female improvement immensely great'. She reflected upon whether a daughter might conscientiously disobey a father, especially in the choice of her own reading, and whether a friend might knowingly lend books to which a father was opposed.[32] Social life among her parents' set could be genteelly frustrating, the men and women 'so distinct, so markedly of different sexes'. In such company, she had to quieten her own desire to 'heterodox wickedness'.[33] She admired Barbara's many plans but felt her own life much more constrained:

> my duty will lead me to a London life where I must attend in a certain measure to horrid fashionable requirements, because I must not let my dear Mother go about alone, to follow any of my own purposes. And should they lose Priestley I must be double to Father & mother & their opinions are not mine. Especially my Fathers.[34]

Though restraints on independent travel grew less as she grew older, that too was still a constant subject of parental concern.[35]

What the two women could share first of all was a common habit of reading and study. They talked, and they wrote endlessly about their reading, as Barbara wrote in 'To Bessie':

> You and I have talked a pace
> Of everything, & every place
> Of everybody live or dead
> On horseback with the leaves o'er head.[36]

Their reading was immensely wide-ranging: classical writers, Locke, Bacon, Butler, the Romantic poets. When Bessie went to stay with her friend in Blandford Square, she noted reading the life of Swedenborg to Barbara at night, while 'B's lovely face looked from behind her screen at me but I said nothing'.[37] They reflected on changing literary and moral standards. Reading *Clarissa Harlowe*, Bessie 'could not conceive how Richardson could have written such a book only a century ago, and in a great measure *for* ladies', for though she found it 'exquisite', she thought it would certainly injure most schoolgirls.[38] Bessie read the work of women writers like Hannah More, Maria Edgeworth, and the contemporary Swedish feminist author, Fredrika Bremer. Barbara introduced Bessie in 1848 to her old friend, Mary Howitt, Bremer's translator, through whom she later met Fredrika Bremer on a visit to England in 1851.[39] They shared their enjoyment of Charlotte Brontë's *Shirley*, of which Bessie wrote: 'full of power & poetry, written by a *woman* I am sure'.[40] In 1848 a work which made a very considerable impression on both women was Tennyson's *The Princess* – that fantasy of the all-female college, ruled by Ida, devoted to the advancement of women, but conquered for a companionate ideal of marriage by an adventurous and persuasive Prince. Bessie at first describes the poem as 'one lovely dream throughout', with Ida 'a very ideal of womanhood' and the Prince worthy even of Barbara. Yet there was disagreement. Barbara saw '*nothing* absurd' in Ida, though Bessie criticized her unyielding dogmatism: 'I heartily love her for her enthusiasm for her sex but she went to the other extreme & *put the men below* instead of *equal*.' Ida had mixed with her zeal 'love of power not right'. Two years later Bessie returned to the poem, and questioned Tennyson's intentions: 'It may mean almost anything according to the eyes of the reader. What does he think was Ida's mistake?'[41]

Such reading included liberal political writing. In April 1847, for instance, Bessie recommended to Barbara an American study of individual rights, E. P. Hurlbut's *Essays on Human Rights and their Political Guarantees*, which had chapters arguing for the extension of representation to women and the reform of the marriage laws; but the Scottish editor, George Combe, strongly disagreed on these points.[42] More important was their developing interest in the field of political economy. By the end of 1849 the two women were reading John Stuart Mill's newly published *Principles of Political Economy* together – 'beautiful lucid Mill', as Bessie called him. As she struggled with the *Principles*, she apparently found Mill 'more enchanting . . . every day' and the section on peasant proprietorship 'delightful'. On 4 November 1849, having spent the day reading Mill and the latest article on

Malthus in the *Westminster Review*, they sat down in the evening to compare their abstracts.[43] Barbara's work was much fuller and more detailed; and it was Barbara who noted in her abstract Mill's comments on the situation of women in his chapter on 'The probable futurity of the labouring classes'. She thought his opinions right and liberal as far as they went, yet wished he would give his opinion on the 'contract of marriage', on those 'unjust laws both of society and country which crush women', that 'tyranny so deeply felt yet borne so silently'. She wished Mill would write 'a Moral Philosophy, a treatise on the Duties of men to one another in their various relations'. Political economy seemed to her 'the shifting stone to "things superior in importance", "considerations much larger & deeper"'.[44]

Reading, of course, was not enough. Neither Bessie nor Barbara could bear frustration silently. Barbara wrote to Bessie in 1847:

> I have a great deal to say to you about *work* & *life* & the necessity of *yr* fixing early on a train of action, *you* I mean, what is so sad so utterly black as a wasted life, & how common! – I believe there are thousands & tens of thousands who like you & I *intend doing*, – *intend working* but live & die, only intending.[45]

Bessie in the same year ended a letter to 'dear Barbarossa' with 'I hope to earn my bread before I die, don't you?'[46] After a visit to an English country house she remarked on the emptiness of the life of an 'English gentlewoman' – where there might be 'cultivation, but no brain work', no manual labour, not even 'house arrangements such as press on our class. . . . It is as if the sinews are taken out of life.' The process of self-education required some purpose: 'What shall I do? What shall I educate myself for?' Bessie could display her confidence, write that she had mental power enough to do 'anything men have ever done'. But at the same time she frequently doubted her own abilities, intellectual and physical – 'so dreadfully unfit, so uneducated . . . engaged in the pursuit of knowledge under mountains of physical difficulty'.[47] She could only constantly compare what lay open to her with the potential for men of her own class. 'Don't you wish you were a man? Sometimes I do, sometimes I am glad I am a woman, that I may help to push on my own sex', Bessie wrote to Barbara in 1848.[48]

That desire for activity, however, was coupled with the knowledge that social convention prevented them following any kind of political career or taking up paid employment. Through their families they watched and sympathized with radical and liberal political ideas and new middle-class political organizations. In 1847 Bessie identified with 'the people who have just learned their power by the victory of the Anti-Corn Law League' and defended her sympathy with 'democracy' as 'the great reality surging up all round us: struggling on the Continent for dear life; here educating themselves and clamouring for extension of suffrage'. They exchanged views on the dissenting battle against Anglican claims to a monopoly over elementary education.[49] They saw with approval the formation of the new Freehold Societies enabling small savers to purchase land.[50] They attended the lectures of the Peace Society and of the Italian Society. Sharing general radical sympathy with nationalist aspirations abroad, they watched the progress of revolutions in France, Germany, and Italy in 1848.[51] Both met Kossuth, and admired Mazzini, while the Leigh Smiths entertained refugees from most European countries.[52] By 1852 Bessie wrote of the possibility of a government which 'though of parties must be seen to represent the first step towards a national party' ending the old dominance of Whig and Tory since 1688 – almost a replaying of the 1830s philosophic radical aspirations to a popular party.[53] Yet their own part in such aspirations remained problematic.

Similarly they had a sense of the power and force of the rapid industrial growth of their world. Bessie wrote in her letters of the excitement of the dominating and dramatic landscape of Birmingham and the West Midlands, of new industries and factories everywhere. On a visit to Glasgow in 1849 she noted a visit to 'Mr Napier's *wonderful* engine foundry', where 'nowhere perhaps is mind more *palpably* shown than here'.[54] Yet they were, of course, excluded from any active part in such developments, developments which were central to the male members of those urban élites, joined by business interests and kinship, of which they were a part. There was another side to such rapid expansion: they were to become aware of women's vulnerability in such a world, in which sudden bankruptcies and financial disasters were commonplace. Women of their own class forced to earn their living could do so only as poorly paid governesses. Barbara could write enthusiastically and ingenuously of the beauty and independence of the life of two sisters forced to support themselves with little money and no relations, who kept a school in one of the worst parts of Edinburgh 'in a place of utter moral darkness', sustained by the good they did.[55] Bessie, writing of the situation of one of her school friends, whose family had lost their money and who had to become a governess, dreamt in such a position not of losing her independence in this way but of earning money as a bookkeeper or manager of a warehouse. Salary and independence were both preferable.[56] They were both aware of the public debate about the situation of the governess. Bessie noted of the latest reports from the Governesses Benevolent Institution that 'the Governess papers are *awful*. I can scarcely read them. How little one knows what privation is.'[57]

In the late 1840s and early 1850s the means by which the two young women might find some occupation and commit themselves to their cause were not clear. Bessie Parkes and Barbara Leigh Smith together first shared occasional writing, which emerged from their friendship and their correspondence; each was able to identify for herself a possible career as a creative artist. Yet the conditions of their lives meant that their political commitment and their creative work were impossible to separate. So too in friendship and support for other women outside the bounds of convention, and in a desire for useful occupation – which could mean only philanthropy – they were able to develop their view of women's situation in mid-nineteenth-century society.

In attempting to give their ideas expression, they did, of course, write; and they began together in 1848 to look for somewhere to place the poems and stories they were accustomed to write for each other and their families. In 1848 they approached two local newspapers with which they had family connections, the *Hastings and St Leonards News* and the *Birmingham Journal*. In a letter to the editor of the *Birmingham Journal*, Bessie asked for his views on the possibility of taking up literature as a profession. In his reply, the editor predictably, patronizingly, and realistically dampened her expectations, pointing to her lack of experience of writing to deadlines, her ignorance of realistic competition. He urged her 'not to cast aside the prospect of domestic happiness' and to consult her father, who was also a former proprietor of the paper. However, she continued to deal with the two editors on behalf of Barbara and herself.[58]

In 1848 she reviewed Mary Howitt's translation of Fredrika Bremer's *Brothers and Sisters*, and a new work by Harriet Martineau for these two local papers, though her abstract of Mill was turned down for publication by the *Birmingham Journal*.[59] In May 1848 Barbara wrote to that journal of the desirability of reading clubs among the poor,[60] and contributed minor items to the *Hastings News*. 'ERP' wrote from London to the *Hastings News* in September 1848 calling for collections of works of art and exhibitions of crafts and trades to be made available to the lower classes, to be introduced into 'a world of rational pleasure'.[61] Two articles signed by 'Aesculapius', probably Bessie, on women's education, appeared in the *Hastings News* in July and August 1848. The author attacked the view that 'women, in the ordinary cant of the day, are supposed to have a mission', that women are 'angels by nature'.[62]

The *Hastings News*, newly founded with a rationalist and philanthropic outlook, was most sympathetic. Bessie contributed both poetry and prose regularly, mostly under the pseudonym 'Bernard'. By mid-1849 she was contributing weekly, often work first written a year or so earlier and exchanged with Barbara. Her poetry could be simply nature poetry, sometimes extremely sentimental. But it could also reflect her immediate personal and political concerns. An early work, 'The Abbess', celebrated sisterhood and female friendship, just as her 'Riding Song' dwelt on the exhilaration of physical activity and exercise.[63] In 'City Scenes' two young women, both beautiful and of similar age, are contrasted in the urban scene. One is wealthy with her fortunate life ahead of her; the other is destined to prostitution and starvation. In 'Two Artists', the one in her tiny room, the other striding the landscape, there is surely a portrait of Barbara and Anna-Mary Howitt.[64]

Her work could have a more direct political message. In 'To Birmingham' she recalled the memory of 'many victories over Feudality', yet also that power of leadership over the mass of the population granted to those with 'master energies'.[65] In 'Progression' she wrote of individual responsibility for the onward and upward march of progress; and in 'Poets of 1848', as in other work, she proclaimed the poet's political mission in such times.[66] Local political issues were touched on. In Hastings in the late 1840s much interest was stirred by the enclosure of old footpaths and rights of way by landowners. Barbara demanded that her friend write 'a stirring poem, a battle against the oppression of the selfish squires'. The result was 'No Thoroughfare', a new poem first published in the *Hastings News*.[67] By 1849 sanitary reform was an issue of major importance in Hastings in the wake of a cholera epidemic in the town, and Bessie's poem 'My Old House' invoked the new truths of public health.[68]

These minor contributions to local life hint at radical political interests, awareness of the position of women in their society, and also some perception of the hardships of their world, of the need for social intervention to mitigate the consequences of social change. Both women continued to write occasionally for the local papers, but also for national periodicals. Bessie contributed an article on Florence Nightingale to *The Leader* in 1856, a translation of Julie d'Héricourt's refutation of Proudhon's ideas on women to *The Reasoner*, and articles on Algeria to *Chambers's Journal* in 1857.[69] But both Bessie and Barbara saw their future not in journalism but in creative work. By 1849 Bessie was writing a novel: in a letter to Barbara she reflected on the situation of women, as she described the central relationships of the novel. She had managed to get her heroine, Florence, to a hill overlooking the fires of the Staffordshire ironworks at night, a place she knew well and had designated for a proposal of marriage, and she wrote:

> I got them there without any impropriety, how in Heaven's name? you will say. Dear Barbara, folks would say Florence is so unnatural for a girl of twenty, yet she only does & says & thinks what you & I do, are we very odd fishes? She would be called so wild and masculine in her ideas. . . . I do think so *totally* differently from all about me, & so must you except your father & the Howitts that I sometimes feel quite mystified.

In the same letter she noted how, increasingly, conventional scales fell year by year from her eyes. The danger was that they might become '*bigotted liberals*', forgetting in their 'desperate' impatience how all around her opinions were slowly changing, especially on the education of women. Already, then, even in 1849, the two women set themselves apart from much contemporary opinion; Bessie wrote that 'we should often be frightened at the good we are preparing *if we knew it*'.[70]

Yet both had come to identify a firmer purpose in their lives. For Bessie it was to be the career of a poet. She continued to write, and published her first volume, mostly poems already printed in the *Hastings News*, in 1852; and she determined 'in the future & nobler sense I have sworn to myself to be a poet'.[71] In *Summer Sketches and Other Poems*, published in 1854, Bessie was more explicitly to explore themes of female friendship and women's new political awareness. It is written in the form of a letter from Bessie to Barbara, an account of two women, together in a remote Welsh cottage, where 'even the

151

flowers are Tory', watching the progress of the women's movement in the United States, ready to challenge orthodoxy. She writes of Mary Carpenter's work, of Margaret Fuller's inspiration, of the life of an unknown schoolmistress. The theme of the rural idyll shared by two women is one which recurs in Bessie's work, as in her children's story, *History of Our Cat Aspasia* (1856). Yet ultimately the two women feel 'the sort of hunger after public things', the thirst for news of a new political movement, as

> A spirit moves
> Amidst the silk of gilded drawing rooms
> And in laborious homes, with equal voice
> It summons us to labour and to prayer, –
> To labour, which is prayer, and which alone
> Can solve the question which the age demands
> 'What is a woman's right and fitting sphere?'[72]

Barbara's energies were put to a different purpose; from 1849 she enrolled in art classes in the first year of the new Bedford College, and pursued a serious artistic career. In Bessie Parkes's papers there is a kind of parable written by Barbara in July 1849, which tells the story of a rich young girl who sought the truths of nature in the Scottish countryside, yet who returned to her studies to learn the language of nature, as Barbara was to do at Bedford College.[73] She was primarily a watercolourist, and mainly a landscape artist. In 1850 she was to have two paintings accepted by the Royal Academy, and in the future her work was to be accepted there seven times, and in many other exhibitions. She was single-minded in her determination; in *Summer Sketches*, Helen (Barbara) replies to Bessie:

> I paint
> From morn to eve, from morn to eve again,
> Striving against the hinderance of time
> And all the weight of custom; and I will,
> I tell you Lillian, that I *will* succeed.[74]

Her painting meant extensive walking and frequent sketching expeditions, which themselves challenged convention. Yet her ambition was not entirely that of the individual artist. Anna-Mary Howitt, her friend and fellow artist, recorded the plans of Barbara (Justina) for 'a beautiful sisterhood in Art', for an Inner Sisterhood of art-sisters bound by their single objective, and an Outer Sisterhood of women, all workers bound to a pure but also a professional life. In 1857 Howitt and Leigh Smith were particularly influential in the founding of the Society of Female Artists, a group which exhibited, and campaigned for the admission of women to the Royal Academy.[75]

By the early 1850s friendship might have a more clear-cut political meaning. In 1850 Elizabeth Blackwell, already a medical graduate, came to Europe for further medical education; she was a cousin of Bessie's suitor Samuel Blackwell. Bessie and Barbara called upon her, impressing her with their unconventional appearance and determination to support her in her medical work. As Elizabeth Blackwell later wrote, this was 'the commencement of a lifelong friendship'. The two did their best to support her efforts to raise funds for a women's medical school but with no immediate success: they parted with her in some sorrow.[76]

Other associations brought the two women to examine those barriers between themselves and a world of sexual experience from which they were formally excluded. Barbara and Bessie were by 1853 both friendly with members of the Pre-Raphaelite circle, especially with Dante Gabriel Rossetti and Lizzie Siddall, with whom they had regular spiritualist seances at the home of the Howitts. That friendship was maintained in the knowledge of Lizzie Siddall's anomalous social situation, as a model, living with Rossetti. When Lizzie appeared seriously ill in 1854, Barbara persuaded Rossetti to allow her to bring Lizzie to Hastings, and after several stays at Scalands, Barbara's Sussex cottage, she seemed to improve.[77]

The relationship between Bessie Parkes, Barbara Leigh Smith, and Marian Evans (George Eliot) is one which merits a more detailed study in its own right. Marian Evans had been supported by Joseph Parkes in her translation of Strauss, and after meeting Bessie in 1851 became a family friend. Both Bessie and Barbara saw much of her, and were deeply impressed by her intellect and her personality. Marian Evans's elopement with George Lewes brought the Parkes parents to ban all contact with her, to urge both Bessie and Barbara to have nothing to do with a woman who had so betrayed her talents and contravened that most fundamental of taboos.[78] Neither obeyed these injunctions, continuing to visit and to support Marian Evans – though even as late as 1863 such visits were difficult for Bessie to make. But the support and friendship of Barbara was immensely valuable to the isolated novelist. It was such events in their own lives which made both write of the hypocrisy of the barriers faced by young

153

middle-class women, of the need to open a world of experience to them that they might understand it.

The most obvious way in which a young middle-class woman might find occupation lay in philanthropic activity of different kinds, which might or might not have radical implications. Bessie and Barbara were engaged in such activity from the beginning of their friendship. They were especially interested in the education of girls. Barbara had been given the title to Westminster Infant School by her father at 21. Even before then, both had done some teaching. Barbara's own education had interested her in progressive educational ideas, and she disagreed with Bessie on religious teaching in schools, which Bessie defended, though she objected to rigid injunctions to children '*to be good*' and the failure to allow children to learn from their own experience.[79] Bessie taught in local schools in Warwickshire, and both patronized the British School (the elementary school run by the British and Foreign Schools Society) in Hastings. On 9 November 1849, while staying with Barbara in Blandford Square, Bessie wrote that she was going to the local British School with Barbara and that 'I think of taking a class there twice a week'.[80] Staying in Stourbridge, in 1851, she wrote to Barbara that she had visited a local girls' school, which had a cheap library, and listened to 'a droll picture of the struggle between the ideas of the Ladies committee and the government inspector' from a Miss Alden 'about 26, ugly, lame and very intelligent'. The ladies' committee were all for 'sewing and morality' and Miss Alden for 'the Government opinions on female education'.[81]

Barbara's views on education were considerably more radical than those of either the ladies' committee or the government inspector, and were inspired partly by her own education. She established her own new school, the Portman Hall, in a poor neighbourhood in Paddington. Bessie wrote to Sam Blackwell that Barbara's intention was to open a school 'for the daughters of mechanics and artisans' and asked him to lay in some mineral specimens for a future museum of natural history. Bessie was 'nearly as much interested in the school as is the founder' and hoped to give lectures on literature and even on gymnastic exercises. Barbara was particularly concerned to secure a good trained teacher, prepared to teach according to 'the principles and methods she had conceived essential for a "people's" school'. Through contacts with the Unitarian journalist and radical William Johnson Fox, she found Elizabeth Malleson, who had trained for six months at a Birkbeck school in Peckham. In November 1854 the school was opened. Girls and a few small boys were taught together there; pupils included Barbara's own nieces, Elizabeth Malleson's sisters, the son of Garibaldi, and the sons and daughters of neighbouring tradesmen. There were no punishments, no uniform, and no specifically religious teaching, though there were moral lessons. The teaching included not only reading, arithmetic, French, drawing, and music, but elementary science, physiology, and hygiene, with particular emphasis on health habits. Both Bessie and Barbara continued to be greatly interested in educational practice at all levels, and had even greater hopes for the school to become 'the germ and [?] the centre of much ... a point of work and mutual interest for an increasing circle of young women of our kind'.[82] However, by the mid-1850s the pressure of other activities meant that they spent less time directly involved in the school.

Interest in education extended to those regarded as delinquent and outcast. In June 1853 Bessie visited with Barbara's aunt and sister the reformatory at Redhill in Surrey, and in July Mary Carpenter's reformatory, Kingswood, for delinquent boys and girls near Bristol, and the ragged school she ran in Bristol. Bessie admired Mary Carpenter's humility: 'I wish B. could see her. B. is as unselfish but relies more on her own strength.' The atmosphere of the school showed the sheltered Bessie very clearly that the task of reform was not an easy one and that the rowdy, high-spirited children, who were dancing and 'hollering', needed something more than a move from their homes and Christian care.[83] But the condition of young women from backgrounds of poverty and slum life did continue to engage her attention.

Running through Bessie's correspondence lies evidence of her consciousness also of the existence of extensive prostitution in London. She wrote in December 1849 to Barbara that 'In the cab we passed two unmistakably miserable creatures; it makes me shudder now, two hours after, to think of them.' Her knowledge of such conditions increased, as she came to take part in missionary work, probably a Unitarian mission in the slums of Westminster. She had been a subscriber to the Unitarian London Domestic Mission since 1847.[84] She was later to write to Samuel Blackwell that one of the reasons for her strong feelings about the law relating to women, and their opportunities for employment, was 'a real knowledge of the relations of the sexes as carried on in Westminster', through visiting a school and accompanying a missionary into crowded streets and homes. There, the marriage ceremony was not customary, and the worse and most squalid kinds of prostitution represented the only feasible way of earning bread. She did not deny that much arose 'from the deba[s]ed nature of the part of my own sex', but a very much greater proportion arose from 'the difficulty of breadgetting and from the improbability of regaining "lost" character in the first instance'. This view recurred in her correspondence, where she reflects on meetings held by 'Unitarian and liberal' women in London, and on the 'feeling which is rising among cultivated women on this subject . . . no longer a tabooed subject of conversation, or of studied blindness'.[85] Her awareness of such consequences of the double moral standard that existed for men and women in sexual matters is clearly set out in her first published writing on women's situation.

In 1854 Bessie Rayner Parkes published her *Remarks on the Education of Girls*, and Barbara Leigh Smith *A Brief Summary in Plain Language of the Most Important Laws of England concerning Women*. They had recently become friendly with Anna Jameson, writer and literary critic, whose early works had highlighted aspects of women's situation. Her approach was in many respects a more cautious one than their own, rooted in her belief of a 'communion of labour' between the complementary but different worlds of men and women. Anna Jameson shared their philanthropic concerns, and indeed claimed a 'maternal' role overseeing the activities of Bessie, Barbara, and Anna-Mary Howitt.[86] Bessie and Barbara were becoming deeply involved in the campaign to secure reform of the married women's property law in 1855 and 1856, a campaign which has been well described recently by Lee Holcombe, and which was fundamental to their view of marriage. By December 1855 Bessie was drafting the wording of the petition which was to go to the House of Commons, trying to make it 'as simple as possible only allowing myself a little rhetoric towards the end'. Anna Jameson distrusted their efforts:

> it will not do as to form & expression. I am afraid it *must* go thro the hands of a man & one of legal experience & ability before it can fulfil its purpose & your hope – who has seen it except us women? it wants the masculine power – the masculine hand – do, dear Bessie, wait for a few days.[87]

Barbara and Bessie did take much advice, from the lawyer Matthew Davenport Hill, and from William Johnson Fox; and they shared with a number of other committee members the work of collecting signatures for the petition. Bessie was able to support Barbara, depressed and miserable in the aftermath of her affair with Chapman, through the labour of much of this work.[88] Their success lay in mobilizing an active committee, in collecting overwhelming evidence of hardship, and in a petition presented to the House of Commons with over 3,000 signatures. They failed, however, in that the resolution presented to the House of Commons in 1856 was withdrawn under pressure, and the bill of 1857 rapidly dropped out of sight, to be overtaken by a divorce bill of a very different kind. The battle for married women's property was to be postponed for a further ten years.

The basis of their personal relationship was by then changing. Carried off by her family to recover from the affair with John Chapman to a winter in Algiers in 1856, Barbara Leigh Smith was joined there by Bessie. She also met Eugène Bodichon there, and returned to Britain in 1857 determined to marry him, though on a basis which preserved her financial independence and her autonomy to continue her art and her politics. The couple were to spend half their time in Algiers, half in England. Bessie's surviving letters at this date betray a certain doubt of the marriage, which was shared by almost all Barbara's friends, and even more unhappiness about Barbara's future absences in Algiers. They do not, however, suggest open hostility.[89]

By this time Bessie also had new friends. In 1855 she had met Matilda Mary Hays, ex-actress, novelist, translator of George Sand, and close friend of the American actress Charlotte Cushman. When the relationship with Cushman foundered, it was Bessie Parkes who attracted her from a circle of women friends in Rome to a new literary career in London.[90] Mary Merryweather, Quaker and philanthropic worker, was equally of great importance to her. Since 1847 Mary Merryweather, recorded as a 'moral missionary' in the 1851 census, had worked for Ellen and Samuel Courtauld among the women and men of the Halstead silk mills in Essex. From Mary Merryweather Bessie Parkes learned about the possibilities of philanthropy and 'sanitary improvement' in an industrial setting. In 1856 she profoundly annoyed the Courtauld family by publicly criticizing their mills in the *Daily News*, contrasting their failings to the successes of the Lowell mills of New Hampshire.[91] With both Hays and Merryweather she enjoyed a period of passionate friendship, which in no way detracted from the political and personal commitments shared with Barbara.

It was Barbara alone who could offer the energy, the conviction, the support, and, especially, the money for a new venture which they shared. On a visit to Edinburgh in October 1856 Bessie Parkes had met Isa Craig, a single woman trying to support herself through poetry and journalism, and together they had noticed a periodical called the *Waverley Journal*, 'published by ladies for the cultivation of the memorable, the progressive and the beautiful'. Bessie, Barbara, and Isa Craig all sent occasional contributions to the periodical, and in January 1857 Bessie and Isa Craig joined the staff of the paper. The new project, developed by Bessie and Barbara together in Algiers, was to exploit this connection with the *Waverley Journal*, to bring it to London and make it into a new kind of paper for women, together with the establishment of a shop in London for the sale of women's books, tracts, and stationery, employing women only, with a club as a co-ordinating centre for women's activities.[92] In April 1857 Bessie Parkes was offered the editorship of the *Waverley Journal*, which she took over on returning to England in June. Barbara made available a considerable sum of money to improve and if necessary purchase the magazine. By August 1857 the first number of the new *Waverley* was out, edited by Bessie, though still under the old ownership. She described it as '*ours* for all practical purposes', though not to be risked for propagandist purposes. She foresaw a 'noble career' for it on women's issues, and wrote to Barbara that she would deal 'unsparingly' with everything connected with 'professional life for women'.[93] Originally devoted to 'the memorable, the progressive and the beautiful', it was now advertised as being a 'Working Woman's Journal' for 'all women who are actively engaged in any labours of brain or hand', paid or philanthropic, artistic or manual. Its intention was to collect material on women's employment and on legal and social reform, while retaining some fiction, poetry, and literary reviews. At the head of her editorial column, Bessie Parkes put a quotation from *Aurora Leigh* which also stands at the head of Barbara Leigh Smith's *Women and Work*:

> The honest, earnest man must stand and work;
> The Woman also, otherwise she drops
> At once below the dignity of man,
> Accepting serfdom.[94]

A new office for the *Waverley Journal* was established at 14A Princes Street, off Cavendish Square, and Isa Craig came from Edinburgh to London to help in the work. So too did Bessie's friend, Matilda Hays, brought from Rome. The paper's outlook undoubtedly came to foreshadow the *English Woman's Journal*. I have located issues for late 1856 and early 1858 only, though in some cases other contents are clear from correspondence.[95] There are a number of features which reappeared in the later paper – most clearly, an 'Open Council' for correspondents. Broadly it had similar preoccupations: interests in philanthropy, education, employment. Already it was building up regular contributors later to appear in the *Engish Woman's Journal*: didactic fiction by Amelia Edwards and poetry by Matilda Hays.[96] Bessie Parkes reviewed important new work, including Elizabeth Barrett Browning's *Aurora Leigh* and Dinah Mulock Craik's *A Woman's Thoughts about Woman*, and increasingly the paper paid attention to the work of Anna Jameson.[97] Mary Merryweather's *Experiences of Factory Life* and Barbara Leigh Smith's *Women and Work* were both first published in the *Waverley*.[98] But attempts to buy the paper with money from Barbara Leigh Smith failed, and its last issues appeared in January 1858. A part of the extended project remained. Already in 1857, at the small office in Princes Street, a small reading room for ladies was established and had over seventy subscriptions by 1858.[99]

The work of Parkes and Leigh Smith published between 1854 and 1857, occasional and imperfect as it is, owed much to the world of political radicalism; yet it also arose from a very different experience from that of masculine dissent. They desired knowledge and experience, so that the individual woman might achieve her own fulfilment. Their ideas were rooted partly in individualist and liberal language, anticipating future continuing progress, to the 'indefinite perfection of the race'.[100] Yet, just as Barbara Leigh Smith had wished for Mill to write a philosophy of moral duties to complement that of rights, there is also infused into this individualistic world some sense of duty, of social responsibility, which seems to spring from a different moral perspective.

For Bessie Parkes, women above all needed access to the *knowledge* possessed by men of their class and kind, to whom women now stood in the same relationship that once did 'democracy towards the upper classes'. Individual fulfilment in a world of civil and religous liberty for women and men required the fullest possible training of women's faculties, both mental and physical. Her pamphlet *Remarks on the Education of Girls* was not narrowly focused on educational issues but directed against the prescriptive literature on 'the Whole Duty of Woman', little books which mapped out and confined women's lives. For Parkes, no books should be closed to women and in particular not those which dealt with the relations of the sexes: 'the younger portions of the sexes are kept apart as they might be from the plague or the cholera'. There should be nothing hidden:

> If women be as pure in nature as they are invariably represented, they will act on pollution like chloride of lime. But there must be no concealment; they must learn to affix the right names to things: they must know what is going on around them; they must read.[101]

They must read even the works of such as George Sand. Timidity and ignorance were not purity. The impact of the argument was considerable, and the name of George Sand invoked by an unmarried woman as a provocation, for which she received a public 'flagellation', as Joseph Parkes referred to it, from reviewers.[102]

In her pamphlet *Women and Work*, first published in the *Waverley Journal*, Barbara Leigh Smith argued that marriage and love should not be seen as a profession, an end in itself: dependence on men for support lowered women's dignity 'and tends to prostitution whether legal or in the streets'. Love would come more easily when women mixed more naturally with men. She related the sexual and financial structures of marriage in a way which could profoundly disturb readers, including reviewers and the Parkes parents. Joseph Parkes criticized her coarseness of language and frank treatment of subjects not properly to be discussed by young unmarried women. Elizabeth Parkes wrote that she did not believe 'the sexual side of the question' was a matter for single women to write upon.[103]

With a desire for knowledge of forbidden matters went the case for physical freedom, an ending of the restraints which crippled women's bodies, as their minds were confined. Bessie Parkes invoked the writings of Mary Wollstonecraft and Elizabeth Blackwell, in her *Remarks* and in the *Waverley Journal*. She called for women to take exercise, to develop their bodies to be as tall, as strong, and as capable of exertion as possible. Incidentally, she criticized the 'peculiar physical ideal of womanhood' which the Pre-Raphaelites were popularizing as 'skinny and ill-expanded corporeal frames'; though their faces were 'thoughtful and refined', they hardly looked strong enough to undertake even domestic duties.[104]

As important in understanding the context of their own lives was an understanding of the science of social and political economy for young women: it was more important in itself for women who were increasingly expected to undertake the detailed relief for social evils; it was well adapted for training the mind in the necessary powers of analysis and judgement; above all, it would equally give women a far more intelligent interest in the condition of their own sex, perhaps 'a consideration of the laws under which they as wives and mothers will one day in all probability live' – and so perhaps promote their reform. Such demands reflected their own interests, yet also the importance of such themes in the politics of their own middle-class families. In the *English Woman's Journal* Bessie was later to call for an understanding of the 'political economy' of marriage in a way which drew together these strands of hidden knowledge.[105]

These elements of education for Parkes and for Leigh Smith were all to contribute to the case for women's individual responsibility and judgement, as a means to fulfilment. For them, a family life which constrained women into beings incapable of any general views, and prevented young women from any acquaintance with the opposite sex, mistook the function of the family. For Parkes, the family was rather 'an aggregate of independent interests' which found within it sympathy and help.[106] Barbara Leigh Smith's view was similar, as her defence of divorce reform suggests. Neither in their work at this period drew rigid boundaries between work and marriage. Their demands were for occupation and employment, as a means to individual fulfilment, for 'WORK ... the great beautifier'. Barbara Leigh Smith pointed out the necessity of training young women, who might work before marriage, and who might if poor need to work after marriage:

Women want work both for the health of their minds and bodies. They want it often because they must eat and because they have children and others dependent upon them – *for all the reasons that men want work*. They are placed at a great disadvantage in the market of work because they are not skilled labourers, and are therefore badly paid. They rarely have any training. It is the duty of fathers and mothers to give their daughters this training.

Indeed, a young woman might choose to work to enhance her marriage, for all experience proved the beneficial effects of women's independence on married life.[107] Bessie Parkes believed that only time and education would allow women to find the work for which they were fitted and for which they should have the fullest liberty of decision. Both women shared the view that certain kinds of work were likely to be more suitable for women, and neither rejected women's domestic orientation. Parkes discussed women's participation in family businesses, art, medicine, philanthropy, and teaching at all levels. Leigh Smith suggested that much work could be carried on at home, and that women might look for work, even if caring for children. Although she also mentioned the importance of medical and philanthropic work, she equally stressed the importance of being paid for one's labour, whether professional or manual.

Yet Leigh Smith discounted at this time (though not in the future) the probability of women entering the masculine spheres of politics, army, and law, for 'women will rather prefer those nobler works which have in them something congenial to their moral natures'. They shared a sense that women would always be likely to express a 'different point of view ... from its [the sex's] maternal relations and the peculiar susceptibility always attributed to women'.[108] Yet that difference could bring with it a much wider responsibility to their sex. Bessie Parkes laid more stress on philanthropy, paid or unpaid, as a means to fulfilment, and on the need for social reform, especially in relation to the squalor and prostitution of large cities. She was greatly interested in Anna Jameson's writing on sisterhoods, Catholic and Protestant.[109] There were, of course, significant differences between the two women, which were to become more marked in later years: by 1858 Bessie was already sympathetic to the Catholic faith to which she was to be formally converted in 1864, perhaps partly drawn by the solutions which it offered to 'active, well-ordered charity'; Barbara never shared that sympathy.

There is a tension which seems to me to run through much of the nineteenth-century middle-class women's movement, between the sharing of liberal ideals and that identification with responsibility to one's sex, which philanthropic work of a certain kind, denounced by John Stuart Mill as a 'sentimental priesthood', could represent. The growing commitment of both Barbara and Bessie to changing the situation of women in their society throughout these years was expressed simultaneously with a desire – often ingenuous – to combat 'the misery in the world & its ignorance', to question dual moral standards. Neither woman thought the question of the suffrage of primary importance in these years. Bessie wrote to Barbara in the first year of the *English Woman's Journal* that she believed there was no 'abstract public for divorce and the suffrage' and that she aimed slowly to change public opinion rather 'than to smash my head & your money against a brick wall'.[110]

Hopes and energies were still high in 1857: the failure of the *Waverley* was followed in February 1858 by the founding of the *English Woman's Journal* edited by Bessie and financed by Barbara. The new *Journal* was to succeed, if only briefly, in drawing together a small but effective group of committed women with wide-ranging interests, as Bessie had hoped throughout the 1850s.

The awakening of self-consciousness and of different kinds of feminist activity cannot be understood by reference to the public record alone: it has to be related to personal histories and to the networks of friendship which underlay the slow growth of that movement. A study of the friendship between Bessie Parkes and Barbara Leigh Smith offers one perspective on a much wider pattern, and undoubtedly confirms the view expressed by Lilian Faderman that close and 'romantic' bonds between women could serve both as powerful emotional support and as inspiration to political activity in a hostile environment. There were complex differences, however, between the two women. No reader of Bessie Parkes's correspondence can be unaware of the centrality of female friendship to her life and political work. From the many, overlapping, circles of female friends described here, to her later career as editor of the *English Woman's Journal*, as a convert to Roman Catholicism in 1864, and after marriage, in 1867, as a mother, her world was supported by the friendships and the values of that separate female sphere. Even in the period discussed here it is clear that for Barbara Leigh Smith such a sphere, though supportive and inspiring, was not enough, in personal or political terms. She was to look for models of political action, not only to those 'independent communities' of women which Martha Vicinus has described but to the voluntaristic political associations of mid-nineteenth-century England, to a powerful liberal culture which took John Stuart Mill as its mentor. The differences between them perhaps go some way towards explaining – though not in simple terms – the contrast in their later careers. After her conversion in 1864, Bessie Parkes increasingly withdrew from political activity, while Barbara

Leigh Smith never ceased to be involved in a wide variety of feminist causes. Nevertheless, the relationship between these two in the years from 1846 to 1858, had spanned a critical period in the emergence of a women's movement in England.

NOTES

I should like to thank the C. and J. B. Morrell Trust for financial assistance, and Kate Perry for all her help on the Girton College archives.

Abbreviations: PPG = Parkes Papers, Girton College; BRP = Bessie Rayner Parkes; BLS = Barbara Leigh Smith (Bodichon).

1   BRP [Poem], PPG, vol. V/1.
2   Carroll Smith-Rosenberg, 'The female world of love and ritual: relations between women in nineteenth century America', in *Disorderly Conduct: Visions of Gender in Victorian America*, New York and Oxford, OUP, 1985; Lilian Faderman, *Surpassing the Love of Men: Romantic Friendship and Love between Women from the Renaissance to the Present*, London, Women's Press, 1985; William R. Taylor and Christopher Lasch, ' "Two kindred spirits": sorority and family in New England 1839–1846', *New England Quarterly*, 36, 1963, 25–41; Martha Vicinus, *Independent Women: Work and Community for Single Women 1850–1920*, London, Virago, 1985; Liz Stanley, *Feminism and Friendship: Two Essays on Olive Schreiner*, Studies in Sexual Politics, 8, Manchester, University of Manchester.
3   For recent work, see: Lee Holcombe, *Victorian Ladies at Work: Middle Class Working Women in England and Wales, 1850–1914*, Newton Abbot, David & Charles, 1973, ch. 1, and *Wives and Property: Reform of the Married Women's Property Law in Nineteenth Century England*, Oxford, Basil Blackwell, 1983; Sheila Herstein, *A Mid-Victorian Feminist, Barbara Leigh Smith Bodichon*, New Haven, Conn., and London, Yale University Press, 1985; Jacquie Matthews, 'Barbara Bodichon: integrity in diversity (1827–91)', in Dale Spender (ed.), *Feminist Theorists: Three Centuries of Women's Intellectual Traditions*, London, Women's Press, 1983; Kathleen E. McCrone, 'The National Association for the promotion of Social Science, and the Advancement of Victorian Women', *Atlantis* (Canada), 8, 1982, 44–66. There is an excellent unpublished thesis by Diane Mary Chase Worzala, 'The Langham Place Circle: the beginnings of the organized women's movement in England, 1854–71', PhD, University of Wisconsin–Madison, 1982.
    On the *English Woman's Journal*, see: Pauline A. Nestor, 'A new departure in women's publishing: the *English Woman's Journal* and *The Victoria Magazine*', *Victorian Periodicals Review*, 15, 1982, 93–106; Jane Rendall, ' "A moral engine": feminism, liberalism and the *English Woman's Journal*', in Jane Rendall (ed.), *Equal or Different: Women's*

Politics 1800–1914, Oxford, Basil Blackwell, 1987.

4   See Herstein, op. cit., ch. 1, and, for the family background, R. W.
    Davis, *Dissent in Politics, 1780–1830: The Political Life of William Smith,
    MP*, London, Epworth Press, 1971.

5   MS by BRP 'The Parkes of Warwick', PPG, vol. I/10; Joseph Parkes to
    BRP, n.d., PPG, vol. II/85.

6   William Thomas, *The Philosophic Radicals; Nine Studies in Theory and
    Practice, 1817–41*, Oxford, OUP, 1979, ch. 6; there is also Jessie Buckley,
    Joseph Parkes of Birmingham, London, Methuen, 1926.

7   Barbara Isabella Buchanan, *Buchanan Family Records*, Capetown,
    Townsend, 1923, 18–27; typescript MS 'Recollections of Julia Smith',
    58–60, William Smith Papers, Add. MSS 7621, Box 2, Cambridge
    University Library.

8   Marie Belloc Lowndes, '*I Too have Lived in Arcadia': A Record of Love and of
    Childhood*, London, Macmillan, 1941, 43.

9   References to BRP's schooling are taken from her MSS recollections,
    'My childhood, my schooldays', signed 2 August 1849, PPG vol. I/1.

10 For instance, BRP to BLS, n.d. [1848] and 30 May 1850, PPG vol. V/48
    and 142.

11 BRP to Samuel Blackwell, n.d., PPG, vol. IX/12.

12 Belloc Lowndes, op. cit., 40.

13 Joseph Parkes to BRP, 5 Sept. 1852, 5 Nov. 1853, and 27 Mar. 1856,
    PPG, vol. II/47, 51, 55.

14 Joseph Parkes to BRP, 24 Sept. 1858, PPG, vol. II/64.

15 Typescript MS, 23 pp., by Marie Belloc Lowndes, 'Before she found
    Arcadia', PPG, appendix A/32/11–12.

16 BRP's diary for Aug.–Dec. 1849 (incomplete), entries for 4–6 Oct.
    1849, PPG, vol. I/4/8–9.

17 ibid., 13–23 Nov. 1849, PPG, vol. I/4/13–14.

18 ibid., 13 Dec. 1849, PPG, vol. I/4/16; BRP to BLS, n.d. [1850], PPG,
    vol. V/47.

19 BRP's diary, 1 Nov. 1849, PPG, vol. I/4/11.

20 ibid, entries for 7 and 24 Oct. 1849, PPG, vol. I/4/9–10.

21 BRP to BLS, 30 April 1848 and 30 May 1849, PPG, vol. V/23 and 30.

22 BRP to BLS, 27 Mar., 15 Apr. and 4 June 1852, PPG, vol. V/60b, 62,
    and 63.

23 BRP to BLS, 11 Sept. 1851, PPG, vol. V/57; draft letter from BLS to
    Lucy Field, n.d., PPG, vol. X/45.

24 BRP to BLS, 3 Aug. 1849, PPG, vol. V/34.

25 BRP to BLS, n.d [1852], PPG, vol. V/145.

26 BRP's entry in diary, 24 Nov. 1849, PPG, vol. I/4/15; BRP to R. Fane, 5
    and 28 Nov. 1849, PPG, vol. IX/109 and 110.

27 BRP to Joseph Parkes, 25 Nov. and 8 Dec. 1849, PPG, vol. II/34 and
    36; Joseph Parkes to BRP, n.d. [Nov. 1849], PPG, vol. II/45.

28 BRP to Samuel Blackwell, 28 July 1854, PPG, vol. IX/6.

29 BRP to Samuel Blackwell, n.d., PPG, vol. IX/15.

30 'Dear I am not a bit tired of JC if only you are happy in him', typescript

copy of letter from BRP to BLS, 29 Aug. 1855, PPG, vol. V/74.
Margaret Crompton also quotes from an unlocated letter from BRP in her MS biography 'Prelude to Arcadia: the early life and friendships of Bessie Rayner Parkes', 'Dear only be happy in JC and I shall be too thankful. I blame myself much for all I allowed myself to say, tho' on the outside commonsense view it seemed right. But I have done with common sense for ever more', PPG, appendix A/70/130.

31   Quoted in Margaret Crompton, 'Prelude to Arcadia', PPG, appendix A/70/130. I have not located the original of this letter.
32   BRP to BLS, n.d [1847], PPG, vol. V/2 and 3.
33   BRP to BLS, 30 May 1850, PPG, vol. V/48.
34   BRP to BLS, n.d. [1848], PPG, Vol. V/142.
35   BRP to Mary Swainson, 23 June 1848, PPG, vol. III/17; BRP to Joseph Parkes, 21 Feb. 1857, PPG, vol. II/58.
36   BLS, 'To Bessie', PPG, vol. V/161.
37   Entry in BRP's diary, 3 Nov. 1849, PPG, vol. I/4/12.
38   BRP to BLS, 29 July 1847, PPG, vol. V/11.
39   BRP to Elizabeth Parkes, 16 Oct. 1851, PPG, vol. II/3; BRP to BLS, 27 May, 20 Nov., and 24 Dec. 1847, 19 Nov. 1848, PPG, vol. V/9, 16, 18, and 28; Margaret Howitt (ed.), *Mary Howitt: An Autobiography*, 2 vols., London, 1889, vol. 2, 84–5.
40   Entry in BRP's diary, 1 Nov. 1849, PPG, vol. I/4/11.
41   BRP to BLS, n.d. [Jan. 1848] and 22 June 1850, PPG, vol. V/19 and 50.
42   BRP to BLS, 27 May 1847, PPG, vol. V/8; E. P. Hurlbut, *Essays on Human Rights and their Political Guarantees*, with a preface and notes by George Combe, Edinburgh, 1847.
43   Entries in BRP's diary, 3 and 4 Nov. and 13 Dec. 1849, PPG, vol. I/4/12 and 16.
44   BLS, 'Abstract of Mill's principles of political economy', Bodichon Papers, Box 3, Girton College.
45   BLS to BRP, n.d., PPG, vol. V/165.
46   BRP to BLS, 29 July 1847, PPG, vol. V/11.
47   BRP to BLS, 24 Aug. 1849, 22 June 1850, and 15 April 1852, PPG, vol. V/35, 50, and 62.
48   BRP to BLS [1848], PPG, vol. V/27.
49   BRP to Mary Swainson, 5 June 1851, PPG, vol. III/23; BRP to BLS, 21 Apr., 16 and 24 Dec. 1847, PPG, vol. V/8, 17, and 18.
50   BRP to BLS, June 1849, PPG, vol. V/31.
51   BRP to BLS, 30 Mar. 1848 and 14 Nov. 1851, PPG, vol. V/21 and 58. 'Bernard', 'Eyes and no eyes', *Hastings and St Leonard's News*, 27 Apr. 1849, refers to attendance at a lecture of Elihu Barrett.
52   BRP to BLS, 25 Nov. 1851 and 27 Mar. 1852, PPG, vol. V/59 and 60b; BRP to Joseph Parkes, 11 Nov. 1851, PPG, vol II/39; Howitt (ed.), op. cit., vol. 2, 78–81.
53   BRP to Mary Swainson, 2 Jan. 1852, PPG, vol. III/25.
54   Entry in BRP's diary, 18 Sept. 1849, PPG, vol. I/4/7.
55   BLS to BRP, n.d., PPG, vol. V/165.

56   BRP to BLS, 13 Feb. 1847, PPG, vol. V/6.
57   BRP to BLS, 30 May 1849, PPG, vol. V/30.
58   BRP to BLS, 22 and 27 May 1847, 23 May, 6 June, and undated letter [1848], PPG, vol. V/9, 24, 25, 26, 27 (and many other references); J. T. Feeny to BRP, 11 Oct. [1847?], PPG, vol. IX/23.
59   BRP to BLS, 3 June 1848, PPG, vol. V/26; entry in BRP's diary, 13 Nov. 1849, PPG, vol. I/4/13; *Hastings and St Leonards News*, 14 July 1848; *Birmingham Journal*, 3 June 1848.
60   'RAB', 'Some ways of doing good at little cost', *Birmingham Journal*, 13 May 1848.
61   *Hastings and St Leonards News*, 1 Sept. 1848.
62   ibid., 28 July and 25 Aug. 1848.
63   Most of the poems mentioned in this paragraph first appear, dated, in a bound volume of MS poems, PPG, vol. I/26. 'The Lady Abbess', 19 Dec. 1847, was then partially reprinted in the *Hastings and St Leonards News*, 22 June 1849; 'Riding Song', 19 Oct. 1847, was reprinted in the *Hastings and St Leonards News*, and in her *Poems*, London, 1852.
64   'City Scenes' was written as 'Hampstead Heath', 2 Oct. 1847, PPG, vol. I/26, and was reprinted first as 'London from Hampstead Heath' and 'City Scenes', *Hastings and St Leonards News*, 7 July 1848, 27 July, and 10 Aug. 1849, and the first part only, amended and excluding the comparison of the two young women, as 'London from Hampstead Heath', in her *Poems*, 1852. 'Two Artists' first appears in *Poems*, 1852.
65   'To Birmingham', Dec. 1848, PPG, vol. I/26, appears in *Poems*, 1852.
66   'Progression', *Birmingham Journal*, 22 Apr. 1848, *Hastings and St Leonards News*, 2 June 1848, identified in BRP to BLS, 23 May 1848, PPG, vol. V/25; 'Poets of 1848', *Birmingham Journal*, 8 Apr. 1848, identified in BRP to BLS, 29 Apr. 1848, PPG, vol. V/22. This could be compared with her 'Rome in 1849' and 'England and Hungary in 1849', printed in *Poems*, 1852.
67   BLS to BRP, n.d. [1848], PPG, vol. V/167; 'No Thoroughfare', first written 21 Sept. 1848, PPG, vol. I/26, and reprinted *Hastings and St Leonards News*, 29 Sept. 1848.
68   'My Old House', *Poems*, 1852.
69   BRP, 'The Nightingale Testimonial', letters to the editor of the *Birmingham Journal*, 5 and 11 Sept. 1855, newspaper cuttings, PPG, vol. XI/11–12; BRP to G. J. Holyoake, 30 Jan. 1857, copies from Holyoake Papers, Manchester, in Girton College Library; Elizabeth Parkes to BRP, 30 Jan. 1857, PPG, vol. II/27.
70   BRP to BLS [1849], PPG, vol. V/133.
71   BRP's MS diary, in bound unpaginated volume, intermittent entries from 21 July 1852 to 31 Dec. 1854, entry for 13 Nov. 1852, PPG, unsorted documents.
72   BRP, *Summer Sketches and Other Poems*, London, 1854, reprinted in the edition used here, Elizabeth Rayner Parkes, *Poems*, London, 1855, 164–5.
73   Bound MS volume, BRP, 'Abstract of sermons, lectures, etc.', fo. 47,

BLS, 'A Parable', noted 'Sent to me July 7th 1849', PPG, unsorted documents.

74 BRP, *Summer Sketches*, in *Poems*, 1855, 177.

75 Anna-Mary Howitt, *An Art Student in Munich*, London, 1853. On BLS's artistic career, see John Crabbe, 'An artist divided', *Apollo*, 113, May 1981, 311–13, and Pamela Gerrish Nunn (ed.), *Canvassing: Recollections by Six Victorian Artists*, London, Camden Press, 1986, 1–25, 40–44.

76 Elizabeth Blackwell, *Pioneer Work for Women*, London, 1895, Everyman edition, London, Dent, 1914, 142–3 and 152. There are frequent references to Elizabeth Blackwell in the correspondence between BRP and BLS. See also BRP's poem 'To E.B at New York', in *Poems*, 1852.

77 Herstein, op. cit., 100; Jan Marsh, *Pre-Raphaelite Sisterhood*, London, Quartet, 1985, 48–51.

78 BRP to BLS, 15 Sept. 1851, 'I was at Coventry last week at Mr C. Bray's and saw Miss Hennell . . . and a very clever Miss Evans whom we must know well. She will be at the Chapmans all this winter', PPG, vol. V/57; Gordon S. Haight, *George Eliot: A Biography*, Oxford, OUP, 1968, 53, 57, 89, 102–6. For the reaction of the Parkes parents to the elopement, see Elizabeth Parkes to BRP, 22 and 23 Sept. 1854, PPG, vol. II/25 and 26; Joseph Parkes to BRP, 5 Oct. and n.d 1854, PPG, vol. II/52 and 53; BRP to BLS [1863], PPG, vol. V/124. An interesting recent discussion of the novelist's relationship to the early women's movement is found in Gillian Beer, *George Eliot*, Brighton, Harvester, 1986, ch. 6.

79 BRP to BLS, 16 and 24 Dec. 1847, PPG, vol. V/17 and 18.

80 Entry in BRP's diary, 9 Nov. 1849, PPG, vol. I/4/11.

81 BRP to BLS [Feb. 1851], PPG, vol. V/55.

82 BRP to SB, n.d., copied in Marie Belloc Lowndes's MS biography of BRP, 'Before she found Arcadia', PPG, appendix B, 150; Herstein, op. cit., 59–64; Elizabeth Malleson, 'Portrait of a school', *Journal of Education*, 18, Sept. 1886, 357–9.

83 Entry for 18 June and 22 July in BRP's MS diary, bound unpaginated vol., PPG, unsorted documents.

84 BRP to BLS, 16 Dec. 1849, PPG, vol. V/41; Annual Reports of the London Domestic Mission Society, Dr Williams Library, London.

85 BRP to SB, n.d., PPG, vol. IX/16.

86 Anna Jameson to BRP, 10 Dec. [n.y.], PPG, vol. VI/40: 'You are a trio of dear girls – & I love you all – & am well content to accept the *maternal* honours which dear Barbara has laid upon me'.

87 BRP to BLS, 27 Dec. 1855, PPG, vol. V/79; Anna Jameson to BRP, n.d. [1856], PPG, vol. VI/14.

88 BRP to BLS, 22 Dec. and [Dec.] 1855, 28 Mar. and 24 July 1856, PPG, vol. V/79–81, 83.

89 BRP to BLS, 14 May 1857, PPG, vol. V/84; Herstein, op. cit., 111–12.

90 Little is known of Matilda Hays. See the references in Patricia Thomson, *George Sand and the Victorians*, London, Macmillan, 1977; *The Letters of George Eliot*, ed. Gordon S. Haight, 6 vols, Oxford, OUP, 1954,

vol. 2, 38; Joseph Leach, *Bright Particular Star: The Life and Times of Charlotte Cushman*, New Haven, Conn., and London, Yale University Press, 1970; Faderman, op. cit., 220–5.

91   For the work of Mary Merryweather, I am indebted to Judy Lown, 'Gender and class during industrialisation: a study of the Halstead silk industry in Essex', PhD, University of Essex, 1984; BRP, 'The home at Halstead', *Daily News*, 21 Oct. 1856; *Courtauld Family Letters 1782–1900*, 8 vols, printed for private circulation, Cambridge, 1916, vol. 8, 3, 777–3, 783; Mary Merryweather, *Experience of Factory Life: Being a Record of Fourteen Years at Mr Courtauld's Silk Mill at Halstead in Essex*, 3rd edn, much enlarged with a preface by Bessie Rayner Parkes, London, 1862.

92   BRP, 'A review of the last six years', *English Woman's Journal*, 12, Feb. 1864, 363–5; *Waverley Journal*, 12, 10 Jan. 1857, notes that Bessie Rayner Parkes and 'Isa' will be joining the staff; BRP to BLS, 19 May 1857, PPG, vol. V/85; BRP to Mary Merryweather, 26 Jan. 1857, PPG, vol. VI/72.

93   BRP to BLS, 14 May 1857, PPG, vol. V/84.

94   Charles Mitchell, *The Newspaper Press Directory . . . for the Year 1858*, London, 1858, 130. The quotation is found in the *Waverley Journal*, 1 and 15 Jan. 1858, and in Barbara Bodichon, *Woman and Work*, London, 1857; it is taken from Elizabeth Barrett Browning, *Aurora Leigh*, 1857, ed. Cora Kaplan, London, Women's Press, 1978, 342.

95   I have located the *Waverley Journal* only for the issues 9 Aug. 1856 to 10 Jan. 1857 (in Glasgow University Library), and 1–15 Jan. 1858 (British Newspaper Library, Colindale).

96   Amelia B. Edwards, 'The conjuror's table', *Waverley Journal*, 4 and 5, 1 and 15 Jan. 1858; Matilda Hays, 'Stanzas', *Waverley Journal*, 1 Jan. 1858.

97   The following items of interest in the *Waverley Journal* have been tentatively identified as by BRP, from internal evidence or from correspondence: review of Aurora Leigh, *Waverley Journal*, 10, 13 Dec. 1856; review of Anna Jameson's *Communion of Labour*, 12, 10 January 1857; review of Dinah Mulock Craik's *A Woman's Thoughts about Woman*, 1857, 5, 15 Jan. 1858. Anna Jameson, 'Girls' schools and the training of working women', was reprinted on 15 Jan. 1858.

98   Barbara Leigh Smith contributed 'The laws of property and earnings of married women', *Waverley Journal*, 6, 18 Oct. 1856, and her articles can be identified as *Women and Work* from Joseph Parkes to BRP, 12 Feb. 1857, PPG, vol. II/57; *Experiences of Factory Life* by M.M. reprinted from the *Waverley*, 'a working woman's journal', London, 1857.

99   BRP, 'The ladies' reading room', 14 Jan. 1860, unidentified newspaper cutting, PPG, vol. XI/33.

100 BRP, *Remarks on the Education of Girls, with Reference to the Social, Legal and Industrial Position of Women in the Present Day*, 3rd edn, London, 1856, 5.

101 ibid., 14.

102 William Caldwell Roscoe, 'Woman', *National Review*, 7, Oct. 1858, 333–61, reviews and specifically mocks Bessie Rayner Parkes's *Remarks* as 'not only nonsense, but nonsense of a very unpleasant sort . . . the

idea of teaching young girls to study the sexual relations with these works [Chaucer, Dryden, Johnson, Fielding, Sand] for text-books is excusable only under the assumption that the lady is a theorist who has not realized the working of her vague ideas'. Joseph Parkes to BRP, 6 Oct. 1858, wrote angrily to his daughter, 'In 1856 you were about as qualified to write publicly on the Education of Girls as an unborn female baby; either by experience or acquired wisdom. And Barbara's exaggerations were certain to be reduced by the experienced and older males to their proper Press dimensions – your El Dorado', PPG, vol. II/64. The same points are made in the correspondence between the Courtauld family, on Parkes's comments on purity, *Courtauld Family Letters*, vol. 8, 3,838–3,841.

103   BLS, *Women and Work*, 9–13; Joseph Parkes to BRP, 12 Feb. 1857, PPG, vol. II/57–8; Elizabeth Parkes to BRP, 13 Feb. 1857, PPG, vol. II/28.

104   BRP, *Remarks*, 8–12; 'Physical training of females', *Waverley Journal*, 7, 1 Nov. 1856.

105   BRP, *Remarks*, 14–17; BRP, 'Domestic life', *English Woman's Journal*, 2, Oct. 1858, 73–82.

106   BRP, *Remarks*, 18.

107   BLS, *Women and Work*, 51.

108   BLS, *Women and Work*, 51; BRP, *Remarks*, 7.

109   BRP, review of Anna Jameson's *Communion of Labour*, *Waverley Journal*, 12, 10 Jan. 1857; BRP to unknown correspondent, PPG, vol. X/33.

110   BLS to BRP, n.d. [1848/9], and BRP to BLS, 5 Jan. 1858 [1859], PPG, vol. V/168 and 86.

Chapter Five

THE MARRIAGE OF TRUE MINDS: THE IDEAL OF MARRIAGE IN THE PHILOSOPHY OF JOHN STUART MILL

SUSAN MENDUS

True to my Welsh Baptist upbringing, I begin with the text – taken from 'the crudest and most illogical' work which the Victorian age produced; a work that rests upon 'an unsound view of history, an unsound view of morals, and a grotesquely distorted view of facts'; a work whose 'practical application would be as injurious as its theory is false'; a work 'unpleasant in the direction of indecorum'; a work, finally, of 'rank moral and social anarchy'.[1] The work is John Stuart Mill's *The Subjection of Women*, and the text is this:

> what marriage may be in the case of two persons of cultivated faculties, identical in opinions and purposes, between whom there exists that best kind of equality, similarity of powers and capacities with reciprocal superiority in them – so that each can enjoy the luxury of looking up to the other, and can have alternately the pleasure of leading and of being led in the path of development – I will not attempt to describe. To those who can conceive it, there is no need; to those who cannot, it would appear the dream of an enthusiast. But I maintain, with the profoundest conviction, that this, and this only, is the ideal of marriage, and that all opinions, customs and institutions which favour any other notion of it, or turn the conceptions and aspirations connected with it into any other direction, by whatever pretences they may be coloured, are relics of primitive barbarism.[2]

Resounding as anything ever uttered from a Welsh pulpit, this is Mill's positive thesis in *The Subjection of Women*: that marriage, properly understood, is the marriage of minds and not of flesh. Throughout the book his main task is a negative one – to deny the prevailing view of women as naturally unequal and inferior to men –

171

and it is this attempt to argue against the legal inequality of women which generated such high emotion in Mill's own day and which accounts for the greater part of modern interest in the book. In this paper I shall not add to the growing literature on Mill's views on legal inequality between the sexes; it is clear what Mill is *against*. He is against the requirement, embodied in Victorian law, that women renounce independence on marriage and submit to the domination of the husband. The scope and extent of women's dependence on their husbands in nineteenth-century Britain cannot easily be exaggerated. Legally, women did not count as persons and were not possessors of property. In her book, *Wives and Property*, Lee Holcombe tells how Millicent Garrett Fawcett had her purse snatched by a young thief in London. When she appeared to testify against him, she heard the youth charged with 'stealing from the person of Millicent Fawcett a purse containing £1 18s. 6d., the property of Henry Fawcett.' Long afterwards she recalled, 'I felt as if I had been charged with theft myself'.[3] The legal requirements governing the situation of married women – their inability to possess property, to vote, to obtain divorce except in the most extreme cases – served to make a woman, in Mill's words, 'the bond-servant' of her husband. She became his slave, except that by contrast with other slaves, 'no amount of ill-usage, without adultery superadded, will free her from her tormentor'.[4] Mill's impassioned invective against Victorian marriage and property laws as they relate to women is important and timely, but it often serves to disguise the fact that *The Subjection of Women* also suggests a positive thesis of what marriage ideally should be. What I wish to do here is to concentrate on this positive thesis. I shall suggest that *The Subjection of Women* is not only a political, legal, and social tract, but also a profoundly *moral* one, central to which are evaluative theses about human nature and the life worth living. My argument will be that Mill is not only the rejecter of Victorian images of women, he is also the creator of an alternative image, and I shall argue that the image he creates is a deeply depressing and distorted one. In brief, my claim will be that Mill employs his text both to object to the legal subordination of women in nineteenth-century Britain, and also to display his own deep-rooted prejudices on the subject of sexuality.

The status of the text

In her highly influential article, 'Mill and the subjection of women', Julia Annas remarks on the fact that philosophical commentaries tend to give Mill's essay rather short measure. She attributes this to the belief that the essay is almost exclusively concerned with women's legal disabilities in Victorian Britain. Taking such commentators to task, Annas points out that legal disabilities reflect social and economic inequalities, and she argues that

> while today there are few ways in which women are under legal disabilities compared with men (though it would be a mistake to think there are none) women are still subject to economic and social discrimination in a variety of ways, and it is extraordinary to think that Mill's essay no longer contains anything interesting or controversial just because there have been a few changes in the law.[5]

This is an important and much-neglected point, but it disguises a curious feature shared both by Annas's article and by the works of the commentators she criticizes: throughout there is an insistence on treating the essay as *sui generis*, relevant no doubt to Mill's activities as a politician and social reformer, but largely unconnected to the wider concerns of his moral philosophy. The impression is of a man with a substantive political belief (that existing sexual inequalities were unjustifiable) and in search of an argument to support that belief.

There is, however, no suggestion that Mill's positive thesis about marriage coheres with the moral doctrines he expounds elsewhere. Thus Annas concludes her piece with the claim that Mill, 'anxious to do justice to all sides of a question he sees to be complex and important, and unwilling to commit himself definitively to one simple line of thought, qualifies an originally bold and straightforward theory to the point of inconsistency.'[6] What is implied here is that Mill simply chose the wrong arguments, but that he could have chosen the right ones. It seems to me, however, that Mill can do no other than he does: if his account is confused and contradictory, then that verdict will have consequences for the whole of his philosophy, and it is simply untrue that he might have got it right if only he had thought more carefully. Where Annas insists that *The Subjection of Women* is not merely an account of legal disabilities, but a piece of social philosophy, I want to insist that it is not merely a piece of social philosophy, but a moral text which coheres in a disturbing manner with Mill's other moral writings. If the argument against legal inequality is central to his political thought, the argument for the ideal of marriage as a marriage of true minds is central to his moral thought and is the inevitable consequence of pursuing that thought to its logical conclusion.

The ideal of marriage in Mill's philosophy

The first move is to establish exactly what Mill's ideal of marriage is. The ideal is stated explicitly in the passage quoted from chapter 4 of *The Subjection of Women*, and what I wish to draw attention to in that passage are the references to the 'path of development' and 'reciprocal superiority'. These terms obviously express Mill's hostility to the Victorian conception of marriage as a partnership based on inequality. However, it seems to me that this is not its only, nor its most significant, import: in addition to objecting to the Victorian requirement that, on marrying, the woman give up her independence and submit to the domination of her husband, Mill is also here proposing an alternative, moral ideal according to which marriage is a route to moral perfection. In the passage immediately following the one quoted at the beginning of the paper, Mill declares that justice under law is required in the interests of moral regeneration. The reason for insisting on legal equality is that this is a necessary precondition of moral improvement, and it is the possibility of moral improvement which really interests Mill. Central to his vision are two notions, explicit in the passage quoted earlier and, I shall argue, fundamental to his moral thought: these are the notions of perfectibility and of complementarity.

PERFECTIBILITY

The notion of perfectibility, and its role in Mill's philosophical thought, may be approached via a discussion of two related problems – the problem of two Mills, and the problem of the interpretation of Mill's account of freedom. Each of these has a bearing on Mill's concept of perfectibility, and each indicates how central that concept is to his moral philosophy. I begin, therefore, with the problem of two Mills.

The problem of two Mills

The story of Mill's early life and education, his rigorous drilling in Greek, Latin, logic, and history, is well known and does not need repeating here: Mill himself says, 'I never was a boy, never played at cricket: it is better to let nature have her way.'[7] Some have suggested that nature did, after all, have her way, for when he was in his early twenties Mill suffered a 'mental crisis', as a result of which he says: 'I found the fabric of my old and taught opinions giving way in many places, and I never allowed it to fall to pieces, but was incessantly occupied in weaving it anew.'[8]

Here are the seeds of the problem of two Mills. To what extent may the later writings be construed as a rejection of his early, Benthamite utilitarian teaching, and to what extent may they be viewed merely as revisions and refinements of the early works? Mill himself appears to be in no doubt. His references to weaving anew the old fabric, and his claim that he never allowed the old to fall to pieces, suggest quite strongly that he saw himself as remoulding Benthamite utilitarianism, but never rejecting it. However, some commentators have denied that this can in fact be done, and they claim that the later writings, particularly those written under the influence of Harriet Taylor, are simply incompatible with the earlier Benthamite doctrines. There are, in other words, two Mills. I shall not here discuss the relative merits of the two Mills thesis, nor shall I spend time counting the number of Mills present in the texts. All that matters for my purposes is that there are, on any account, differences between the earlier and the later doctrines. Mill himself admits as much, and it is, I think, instructive to consider the nature and extent of these differences, since they bear upon the problem of perfectibility which is the immediate topic of concern here.

Three aspects of the distinction between Benthamite utilitarianism and Mill's mature moral and political philosophy are relevant:

1 his explicit objections to Bentham, as given in his essay on Bentham;
2 his distinction between higher and lower pleasures, as stated in *Utilitarianism*;
3 his distinction between animal and human characteristics, described in *A System of Logic*.

In his essay on Bentham, Mill tells us that for Bentham 'man is never recognised . . . as a being capable of pursuing spiritual perfection as an end; of desiring for its own sake the conformity of his own character to his standard of excellence'.[9] Against this, Mill insists that morality consists of two parts – the regulation of outward action, and the individual's own training of himself, his own character, affections, and will. In this latter department, Mill says, Bentham's system is a complete blank. Indeed, he goes further and suggests that even the regulation of outward actions will be imperfect and halting without consideration of excellence of character. Thus he concludes:

> A moralist on Bentham's principles may get as far as this, that he ought not to slay, burn or steal; but what will be his qualifications for regulating the nicer shades of human behaviour, or for laying down even the greater moralities as to those facts of human life which are liable to influence the depths of the character quite independently of any influence on worldly circumstances – such, for instance, as the sexual relations, or those of family in general, or any other social and sympathetic connexions of an intimate kind? The moralities on these questions depend essentially on considerations which Bentham never so much as took into the account; and when he happened to be in the right, it was always, and necessarily, on wrong or insufficient grounds.[10]

The message here is perfectly clear: Bentham's shortcoming lies in his persistent reference only to external actions – to what are basically police matters. On questions of human excellence and of human character, his philosophy is bankrupt. The fact that he simply took desires as brute – to be satisfied wherever possible, but never to be improved, refined, or made more noble – is, according to Mill, the great defect of his moral philosophy. Mill talks of Bentham as a man with only one eye: he saw a certain part of the truth, and is to be commended for that part which he saw. However, this fact should not blind us to the omissions in Bentham's writings, which render his account inadequate. It is important to note here that the areas in which Bentham is held to be particularly culpable are those of sexual relations and the family. What is crucial about these aspects of life is that they are areas where public action is not necessarily or normally in evidence, yet at the same time they are precisely the areas where excellence of character may be found and developed. Here, then, in the essay on Bentham, we find an indication of the differences between the early and the later Mill. Where Benthamite utilitarianism differs from Mill's own favoured version it is in the failure of the former to make reference to that perfectibility of character essential to the latter.

References to the notion of perfectibility are scattered throughout Mill's writings. For example, *Utilitarianism* contains references to a now notorious distinction between higher and lower pleasures: mindful of the criticism that utilitarianism is the philosophy of swine, Mill urges that this criticism is well founded only if we assume that the pleasures of men are indistinguishable from the pleasures of swine. This, he declares, is not so: it is, famously,

> better to be a human being dissatisfied than a pig satisfied; better to be Socrates dissatisfied than a fool satisfied. And if the fool, or the pig, are of a different opinion, it is because they only know their own side of the question. The other party to the comparison knows both sides.[11]

In the passage immediately following the one just quoted, Mill goes on to warn that 'capacity for the nobler feelings is in most natures a very tender plant, easily killed, not only by hostile influences, but by mere want of sustenance.'[12] Here, the teleological implications of Mill's thought are clear: human nature may flourish if properly nurtured, but otherwise will wither away and die. Part of the purpose of moral philosophy – the part almost wholly ignored by Bentham – is to say something about the proper conditions for human flourishing and the development of excellence. We must not suppose that morality consists exclusively in the satisfaction of wants, for wants may be better or worse, higher or lower, and utilitarianism will indeed degenerate into the philosophy of swine if we forget the requirements of perfectibility and the cultivation of excellence. If all this is borne in mind, the question which now arises is 'In what does human excellence consist?' We have seen that Mill is concerned to argue for the importance of moral excellence and the development of nobler feelings. How, then, are we to judge which are the nobler feelings and which the baser?

An indication of the response to this question is provided in *A System of Logic*, where Mill makes two points crucial to the present discussion. First, he claims that man is a natural kind separated from the kind animal by the specific determinants of rationality and having a certain external form. Natural kinds which reflect specific distinctions in this way are, says Mill, 'parted off from one another by an unfathomable chasm, instead of a mere ordinary ditch with a visible bottom'.[13] Of course, man shares characteristics with animals, but in respect of that which makes man mankind, these characteristics

177

(rationality and having a certain external form) are central. The second crucial point which concerns us is Mill's insistence in *A System of Logic* that the sciences of human nature and society are distinguished by the fact that their subject-matter is changeable:

> The circumstances in which mankind are placed, operating according to their own laws and to the laws of human nature, form the characters of the human beings; but the human beings, in their turn, mould and shape the circumstances for themselves and for those who come after them.[14]

Putting these two together, we might expect Mill to argue that human progress and perfectibility will consist in the development of the human (as against the animal) characteristics. Having made the distinction between what is merely animal and what is essentially human, and having urged that the central feature of the science of human nature is that it deals with a pliable subject-matter, Mill is well placed to argue that the perfectibility of character ignored by Bentham consists precisely in fostering and encouraging the human, while minimizing the animal. And this is indeed his claim. In *Principles of Political Economy* he goes so far as to assert that 'Civilisation in every one of its aspects is a struggle against the animal instincts' and that 'society is possible precisely because man is not necessarily a brute'.[15] What, then, are these animal instincts and brutish impulses which must be guarded against if civilization is to advance? Chief among them is the sexual impulse, and time and again we fnd Mill speaking of this as 'brutish', 'swinish', 'lower'. Referring to his relationship with Harriet Taylor, Mill remarks:

> we disdained, as every person not a slave of the animal appetites must do, the abject notion that the strongest and tenderest friendship cannot exist between a man and a woman without a sensual relation, or that any impulses of that lower character cannot be put aside without regard for the feelings of others, or even when only prudence and personal dignity require it.[16]

His references to sexuality as 'lower' and 'animal' are, however, not confined to the rather personal (and understandably defensive) passages in which he discusses his relationship with Mrs Taylor. In a letter to Lord Amberley he declares that the possibility of progress depends upon the reduction of sexuality, and that no great improvement in human life can be looked for so long as 'the animal instinct of sex occupies the absurdly disproportionate place it does therein'.[17] Likewise, in *Principles of Political Economy* he speaks of sex as 'a degrading slavery to a brute instinct' and calls upon the existence of impulses 'superior to mere animal instincts' to ensure that men do not 'propagate like swine'.[18] In all these cases Mill urges that there is a distinction between human and animal characteristics and suggests that man's animality is lower than his humanity, and that his animality can and should be suppressed. It is important to note here that, in urging the suppression of the sexual impulse, Mill is not merely appealing to Benthamite considerations such as that too large a population will flood the market with labour and result in poverty: consequentialist arguments of that sort do not require that sexuality be considered 'lower', or 'swinish', or 'brutish', yet what is central to Mill's case is precisely the claim that the sexually incontinent not only harm others, by flooding the market with labour, but also harm their own characters, much as the drunkard harms his own character quite independently of any consequentialist harm he visits on others.[19]

I began by asking how we can know what, for Mill, constitutes the better, higher, or nobler. The answer is that the distinction between the higher and the lower is premised on a distinction between human and animal characteristics, with sexual impulses and instincts firmly consigned to the latter category. This distinction is set against the background of Mill's objections to Bentham as neglecting considerations of spiritual perfection and self-education. Mill's post-Benthamite moral philosophy may thus be read as an extended argument for self-improvement and the rejection of what is purely animal – in particular, the suppression of all that is sexual or physical. Since the animal characteristics simply are what they are, and are incapable of being refined or developed in any way, it follows that Mill's rejection of sex is a natural and unavoidable consequence of his philosophical thought. His conception of marriage as properly the path of development, the route by which capacities may be refined and the nobler feelings cultivated, is characteristic of and essential to all his thought.

So far, I have said something about the problem of two Mills – about the ways in which Mill's moral philosophy differs from Bentham's, and about the consequences that appears to have for Mill's view of marriage – but earlier in the paper I said that the notion of perfectibility was associated with two problems in Mill's philosophy. The first of these is the problem of the distinctions and differences between Mill's earlier and later thought. The second, associated, problem is that of the compatibility between the notion of perfection, or moral self-education, and Mill's championship of the cause of liberty in his essay *On Liberty*. I turn now, therefore, to this second problem.

Freedom

Mill's commitment to the possibility of human development and self-improvement is not an unmixed blessing. While it might serve to distinguish his moral philosophy from 'the philosophy of swine', it also carries with it the implication that freedom is merely an instrumental good, to be allowed when and in so far as it will contribute to human advancement. The passage from *The Subjection of Women*, quoted at the beginning of the paper, reinforces the suspicion that Mill's commitment is simply to freedom as an instrumental good, for he tells us there that ideals of marriage distinct from his own are 'relics of primitive barbarism', and this suggests quite strongly that he believes that ultimately barbarism will give way to civilization and sexuality will yield to intellect. However, if this is Mill's view in *The Subjection of Women*, then it appears to be quite at odds with his stated position in his essay *On Liberty*. *On Liberty* is standardly seen as Mill's *tour de force* against the tyranny of the majority and in favour of unbridled individuality, even eccentricity. The motto of the essay is Wilhelm von Humboldt's statement that 'the grand, leading principle towards which every argument unfolded in these pages directly converges, is the absolute and essential importance of human development *in its richest diversity*'.

Appeal to diversity is omnipresent in the pages of *On Liberty*; again and again Mill inveighs against the tyranny of public opinion, against the despotism of custom, and against 'the Chinese ideal of making all people alike'.[20] Yet, we may ask, would he not himself make all people alike by insisting on this one true ideal of marriage and by dismissing as barbaric all other ideals? Crudely put, Mill's problem is this: if he thinks freedom an intrinsic good – a good in itself – then he must allow that people may express their freedom by subscribing to ideals of marriage contrary to his own. (They may, for example, genuinely believe that marriage is an institution whose purpose is to ensure regular and reliable sexual gratification. Far from leading them to reject this ideal, freedom may simply serve to encourage it.) On the other hand, if Mill thinks that freedom is an instrumental good, justified by its contribution to human advancement and improvement, then he must allow that certain freedoms are impermissible, namely those freedoms which do not in fact contribute to human advancement and improvement. One thing seems certain – he cannot have it both ways. Or can he? Two preliminary points need to be made here.

First, the earlier discussion has shown only Mill's belief in human development, and, as the quote from von Humboldt illustrates, nothing in that entails commitment to uniformity. Indeed, in *On Liberty*, Mill implies quite the reverse when he says:

> there is no reason at all that human existence should be constructed on some one or some small number of patterns. If a person possesses any tolerable amount of common sense and experience, his own mode of laying out his existence is best, not because it is the best in itself, but because it is his own mode. Human beings are not like sheep, and even sheep are not undistinguishably alike.[21]

So from the belief in human development nothing follows about conformity or uniformity. The analogy between human flourishing and the flourishing of plants in nature is instructive here. There may be no more reason why two different persons should flourish in the same moral climate than why the daffodil and the orchid should flourish in the same physical climate. (I shall return to this point later.)

Second, even if Mill is in fact (though not in logic) committed to a single ideal of marriage, he need not be committed to the diminution of freedom involved in the forcible imposition of that ideal: marriage for the purpose of sexual gratification is indeed ignoble, base, and dehumanizing, but barbarians must be allowed to wallow in their own barbarism.

So Mill's belief in development does not entail a single ideal, and even if he in fact subscribes to a single ideal he is not thereby committed to the legitimacy of forcibly imposing the ideal. However, even if his thesis does not lead him to a single ideal, it does nevertheless rule out a substantial number of ideals. In particular, his distinction between higher and lower pleasures, based on the contrast between human and animal characteristics, rules out the possibility of construing marriage as primarily a sexual relationship. Perhaps we are not compelled to think of marriage as the marriage of intellects, but we must not think of it as the marriage of bodies. Anyone who did think of it in this way would be like the fool who prefers pushpin to poetry or like the pig satisfied with his swinish pleasures. Of this Mill is in no doubt, and he tells us that 'one of the deepest seated and most pervading evils in the human mind is the perversion of the imagination and feelings resulting from dwelling on the physical relation and its adjuncts.'[22] But this is a problematic conclusion for Mill: if there is a correct ideal of marriage (as he clearly thinks there is), and if failure to embrace this ideal constitutes a pervading evil and a perversion (as he clearly thinks it does), then why freedom? For it is hard to see what the positive value of freedom could be where freedom is only freedom to submit to one's animal instincts. Mill may think that barbarians should be allowed to wallow in their barbarism, but it could hardly be a virtue to allow them to do so. In brief, what justifies construing freedom as a virtue is Mill's optimism. Throughout the whole of his writings he displays a touching faith in the propensity of individuals to seek their own self-development and improvement. Hence his claim that 'the only unfailing and permanent source of improvement is liberty, since by it there are as many possible independent centres of improvement as there are individuals.'[23] Commitment to human perfectibility is commonly associated not with liberal political theories of the sort Mill espoused, but with authoritarian, even totalitarian, theories according to which any amount of interference with individual liberty is justified simply by appealing to subsequent gratitude for improvement. Mill escapes the authoritarian implications of his own writings only by coupling a belief in human perfectibility with optimism about human nature. This is most clearly seen in his views on population policy, where he envisages that men and women (but particularly men) will gradually refine their feelings to a point where affinity of intellect and taste will replace sexual passion as the main impulse to marriage. Population policy will not be needed, as people will come to see for themselves that abstinence is superior to sex, just as the wise man sees that poetry is superior to pushpin. As Geoffrey Smith puts it in a recent article:

> Mill simply takes it for granted most of the time that – at least in the long run and for the great majority of people – a policy of tolerance, encouragement of social variety and concerned, non-coercive intervention will trigger, not any arbitrary range of self-regarding desires, but a very specific desire: that for individual self-improvement.[24]

In the case of marriage, the desire for self-improvement will issue in the recognition of the true ideal of marriage as a marriage of minds. For there can be no self-improvement without the recognition of this, but only a slow decline into animality and sensuality.

I began by pointing to a tension between Mill's belief in individual freedom and his belief in perfectibility, and I asked whether he could have it both ways. The burden of the preceding discussion is to suggest that, in a sense, Mill can have it both ways: he can resist the authoritarian implications of the belief in human improvement and cling on to the ideal of freedom as an intrinsic good if, and only if, he is willing to adopt an optimistic view of human nature, according to which freedom and perfectibility are inextricably linked. And he is (in general) prepared to adopt such a view, stating that 'the only unfailing and permanent source of improvement is liberty'. But, even if Mill can reconcile the apparently conflicting claims of freedom and perfectibility, he is still left with the problem of diversity. Von Humboldt had advocated the essential importance of human development *in all its richest diversity*. But, if freedom and development can be made to march together, then they appear to march not towards diversity but towards uniformity – towards a single ideal of marriage which is intellectual, refined, and largely asexual. If there is human development, and if people are free, then, Mill implies, they will freely choose a single ideal, but how much room for diversity is allowed by this single ideal? The answer lies, I think, in the second of the two notions mentioned in the original quotation from *The Subjection of Women*, the notion of complementarity, and I turn now to that.

COMPLEMENTARITY

Mill's essay on Bentham, mentioned earlier in discussing the differences between Benthamite utilitarianism and Mill's utilitarianism, was published shortly before his essay on the poet Coleridge. Mill speaks of Bentham and Coleridge as 'the two great seminal minds of England in their age', and his aim in the essays is to draw attention to the differences and similarities between the two, the ways in which they complement one another, the ways in which, for example, Coleridge may make good the defects and omissions in Bentham and vice versa. He remarks:

183

For among the truths long recognised by Continental philosophers, but which very few Englishmen have yet arrived at, one is, the importance, in the present imperfect state of mental and social science, of antagonistic modes of thought: which it will one day be felt are as necessary to one another in speculation, as mutually checking powers are in a political constitution.[25]

Mill's belief in the importance of complementarity goes back to his early mental crisis. In the *Autobiography* he tells us that he was released from depression partly by reading the poems of Wordsworth, which appealed powerfully to his emotions and expressed 'not mere outward beauty, but states of feeling and of thought coloured by feeling, under the excitement of beauty'.[26] His emergence from the mental crisis brought with it a reluctance to place total faith in powers of analysis and intellect. He searched now for people – poets, writers, artists – who could make up the deficits in his own character and early education by providing emotion and intuition to complement his own rationality. He turned first to Carlyle: 'the good his writings did was not as philosophy to instruct, but as poetry to animate'.[27]

I did not deem myself a competent judge of Carlyle. I felt that he was a poet, and that I was not; that he was a man of intuition, which I was not, and that as such he not only saw many things before me, which I could only, when they were pointed out to me, hobble after and prove, but that it was highly probable he could see many things which were not visible to me even after they were pointed out. I knew that I could not see round him, and could never be certain that I saw over him; and I never presumed to judge him with any definiteness until he was interpreted to me by one greatly superior to us both – who was more a poet than he, more a thinker than I – whose own mind and nature included his and infinitely more.[28]

Of course, the one greater than them both was Harriet Taylor and, in speaking of her, Mill again refers to the notion of complementarity: what was important about Harriet (as about Carlyle) was that she was able to make good the defects in Mill's character with respect to feeling, emotion, intuition. She was a poet, where Mill was only a thinker. It is in these references to complementarity that room is made for diversity within the single ideal of marriage. Mill's ideal of marriage is unswervingly the ideal of a marriage of true minds. The diversity he recommends is not the diversity of lower as against higher, or animal as against human characteristics. Rather, proper diversity is to be found in the marriage between the poet and the thinker, the emotional and the rational, the intuitive and the intellectual. Moral self-development will best be effected by the joining of equal but complementary partners, who may thus inform and educate one another. Just as Bentham had only one eye without the insights of Coleridge, so Mill had only one eye without the insights of Harriet (or so he thought). Remarking on the actual (as against the supposed) relationship between Mill and Mrs Taylor, Phyllis Rose says:

> I speak with great trepidation about 'facts' in such matters, but, speaking loosely, the facts in the Mills' case – that a woman of strong and uncomplicated will dominated a guilt ridden man – were less important than their shared imaginative view of the facts, that their marriage fitted their shared ideal of a marriage of equals.[29]

What Mill saw in his relationship with Harriet Taylor was a complementarity of powers and talents which fitted her to lead him in the path of development. The diversity between them thus effected a move to moral and spiritual perfection. This is the true and only genuine diversity allowed for by Mill's ideal of marriage – the diversity of complementary characters who may lead one another towards truth and towards individual self-fulfilment. Indeed, I would go so far as to say that this is the only diversity allowed for in society either: Mill's dream of a world of individuals and eccentrics is really a dream only that the world will contain Coleridge as well as Bentham, Carlyle as well as himself – not a dream that the world will contain Barry Manilow or Samantha Fox or any of the darker, lower, and less acceptable examples of individuality. Of course, this is not wholly wrong: I do not myself subscribe to the view that the world is a richer place for the presence in it of diversity of all and any sort. The world we live in may well be more diverse if it contains racists and fascists, but I cannot myself see that it is the richer or better for that diversity. Nevertheless, we may wonder whether there is in Mill's account sufficient room for diversity. Even if we do not want the diversity which racism and fascism bring with them, we may understandably want something more than merely the choice between Coleridge and Bentham.

The question of exactly how much diversity Mill's theory allows is a complex and controversial one: at one level, a great deal of diversity is to be tolerated. Mill recognizes that we are not yet far progressed on the road to moral improvement, and insists that we cannot forcibly impose any ideal on the unwilling. So the diversity he actually countenances in the actual world is great, even if the ideal amount of diversity in the ideal world would be much smaller. For the purposes of this paper, however, I wish simply to draw attention to an important and, I think, ironic feature of Mill's doctrine. This is the way in which his complementarity thesis informs his view of women generally and makes *The Subjection of Women* a more radical and a less attractive text than is normally allowed.

Complementarity and the 'woman question'

Earlier in the paper I made reference to Julia Annas's discussion of Mill's *The Subjection of Women* and her claim that the book is important for its recognition of the social and economic inequalities in Victorian society, as well as for its objections to women's legal disabilities. Annas argues that Mill goes badly wrong in vacillating between different kinds of argument against inequality: in particular, she says, Mill is never clear whether he is adopting a reformist approach, according to which women are in fact rendered miserable and wretched by their inequality, or whether he is adopting a radical approach, according to which the very fact that women are not miserable and wretched is proof positive that changes must be made. This latter argument is akin to the claim that, where slaves do not object to servitude, that fact itself shows what is wrong with slavery. And Mill himself appeals to this analogy in *The Subjection of Women*. In his more radical moods, Mill insists that woman's true nature cannot really be known, so deformed is it by prevailing social standards and expectations. Yet, apparently forgetful of his own earlier claims, he goes on in chapter 3, to tell us that women are (by nature) capable of intuitive perception of situations, they have a natural bent towards the practical, and they can bring 'rapid and correct insight into present fact'.[30] Annas is appalled:

> Here is the oldest cliché in the book: women are intuitive while men reason. If any cliché has done most harm to the acceptance by men of women as intellectual equals, it is this, and it is distressing to see Mill come out with it. It is even more distressing to find him patronizingly recommending to any man working in a speculative

subject the great value of an intuitive woman to keep him down to earth.[31]

However, this seems to me not the only nor the most plausible explanation of what Mill was about in the relevant passages of *The Subjection of Women*. We have seen that the distinction between intellect and emotion, rationality and intuition, thought and poetry, is not a simple male/female one in his philosophy. The argument about complementarity applies quite generally, and it is a consequence of this that when Mill appeals to it he need not be construed as always placing women on the emotion side of the dichotomy, nor that, when he does so place women, it is in any patronizing or disreputable fashion. The mistake in Annas's interpretation of Mill lies in her failure to see that the complementarity thesis pervades his thought, and is not simply a feature of *The Subjection of Women*. What Mill finds lacking in Bentham and in his own earlier thinking is precisely a sense of the importance of something other than analysis and intellect. In fact, this defect was made good for Mill by his association with Harriet Taylor, but, before ever he met Harriet, the defect was partway to being remedied by his friendship with Carlyle and his reading of Wordsworth. It is a contingent fact of Mill's life that the emotional and intuitive facets were provided for him by a woman, but they might just as well have been provided by a man and would have been none the better or worse for that. (See, for example, the cooling of the relationship between Carlyle and Mill after the latter's meeting with Harriet Taylor. Mrs Taylor took over the function which Carlyle had been performing, much to the dissatisfaction of both Thomas and Jane Carlyle.)[32]

If the mistake of Annas's interpretation lies in her failure to see that the reason/emotion dichotomy is not to be understood as a male/female one, the irony of her interpretation lies in the fact that Mill's complementarity thesis in a sense foreshadows radical feminist accounts of the inadequacy of 'male' conceptions of reason and its powers. In *The Dialectic of Sex* the radical feminist writer, Shulamith Firestone, concedes that women are indeed intuitive rather than rational, emotional rather than logical. Yet, she insists, what is often wrong with science is precisely that it ignores the emotions. She advocates 'emotional science' as a corrective to the overvaluing of technology and its powers, much as Mill praised the corrective influence of the poet in Carlyle, and subsequently in Harriet Taylor.[33] As Alison Jaggar puts it:

Radical feminists glorify women precisely for the same reasons that men have scorned and sometimes feared them; in so doing they give special value to the psychological characteristics that have distinguished women and men. By grasping the nettle so firmly, radical feminists intend not only to crush the sting, but even to produce some celebratory wine.[34]

Similarly, I think, in Mill. The appeal to women's nature as emotional and intuitive is far from patronizing; it is (rightly or wrongly) eulogistic.

In conclusion, I want to use some of the points made earlier to suggest that there is a misperception in our present-day assessment of Mill's *The Subjection of Women*. At the very beginning of this paper I quoted some Victorian critics of Mill: the objection that his text rests upon 'an unsound view of morals' and that it is a work of 'rank moral and social anarchy'. By contrast with this nineteenth-century assessment, modern commentators frequently praise Mill as being ahead of his time and attribute the original unpopularity of *The Subjection of Women* to the fact that it was too radical for its day. I have mentioned one way in which the text is indeed radical, but the overwhelming impression left by it is, I think, morally depressing. In this sense, Mill's contemporaries were more nearly right in their judgement than are twentieth-century feminists. They were right to construe *The Subjection of Women* as essentially a moral tract – not merely a legal one, nor even a social and political one – for embedded in it is commitment to a particular positive ideal of the marriage relationship, which we ignore at our peril. If the weakness of Mill's contemporaries lay in their refusal to countenance the relationship of marriage as a relationship between legal equals, their strength lies in their insistence on seeing it as something other than a legal relationship of any sort. By contrast, modern commentators are so impressed by Mill's objections to legal, social, and economic inequalities that they fail to see the moral ideal by reference to which his objections are voiced. Briefly, the point is this: Mill is so concerned to emphasize the inequality in Victorian marriage contracts that he never stops to ask whether marriage as an ideal is a contract at all, but simply assumes that it is so. His claim is that it must be a contract between equals, and legally this is surely right. Yet in his enthusiasm for this notion he forgets the social and economic circumstances which meant that it could be no such thing for the vast majority of Victorian women, and he also forgets that questions about legality are distinct from questions about ideals. Mill's contemporary, James Fitzjames Stephen, saw this clearly when he pointed out the consequences of taking literally Mill's view that divorce should be freely available. 'If this were the law,' he says, 'it would make women the slaves of their husbands.'[35] And so it would have done in Victorian Britain. If not coupled with extensive social and economic changes, mere changes in the law of divorce would have been disastrous for women, and it is a sign of Mill's persistent unworldliness that he fails to see this. This failure is positively bizarre when considered in its contemporary context: other writers were insistent on the need to open up new professions to women, and the consequences of women's containment in the domestic sphere were constantly pointed out to Mill by feminists of the day. Yet he remains curiously silent on the issue.[36]

More important, however, than Mill's unworldliness about the actual situation of women in Victorian Britain is his genuine belief in the lower, animal nature of sexuality and his commitment to substituting the intellectual for the physical. This feature of his account (also favoured by some modern feminists) found some support among feminists of the day, but Victorian feminists were also often worried by the ways in which sex thwarted women's independence and advancement: for women, sex meant children – lots of children – and inevitably children meant loss of independence, frequently loss of health, and almost certainly containment in the home. By contrast, what concerned Mill was sex itself. He construed it as animal, ignoble, debasing, dehumanizing, and to be avoided wherever possible. In his 1832 *Essay on Marriage and Divorce* he declared the marriage laws to be made 'by sensualists, for sensualists, to bind sensualists',[37] and it was this sensualism which was the target of Mill's real attack. The marriage laws were objected to primarily because they made women sexual slaves. If the disease is sex, the cure is certainly abstinence, and Mill embraced the cure with all the zeal at his disposal. Of course, this dephysicalizing of human nature fits in well with liberalism generally. It is a curious and troublesome feature of liberalism, often remarked upon by its critics, that it fails to take serious account of the practical circumstances of people's lives, construing these as merely contingent factors, unassociated with one's essential nature as a rational agent. Mill adopts this view in spades: not only does he ignore the practical circumstances of women's lives, which were such that mere changes in law (about the

franchise or about divorce) would be at best irrelevant and at worst
catastrophic; he also presents an ideal of marriage which sometimes
appears to aim at the complete denial of the physical – as though
sexuality were an unfortunate by-product of our animal nature, to be
avoided and discouraged wherever possible. Freud referred to Mill's
Autobiography as 'so prudish or so ethereal that one could never gather
from it that human beings consist of men and women, and that this
distinction is the most significant one that exists.'[38] The ethereal
quality pervades much of Mill's writing and informs the greater part
of his moral thought. His ideal of marriage is not only deeply
depressing; it is also dangerous: to set one's faith on a great day when
there will be no more sensualism, and to behave as though that day
might be tomorrow (or, at any rate, next week), is to display a view of
human nature just as impoverished as Bentham's and much less
realistic.

NOTES

An earlier draft of this paper was presented to the Women's Studies
Workshop and to the Political Theory Workshop, both at the University of
York. I am grateful to all who participated in those meetings for their helpful
and incisive comments. My thanks also go to the Trustees of the C. and J. B.
Morrell Trust, which funded my research during the academic years 1985–7.

1 References are to contemporary criticism of Mill's *The Subjection of Women*, and as quoted in M. St John Packe, *The Life of John Stuart Mill*, London, Secker & Warburg, 1954, 495ff.
2 John Stuart Mill, *The Subjection of Women*, London, Virago, 1983, 177.
3 Lee Holcombe, *Wives and Property*, Oxford, Martin Robertson, 1983, 3.
4 Mill, *The Subjection of Women*, 59.
5 Julia Annas, 'Mill and the subjection of women', *Philosophy*, 52, 1977, 179.
6 ibid., 194.
7 As quoted in William Thomas, *Mill*, Oxford, Oxford University Press, 1985, 5.
8 John Stuart Mill, *Autobiography*, ed. J. Stillinger, Oxford, Oxford University Press, 1969, 94.
9 *Mill on Bentham and Coleridge*, ed. F. R. Leavis, Cambridge, Cambridge University Press, 1980, 6.
10 ibid., 71.
11 John Stuart Mill, *Utilitarianism*, ed. Mary Warnock, Glasgow, Fontana, 1962, 260.
12 ibid., 261.
13 John Stuart Mill, *A System of Logic*, in *Collected Works*, vol. 7, Toronto, University of Toronto Press, 1973, 123.

14 ibid., vol. 8, 913.
15 Mill, *Collected Works*, vol. 2, 367. Mill's distinction between humanity and animality is discussed in some detail in John M. Robson, 'Rational animals and others', in John M. Robson and Michael Laine (eds), *James and John Stuart Mill: Papers of the Centenary Conference*, Toronto, University of Toronto Press, 1976, 143–60.
16 *The Early Draft of Mill's Autobiography*, ed. J. Stillinger, Champaign, University of Illinois Press, 1961, 171.
17 As quoted by L. S. Feuer, 'John Stuart Mill as a sociologist' in Robson and Laine (eds), op. cit., 101.
18 Mill, *Collected Works*, vol. 2, 157; see also 156–8, 352, 358.
19 ibid., vol. 2, 368. See also G. W. Smith, 'J. S. Mill on freedom', in Z. Pelczynski and J. Gray (eds), *Conceptions of Liberty in Political Philosophy*, London, Athlone Press, 1984, 210.
20 Mill, *On Liberty*, Harmondsworth, Penguin, 1974, 138.
21 ibid., 133.
22 *Autobiography*, 65.
23 Mill, *On Liberty*, 136.
24 Smith, op. cit., 197.
25 *Mill on Bentham and Coleridge*, 9.
26 *Autobiography*, 89.
27 ibid., 105.
28 ibid., 106.
29 Phyllis Rose, *Parallel Lives: Five Victorian Marriages*, Harmondsworth, Penguin, 1985, 15.
30 Mill, *The Subjection of Women*, 105
31 Annas, op. cit., 184.
32 Rose, op. cit., 117.
33 Shulamith Firestone, *The Dialectic of Sex: The Case for Feminist Revolution*, New York, William Morrow, 1970.
34 Alison Jaggar, *Feminist Politics and Human Nature*, Brighton, Harvester, 1983, 97.
35 James Fitzjames Stephen, *Liberty, Equality and Fraternity*, ed. R. J. White, Cambridge, Cambridge University Press, 1967, 195.
36 See Jane Rendall, *The Origins of Modern Feminism: Women in Britain, France and the United States, 1780–1860*, Basingstoke, Macmillan, 1985, 284–291.
37 In Alice Rossi (ed.), *Essays on Sex Equality*, Chicago, University of Chicago Press, 1970, 70.
38 As quoted by Feuer, op. cit., 101.

Chapter Six

WOMEN'S BIOLOGICAL STRAITJACKET

ANNE DIGBY

In discussing women's past encounters with the medical profession, feminist historiography has focused mainly on the mid- and late nineteenth century, but attention is now beginning to shift towards more detailed examination of an earlier era, in an attempt to understand how and why these extreme positions came to be adopted.[1] This paper contributes to this discussion through an analysis of some of the medical texts of Georgian and Victorian Britain which indicates some significant developments in their depiction of middle-class women. These changing perceptions about female nature were most conspicuous in gynaecological and psychiatric literature; attention is focused here on these rapidly expanding specialisms and upon the networking of assumptions between them.

The extent to which these two medical areas had converged is suggested by an extract from a standard textbook published towards the end of our period in 1892. The *Dictionary of Psychological Medicine* stated:

> The correlation of the sexual functions and nervous phenomena in the female are too common and too striking not to have attracted attention at all times; but, it may confidently be affirmed, that it is only within quite recent years that we have had adequate knowledge to enable us to discuss the problems arising out of these relations with scientific precision. Gynaecology, and our knowledge of the anatomy and physiology of the nervous system have advanced . . . so that now we have the clearer and reciprocal light shed by better knowledge.[2]

As part of an analysis of a pyschiatric 'illness' – climacteric (menstrual) insanity – this assertion has a twofold interest as the starting-point of this paper. First, it drew attention to a crucial link that had been forged between the developing studies of gynaecology and psychiatry. Second, it illustrated this neatly in the description of a female mental illness that had not been perceived before male gynaecologists investigated women's reproductive system.

The evolution of medical views on their physical and psychological nature created an image of women as frail and unstable. Already by 1700 there existed in medical literature a stereotype of woman as a medically unique but inferior being, whose health was determined by her femininity, and in which the central feature was periodic menstruation. These stereotypes were useful to doctors in that they could 'explain' matters on which they were medically ignorant.[3] But not all medical men accepted these ideas, and alongside them an alternative and less deterministic view of women existed.[4] However, during the eighteenth and nineteenth centuries natural events in women's lives – menarche, pregnancy, childbirth, and the meno-pause – were subjected to much more intensive scrutiny by doctors. A comparison of medical texts in the two eras suggests the extent of the intellectual change in professional opinion that occurred as a result. By the mid-nineteenth century a set of interlocking ideas were held which also justified the male doctor's professional position. Poovey has summarized this aptly: 'This set of assumptions – that woman's reproductive function defines her character, position and value, that this function influences and is influenced by an array of nervous disorders – mandates the medical profession's superintendence of women.'[5]

The first part of this paper analyses gynaecological literature with its increasing stress on the dominance of the female reproductive system; and the second part investigates the way in which psychiatric accounts in turn translated these assumptions into theories relating female insanity to the reproductive cycle. The implications that this man-made biological straitjacket had for women's lives are examined in the third section, where 'natural laws' are seen to have been transformed into social conventions that reinforced restrictive gender roles. Here the illustrative case study is taken of attempts to improve female secondary and higher education (and thus to widen women's opportunities for professional careers, including that of medicine), and of the immediate medical backlash which this produced. The paper concludes with a brief evaluation of the causes and significance of this construction of gender dichotomy.

Within our period some of these discoveries in gynaecology and psychiatry had a beneficial result in alleviating female suffering, while others enlarged understanding and resulted later in further therapeutic advances.[6] But there was also a darker side to this process, and one that is ignored in the standard perspectives of medical histories with their inbuilt Whiggish bias towards recording medical 'progress'. This paper explores part of the darker penumbra surrounding a few of these notable advances, by investigating what was a significant strand of argument within a larger medical literature. It does so through analysing standard works whose popularity and influence within the profession was frequently shown by the books having gone through several editions. Their authors were men of reputation, typically holding teaching posts in leading medical schools, so that their professional opinions were also widely disseminated to each generation of doctors. And, beyond the medical arena, it is relevant to note that these specialist views were accorded increasing weight in public debate. Their prominence by the late nineteenth century in the educational debates about overwork revealed doctors' self-confidence and stature on this public social platform.

Much of this Victorian medical literature exhibits a striking contrast between its sound empirical observation and the extreme inferences that were drawn from it. Even allowing for the fact that some of these subjects are still problematic today, and also that bizarre theories may occur in the early stages of enquiry into complex fields, it appears that an allegedly positivistic age produced a pyramiding of assumptions leading to strange conclusions. Significantly, it was the female who was the prime focus of this medical attention. This paper is not concerned with the related issues of how far social factors led women to collude with medical diagnoses (as in 'hysteria'), or whether physical factors such as restrictive dress or dietary deficiencies accentuated problems during menstruation or pregnancy at that time. Rather, its subject is the gaze which the medical profession turned on the Georgian and Victorian woman. That this medical gaze had political significance in marginalizing women in society has been shown in a recent study of Victorian psychiatry.[7]

Women were sensitized to this weight of professional opinion about their alleged frailty and the limitations that this might be expected to impose on lifestyle and aspiration. Not all accepted medical opinion uncritically, and some were sceptical about medical authority and expertise.[8] But, for a minority at least, fear of overwork with related fatigue and ill-health were recurrent concerns. Two notable examples were Bessie Rayner Parkes and Beatrice Webb, who, despite their achievements in the public sphere, were both preoccupied with these anxieties in their private lives.[9] Women could be encouraged to imagine that they suffered from 'female illnesses'. By the late Victorian period the excesses of some gynaecologists in this respect were attracting censure from their colleagues. T. C. Allbutt, in a sensational Goulstonian Lecture to the Royal College of Physicians in 1884, stated that women could become 'entangled in the net of the gynaecologist'. 'Arraign the uterus', as some of his professional brethren had done, 'and you fix in the woman the arrow of hypochondria, it may be for ever', he suggested.[10] The pressures for doctors to do so were evident, since, in a profession where overcrowding was leading to increasing competition, and static or decreasing income, gynaecology offered lucrative opportunities to expand medical practice among affluent women. In their enthusiasm to increase their practice some doctors attracted censure from their colleagues in carrying out unnecessary operations. The most notorious example was that of the clitoridectomist, Isaac Baker Brown, who was expelled from the Obstetric Society because of the manner in which he carried out surgical operations for psychological purposes. Similarly, oophorectomy became discredited as a cure for 'ovarian epilepsy', and this removal of ovaries was recognized as being 'followed by more serious nervous penalties than those for which it had been used as a remedy'.[11] But within such extremes much profitable practice remained, not least because of the useful alliance that was being forged between gynaecology and psychiatry. An American doctor observed how 'the boundary lines which divide the gynaecologist and the psychologist often touch and cross each other.'[12] As we shall see, this networking of perceptions had both a reinforcing and a self-validating tendency, whose consequences were of more than theoretical interest, since such ideas were rapidly translated into practical medical treatment.

GYNAECOLOGY AND OBSTETRICS

In 1797 one of the most articulate female midwives, Martha Mears, found it necessary to speak out against current representations of the pregnant woman:

A state of pregnancy has too generally been considered as a state of indisposition or disease: this is a fatal error and the source of almost all the evils to which women in childbearing are liable. . . . We must hasten to convince the timid female, that the very state, at which she has been taught to tremble, brings her nearer to the perfection of her being; and, instead of disease, affords a much stronger presumption of health and security. . . . Those changes, which most pregnant women soon experience, are happily designed as notices of their situation, not as symptoms of infirmity. What physicians term irritability, at that time, is but an increased sensibility of the womb, after it has received its precious deposit.[13]

Mears was protesting about some of the assumptions and concepts being developed in the rapidly expanding field of gynaecology and obstetrics. These male specialisms were a product of the increasing intervention of male practitioners in the traditionally female-dominated preserves of pregnancy and childbirth. The growing medical practices of male accoucheurs in Georgian Britain, and the establishment of numerous lying-in wards in charities and hospitals, meant there was an abundant supply of clinical material for male practice and observation.[14]

Following on from this came a proliferation of gynaecological handbooks of ever-increasing length and detail, and with a growing stress on the morbid character of what had earlier been considered natural functions. For example, Dr Gooch, who was Physician to both the Westminster and London Lying-In Hospitals, wrote in 1829 *An Account of Some of the Most Important Diseases Peculiar to Women*, in which the concept of the 'irritable uterus' – earlier disliked by Mears – was taken as established fact. He stated revealingly: 'the account of the irritable uterus I consider as a new map of a district which had not been laid down before, and like all new maps [is] an imperfect one.'[15] Effectively, a new female atlas had been started in which provisional frontiers of new countries of frailty, disease, and nervous instability were charted. The detailed topography of these new territories was only to be filled in by the gynaecological, obstetric, and psychiatric explorations of later nineteenth-century specialists. By the end of this Victorian period two authorities within the field reflected that advances in gynaecology had been 'perhaps more remarkable than in any other branch of medicine', but that 'adventurousness' and 'unbalanced zeal has had its inevitable result of injudicious practice, which is to be regretted'.[16] The extremes of this zealousness we have noted were in the operations of clitoridectomy and oophorectomy, and these will not receive attention in this paper, since they have been discussed elsewhere.[17] The focus here is on the cumulative constructions of powerful images during Victorian times of women's nervous instability, arising from their reproductive function.

A comparison of Victorian gynaecological literature with that of the mid- and late eighteenth century is instructive, since it shows how earlier suggestions that some women were liable to particular problems during menstruation were generalized and extended. It is interesting to discover that in 1652 Nicholas Fontanus in the *The Woman's Docteur* had used classical authorities as the basis for a suggestion that female disease proceeded from 'the retention or stoppage of menstruation'.[18] However, the significance of this argument was not fully appreciated until a changed social context gave it resonance. In the eighteenth century an authority like Thomas Denman, for example, suggested merely that *some* women *might* suffer from 'various hysteric and nervous affections', but with characteristic robustness he tended to play down the association of menstruation and disease.[19] The supposed connection of menstruation and hysteria was later developed more fully by writers in Scotland, then the centre for the most advanced medical studies in Europe. Alexander Hamilton, Professor of Midwifery at Edinburgh, suggested that female hysteria 'occurs most frequently about the time of the periodical evacuation' between the ages of 15 and 45.[20] And John Burns, later Professor of Midwifery in Glasgow, wrote that 'all women, at the menstrual period, are more subject than at other times to spasmodic and hysterical complaints.' He argued that, 'as the female system is more irritable during menstruation than at other times', women should avoid 'indigestible food, dancing in warm rooms, sudden exposure to cold', and so on, lest their periods stop or 'troublesome affections' develop.[21]

This image of the female – periodically predisposed to hysteria and other complaints – found wide currency in Victorian literature, where its self-evident truth precluded much intellectual scrutiny being given to it. It was not until the closing decades of the nineteenth century that a further dimension was added. John Thorburn, Professor of Obstetric Medicine at Victoria University, Manchester, suggested that menstruation implied 'an increased liability to all forms of explosive nerve disease'.[22] The eminent Scottish psychiatrist, T. S.

Clouston, developed this line of argument in more extreme terms:

> The regular normal performance of the reproductive functions is of
> the highest importance to the mental soundness of the female.
> Disturbed menstruation is a constant danger to the mental stability
> of some women; nay, the occurrence of normal menstruation is
> attended with some risk in many unstable brains. The actual
> outbreak of mental disease, or its worst paroxysms, is coincident
> with the menstrual period in a very large number of women
> indeed.[23]

It was significant that this explicit linkage of menstruation and female
insanity was contemporaneous with highly charged debates over
women's suitability for more advanced education and training, a
topic to which I return in the third section of this paper.

An illuminating contrast can be drawn between medical view-
points during the Georgian and Victorian ages on the menarche and
menopause, where the shift in viewpoint that we have noted on the
subject of menstruation was even more strikingly displayed. Denman
in the 1790s had concluded:

> It is not however proved that more women suffer at the time of
> puberty than men, though there may be some difference in their
> diseases; nor is it decided that those diseases, which occur at the
> time of the final cessation of the menses, are more frequent or
> dangerous than those to which men are more liable at an equivalent
> age.[24]

By the Victorian era the nervous and mental instability associated
with menstruation was viewed by British doctors as being in a
particularly acute phase at either the beginning or end of women's
reproductive life. These assumptions were also shared by the medical
profession in the United States.[25] And American alienists, typified by
Isaac Ray, were as ready as their British colleagues to link women's
reproductive system to a descending sequence of nervous instability,
'With women it is but a step from extreme nervous susceptibility to
downright hysteria, and from that to overt insanity.'[26] Similarly, in
Britain John Thorburn stated that puberty and the climacteric were
common starting-points for neurasthenia, and a variety of other
complaints. During the menopause, he asserted, 'every form of
neurasthenia, neuralgia, hysteria, convulsive disease, melancholia, or
other mental affliction is rife.'[27] The menopausal woman – like her

adolescent counterpart – was given invalid status. 'The woman who has arrived at this period should be as carefully guarded against noxious influences as the young adolescent girl.'[28] Puberty and the menopause held other dangers too; David Davis, Professor of Obstetric Medicine at University College, London, suggested that it was at these times that nymphomania was most often experienced.[29] Predictably, the Latin name given to this state was *furor uterinus*.

In a popular handbook first published in the opening years of Victoria's reign, and subsequently to go into fourteen editions, Thomas Bull advised mothers that 'there is no organ in the body, with the exception of the stomach, that exercises a more extensive control over the female system than the womb'. He suggested that on the quickening of the foetus the mother could fall into a hysterical paroxysm, and he listed nine morbid conditions from which she might expect to suffer during pregnancy.[30] Bull, as Physician-Accoucheur to the Finsbury Midwifery Institution, stated that his intention was the 'exposure of popular errors' in connection with pregnancy and childbirth, but it appears rather that he was substituting the new orthodoxy of the specialist gynaecologist for traditional beliefs. That such specialist orthodoxy was now enshrined in a very popular handbook indicated its potential influence.

To generalized Georgian beliefs on female frailties were added assertions by a series of medical writers that suggested first that pregnancy disordered the brain, and, later on, that these disorders were akin to insanity. The founder of the Westminster Lying-In Hospital, John Leake, stated confidently in 1782 that pregnant women's imaginations would *not* cause foetal damage as was popularly supposed, since

> A woman's mind, from the delicacy of her frame and the prevalence of her passions, is liable to so many excesses and inordinate notions that had such causes been productive of marks or monsters, they would certainly have been much more frequent.[31]

A decade later, Thomas Denman delineated greater mental frailty in the pregnant woman: 'the functions of the brain are often disturbed in the time of pregnancy, by which headaches, drowsiness, and vertiginous complaints are occasioned.'[32] Writing a century later, the observations of W. S. Playfair, Professor of Obstetric Medicine at King's College, London, indicated a significant extension in professional opinion:

There are many disorders of the nervous system met with during the course of pregnancy. Among the most common are morbid irritability of temper, or a state of mental despondency and dread of the results of labour, sometimes amounting almost to insanity, or even progressing to actual mania. These are but exaggerations of the highly susceptible state of the nervous system generally associated with gestation.[33]

This enlargement of morbid states associated with pregnancy, from everyday headaches or irritability to certifiable cases of insanity, paralleled the changing perspectives of Georgian and Victorian practitioners that we have seen also occurred on menstruation, puberty, and the menopause.

PSYCHIATRY

Traditionally, women's mental state had been seen as influenced by her uterus, and an interpretation of the wandering womb causing nervous disorder can be found as early as Plato. The development of more advanced pathological studies in seventeenth-century England led some, including Thomas Willis, to exonerate the womb from fault in hysterical women, and to see hysteria as originating in the nervous system.[34] Old ideas died hard, however, and William Battie, the physician of the newly established St Luke's Hospital, reflected in 1758 that 'the stomach, intestines and uterus are frequently the real seats of madness, occasioned by the contents of those viscera being stopt in such a manner as to compress the many nervous filaments.'[35] Both William Falconer[36] and the esteemed William Cullen[37] (Professor of the Practice of Physic at Edinburgh) were confident in the late eighteenth century that there was a relationship between the uterus and female nervous disorder, although they were singularly honest in admitting ignorance about the nature of this connection.

By the turn of the nineteenth century a more analytical approach, which favoured subdivision and categorization, was evident in psychological medicine. One result of this was that women's psychiatric experience was more likely to be seen as distinct from that of men. At this time it became axiomatic that 'women, most assuredly, are more liable to insanity than men.'[38] John Haslam, Apothecary at Bethlem Hospital, concurred with this view on the basis of admission figures from his asylum, and explained why he thought this was the case:

The natural process which women undergo, of menstruation, parturition, and of preparing the nutriment for the infant, together with the diseases to which they are subject at these periods, and which are frequently remote causes of insanity, may, perhaps, serve to explain their greater disposition to this malady.[39]

Several distinctive forms of female insanity were being diagnosed by this time, and these were associated with women's reproductive system, since they were linked with pregnancy, with parturition, and with lactation. The least common occurrence was thought to be mental illness during pregnancy, and there was little writing on the subject. However, *The Domestic Guide in Cases of Insanity*, published in 1805, was in no doubt that such cases arose from 'the force of the imagination' and from 'apprehension'.[40] Doctors described cases of 'painful, protracted', or 'unfortunate' parturitions which had resulted in madness.[41] John Ferriar, respected Physician of the Manchester Asylum, attributed the 'morbid susceptibility of the brain' after childbirth to 'the frequent changes or disturbances occurring in the balance of the circulation from the varying and quickly succeeding processes' at this time.[42] He emphasized the vulnerability of women during pregnancy and childbirth:

> I am inclined to consider the puerperal mania as a case of conversion. During gestation, and after delivery when the milk begins to flow, the balance of the circulation is so greatly disturbed as to be liable to much disorder from the application of any exciting cause. If, therefore, cold affecting the head, violent noises, want of sleep, or uneasy thoughts, distress a puerperal patient before the determination of blood to the breasts is regularly made, the impetus may be readily converted to the head, and produce either hysteria or insanity.[43]

Writing some years later in 1810, the eminent obstetrician Thomas Denman in his *Observations . . . on Mania Lactea* attributed an 'aberration of the mental faculties' during breastfeeding to the breast 'in a state of unusual irritation extending its influence to the brain'.[44]

We can see, therefore, that even before that Victorian period on which feminist studies have concentrated[45] certain characteristically female mental illnesses had been isolated. In addition, there was women's alleged disposition to hysteria – particularly at times of menstruation – discussed in the preceding section of this paper; during the Victorian period this was to be converted from a disposition

to a disease and become hysterical insanity. And Victorian mad-
doctors were later to specify as disease entities pubescent insanity,
climacteric insanity, and ovarian or uterine insanity. Such were the
fruits of the alliance between gynaecology and psychiatry, where
advances in clinical knowledge in the former often proved useful to
those working in the latter. Lacking scientific status in their work, but
operating in an increasingly positivistic age, asylum doctors were
eager for scientific legitimation. An increasingly fine nosology of
mental diseases, and strikingly detailed classifications of the causes
of insanity, may be seen as attempts to achieve greater authority by
Victorians working in the difficult field of mental illness. Increasing
interest in women's reproductive systems facilitated this process. For
example, irregular or suppressed catamenia (i.e. menstrual periods),
puerperal disorders, protracted or suddenly subsiding lactation, and
hysteria were among predisposing or exciting causes of female insanities listed early in the Victorian period by asylum doctors. Thirty
years later, uterine irregularity and climacteric changes were also to
be found, and, before the end of our period, ovarian disorders and
puberty were listed in addition.[46]

Girls were deemed to be 'more liable' to pubescent (alternatively
developmental or adolescent) insanity than boys, according to an
authoritative study by the neurologist, Henry Maudsley. In his view
the onset of menstruation was momentous: 'how large a space in her
nature the reproductive function fills and how mightily its fulfilment
belittles other interests.'[47] For Maudsley, as for other alienists, female
adolescent insanity was either closely associated with or indistinguishable from hysterical insanity, since both had their origin in the
female reproductive cycle.[48] The legitimacy of this connection was
explicitly affirmed without the need for any kind of scientific proof in a
standard Victorian textbook on psychological medicine of 1874,
which quoted approvingly from Professor Laycock's *Treatise on the
Nervous Diseases of Women*:

> Women in whom the generative organs are developed or in action
> are those most liable to hysterical disease. Indeed, the general fact
> is so universally acknowledged, and so constantly corroborated by
> daily experience, that anything in the nature of proof is
> unnecessary.[49]

Asylum doctors were very clear about the characteristics of female
hysterics and obviously enjoyed the opportunity to describe in detail

the character of their moral perversity. The Physician-Superintendent of the Royal Edinburgh Asylum described them:

> The fasting girls, the girls with stigmata, those who see visions of the Saviour and the saints and receive special messages in that way, the girls who give birth to mice and frogs, some of those who fall into trances, and those who live on lime and hair are all cases of this disease.

Revealingly, he saw them having 'a morbid ostentation of sexual and uterine symptoms' and 'a morbid concentration of mind on the performance of female functions'.[50] Aptly, Showalter has suggested that such passages are informed by the Victorian male psychiatrist's apparent fear of female sexuality.[51]

It was surely significant that the emphasis on this link between puberty and hysteria (and, as we have seen earlier, between menstruation and insanity) was greatest in the period from the 1870s to the 1890s, when the debate over the suitability of girls for secondary schooling was at its fiercest. Possibly because of the social implications of these beliefs about female hysteria and pubescent insanity, doctors were loath to question these ideas. The authoritative *Dictionary of Psychological Medicine* commented tartly in 1892 that 'even among physicians, many have not yet been able to discard the idea that the uterus, or at least the genital apparatus of the female, is more or less the cause of this disease.'[52] Instead it suggested that hysteria should now be considered as much a male as a female condition (as, indeed, Cullen and Falconer had argued a century before), and that the reproductive organs were only one cause among many. However, customary views were too seductively convenient to be rejected quickly, as this later example suggests:

> That their perverted moral state is somehow connected with the action of the reproductive organs on an unstable nervous system seems probable because it is mostly met with in unmarried women, is prone to exhibit erotic features, and is sometimes cured by marriage.[53]

By this time there was available an equally nebulous diagnosis, in addition to that of hysteria – that of 'nervous exhaustion'. An American commentator gave a cogent explanation of the 'catch 22' situation this provided:

> A clear distinction should be made in the study of etiology, between insanity caused by active disease of the sexual organs, and insanity arising from brain exhaustion produced by prolonged or excessive functional activity of these organs while *free from any disease*. We incline to the belief that as many or even more cases of insanity can be traced to the latter. (my italics)

He was confident that 'many authorities' believed that 'the normal functional activity of the reproductive organs' could lead to female insanity.[54] And in Britain Professor Playfair, in a discussion of the female neurasthenic invalid, emphasized how 'the highly sensitive nervous organisation of the female sex' was related to their reproductive system, and that the origin of such functional neuroses commonly lay in 'some definite morbid condition of the uterus or ovaries'.[55] Such cases lay within the shadowy borderlands of insanity – more prone to be given Weir Mitchell's 'rest cure' than asylum treatment.

The patronizing tone of much of the discussion on female cases of hysteria, nervous exhaustion, and neurasthenia was very obvious but was relatively inoffensive when compared with the condescension and sly, sexist humour in descriptions of climacteric insanity. This was sometimes revealingly referred to as 'old maid's insanity'. Maudsley saw one characteristic of it as formless fears and delusions: 'an old maid is perchance in agitated distress because she ought to have accepted an offer of marriage which was made thirty years ago'.[56] In this context it was associated with delusions which were seen as having a sexual colouring. Charles Mercier's *Textbook of Insanity* of 1902 described confidently how 'an old maid thinks she has been seduced, she has been unchaste, she is engaged to this man or that, to whom perhaps she has never spoken.'[57] That such women existed in a biological straitjacket in the eyes of the Victorian medical profession was expressed most dogmatically – and with unconscious poignancy – in this view that ovarian or old maid's insanity usually occurred in 'unprepossessing old maids' who had been

> severely virtuous in thought, word and deed, and on whom nature, just before or after the climacteric, takes revenge for too absolute a repression of all the manifestation of sex, by arousing a grotesque and baseless passion for some casual acquaintance of the other sex whom the victim believes to be deeply in love with her.

The alienist commented, with ill-concealed anti-feminism, that this was 'so like a trick played on that higher being, which they had always cultivated, by a lower and more animal nature that they had always repressed'.[58] Others cited the possibility of delusions of pregnancy in climacteric insanity and referred to the historical precedent of Joanna Southcott.[59]

There was some concern that this kind of exclusive concern with the spinster was unjustified; reservations were expressed that the disease could arise in any woman as a result of 'defective or irregular menstruation in early life'.[60] Whatever the marital status, melancholia appeared to have been seen as the characteristic state; one alienist attributed this to the menopause's providing 'a startling intimation of mortality and an occasion of sadness'.[61] However, interpretations varied as to whether this illness was more properly described as one form of uterine or ovarian insanity rather than as climacteric insanity. And, among those prefering the latter, some saw it as a disease affecting men as well as women – a developmental insanity related to age rather than gender.

With such entrenched views on the dominance of the reproductive system over women's mental state, a certain air of bafflement can be detected in Victorian doctors' discussions of the insanity of pregnancy (alternatively called 'insanity of reproduction'). All conceded that this was rarely found, yet, in relation to their beliefs about the vulnerability of the female to the vagaries of the uterus, pregnancy should have produced greater mental instability than in fact occurred.

> It is remarkable that although all women are so liable during pregnancy to emotional disturbances, unprovoked 'hysterical' laughing and weeping, 'longings', caprices of all kinds, and other mental disturbances; yet disturbance to the point of actual insanity is rare in pregnancy.[62]

As a result, much was made of the *morbid* nature of pregnant women's cravings, and to the danger of dipsomania: 'If the longing be for alcohol there is no knowing to what this may lead.'[63]

Puerperal insanity occurring after childbirth was recognized as both more frequent and more serious an illness than the insanity of pregnancy. Puerperal madness had been extensively discussed before the Victorian era by Burrows, Gooch, Haslam, and Ferriar in Britain; Rush in America; and Esquirol and Sauvages in France. In early discussions, particularly, the term was also often used to include the insanities of pregnancy and of lactation, later seen as distinct mental illnesses. James Cowles Prichard, writing in 1835, was typical in being uncertain whether puerperal insanity was a result of the delivery of the child or of the irritation accompanying the flow of milk.[64] Many women who suffered this type of attack were treated at home: one estimate was that one-quarter of confinements were complicated in this way, while only one in fourteen of female asylum admissions were accounted for by puerperal insanity.[65] W. S. Playfair explained that this was because 'only the worst and most confirmed cases find their way into these institutions'.[66] In more serious cases, doctors suspected that there was a septic element in its causation – 'the vitiation of the blood by the absorption of septic matter from the uterus'[67] – and that 'the uterus must be examined, and, if necessary, cleaned out'.[68]

In both theoretical and practical terms, puerperal insanity tended to merge into the insanity of lactation. Those wishing to have theoretical tidiness suggested seemingly arbitrary dividing lines that occurred four, six, eight, or twelve weeks after childbirth. Insanity of lactation appeared far less problematical in either causation or treatment than puerperal insanity. There was agreement that it was an insanity of exhaustion, often linked to anaemia, and resulting from breastfeeding being prolonged beyond the strength of the mother. There was good evidence adduced to suggest that the condition was more common among *poorer* mothers, owing to their hard lives, malnutrition, and frequent pregnancies. But this discussion was exceptional in psychiatric literature in focusing on working-class women.

While an increasing proportion of the text in manuals on psychological medicine was being devoted to descriptions of these female diseases, and thus an impression of their importance was being conveyed, information on their actual incidence was minimal. Further, the statistics that were presented did not correlate at all precisely with those in other texts. There was a rudimentary consensus about the relative importance of such diseases, with insanity of pregnancy the rarest, insanity of lactation occupying the middle ground, and insanity of childbirth seen as the most frequent mental illness. Aggregating all three states under 'puerperal insanity' produced estimates which varied from 5 to 25 per cent of cases of female asylum admissions,[69] but with most around the 8–12 per cent range. (A comparable proportion is evident in analysis of the 'puerperal factor' in the causation of insanity.[70]) Only a single estimate of insanity of the climacteric was found, and this suggested that it comprised about 3–4 per cent of women suffering from nervous disorders.[71] Significantly, no attempt seems to have been made by contemporaries to qualify that highly ambiguous category of female asylum admissions – the hysterically insane.

Modern research by Charlotte Mackenzie on female admissions to Ticehurst gives us some valuable quantitative information on this and related topics. Ticehurst was a small private asylum in Sussex that catered for an exclusive upper-class clientele, and its female patients had been assiduously attended by the male medical profession before their admission. Their certification reflected this, for the period 1845–85 that Mackenzie has analysed, since 45 of the 194 female admissions (23 per cent) had gynaecological symptoms or diagnoses attributed to them. Of this group of 45 patients, 15 of them (8 per cent of female admissions) were seen as hysterical; 10 were diagnosed as cases of hysterical mania; 2 as cases of hysteria; in a further 2 cases hysteria was given as the alleged cause of insanity; and finally one case of mania was alleged to have been the result of 'uterine hysteria'. That Ticehurst, with 23 per cent of its admissions coming under the broad heading of 'puerperal insanity', was at the higher end of the range as far as asylum cases of this nature were concerned need not surprise us. The typical status of Ticehurst patients was that of 'gentlewoman' or 'lady', and as such they were particularly likely to have received the attentions of the specialist gynaecologists, as, indeed, their certification indicated.[72]

The statistics of female cases demonstrated that only a small minority of women patients were there because of any perceived link between their illness and their reproductive system. There was a striking disproportion between these hard, quantitative data and the soft, qualitative descriptions in contemporary manuals, and thus between rhetoric and reality.

A comparable discrepancy is apparent when we look at female recovery rates in Victorian asylums, since although women were seen as psychologically more vulnerable than men they were also more liable to achieve a 'recovery' from their mental illness. Asylum recovery tables invariably showed females several percentage points ahead of males in tables of recoveries. Prognosis for those patients suffering from the female insanities we have been discussing were good: three-quarters of those suffering from insanities of pregnancy, childbirth, and lactation were expected to recover.[73] A domestic manual explained this fortunate circumstance: 'There is generally a consolation in female cases, from the principal cause being apparent; and when this is properly attended to, a cure is more easy.'[74]

'The reproductive organs are frequently the seat of disease or abnormal function', commented one standard Victorian manual on psychological medicine in 1874. It went on to suggest that 'androgynous character is often accompanied by mental imbecility' and asked rhetorically: 'is not this a cogent reason why the women who have invaded the sphere of man's work and duty have as a rule proved such miserable failures?' To prevent more women advancing into traditional male territory, including that of medicine, and thus undercutting this type of argument by force of empirical evidence, some members of the medical profession participated in a sustained campaign to obstruct improvements in female secondary and higher education. Prominent in their battery of arguments were references to the psychological frailty of women, which have been analysed in this section, and to the problems of disturbed menstruation that were alleged to occur if women engaged in sustained intellectual study.[75]

WOMEN'S EDUCABILITY

The bitter debate which surrounded the development of improved opportunities for middle-class girls in secondary and higher education from the 1870s is familiar in outline.[76] Two important aspects of this discussion have not been sufficiently emphasized hitherto: the continuity between these extended late Victorian and Edwardian arguments and earlier specialist, medical writing; and the relevance of doctors' preceding views on the psychological, as well as the physiological, nature of women. Prominent in the education debate were four doctors – Clouston, Maudsley, Playfair, and Thorburn – whose extreme opinions on women's biological destiny have been analysed earlier in this paper. The translation of their arguments to the political arena also needs underlining; no longer content with the specialist pages of medical journals, they promoted their views in popular journals that would find their readership in middle-class households. Having mapped new territories in psychiatry and gynaecology, these medical men were keen to exploit their colonized territory, and restrict the opportunities of their 'captive' subjects – women. This case study of female educability also brings out the significance of chronology: hostile pronouncements were precisely

WOMEN'S BIOLOGICAL STRAITJACKET

correlated with specific developments in women's education so as to achieve maximum impact.

Allegations of the pathological effects of more advanced education on women had begun in the United States, but the main arguments were swiftly translated to the British scene in an article, 'Sex in mind and education', which was published by Henry Maudsley in 1874. Maudsley followed the assertions of Dr Clarke of Harvard University in his book, *Sex in Education*, in stating that attempts to 'assimilate the female to the male mind' would not only fail but seriously injure women's health, since their periodic functions disqualified them from uninterrupted effort either in early education or in later careers.

> If it be the effect of excessive and ill-regulated study to produce derangement of the functions of the female organization, of which ... there is great probability, then there can be no question that the subsequent ills mentioned are likely to follow. The important physiological change which takes place at puberty ... may easily overstep its health limits, and pass into pathological change. ... nervous disorders of a minor kind, and even such serious disorders as chorea, epilepsy, insanity, are often connected with irregularities or suspension of these important functions.[77]

These allegations were made in the *Fortnightly Review*, a magazine whose extensive general readership gave his ideas much greater influence than if they had been made in a specialist medical journal with restricted circulation.

Such assertions, if unchallenged, would have threatened the viability of the new high schools being opened by the newly created Girls Public Day School Company, and weakened existing establishments such as the North London Collegiate School. Miss Buss, redoubtable headmistress of this school, persuaded Elizabeth Garrett Anderson to respond to Maudsley's assertions.[78] As the first woman to qualify as a doctor in Britain, she knew at first hand the medical profession's hostility to female education and professional advancement. She was able to assert authoritatively, as a doctor, that it was:

> A great exaggeration to imply that women of average health are periodically incapacitated from serious work by the facts of their organization. *Among poor women, where all the available strength is spent upon manual labour, the daily work goes on without intermission, and, as a rule, without ill effects.* ... With regard to mental work it is within the

209

experience of many women that that which Dr Maudsley
speaks of as an occasion of weakness, if not of temporary
prostration, is either not felt to be such or is even recognised as
an aid, the nervous and mental power being in many cases greater
at those times than at any other. . . . The case is, we admit,
very different during early womanhood, when rapid growth and
the development of new functions have taxed the nutritive powers
more than they are destined to be taxed in mature life . . . [but]
the assertion that, as a rule, girls are unable to go on with an
ordinary amount of quiet exercise or mental work during these
periods, seems to us to be entirely contradicted by experience.[79]
(my italics)

Significantly, Garrett Anderson brought into the discussion the
experiences of working-class women which male doctors had omitted.
Her cogent rebuttal of each of Maudsley's arguments, clear analysis
of the marked differences between the educational systems of the USA
and Britain, and persuasive appeal to the everyday experience of
parents, provided such a forceful refutation that the 'sex in body and
mind' case against advances in female education was silenced for a
time.

In the 1880s anxiety about overwork by schoolchildren gave a fresh
opportunity for critics of female secondary and higher education to
voice their anxieties and also provided new ammunition for their 'sex
in mind and body' polemic. T. S. Clouston's *Female Education from a
Medical Point of View* reopened the debate in 1882, in the same year
that the Church Company was created to found Anglican high
schools for girls. As a result of his enquiries in 'advanced schools for
young ladies', he had found that 'competition is terrific' and that the
most ambitious would, before examinations, 'work twelve and
fourteen hours a day, and take no exercise to speak of'. A farrago of
allegations followed on the health dangers to which such female
pupils made themselves liable: anaemia, stunted growth, nervous-
ness, headaches, neuralgias, morbid cravings for alcohol or drugs,
hysteria, inflammation of the brain, and even insanity.[80] These
conjectures had obvious roots in the medical depiction of the nervous
and hysterical female that we have discussed earlier, but a significant
addition was made, in that Clouston hinted that

The most important effect of all I cannot very well enter on in
detail, for it relates to woman's highest function, that of
motherhood. But that this is affected, and most seriously, by over-

education in bad methods and under bad conditions, no physician will deny. If the end of mind-culture is to be that its victim . . . is to have fewer offspring, and those she has are to be of a puny kind, the risk will be recognised by all thoughtful persons as too severe to be deliberately run for our daughters.

These arguments were disseminated widely, since Clouston reprinted them in the *Popular Science Monthly* in 1883 and 1884.

John Thorburn, Professor of Obstetrics at Manchester, extended Clouston's arguments to the realm of higher education in 1884, in a lecture delivered only a week after the University of Oxford had recognized women there. He warned that if a woman did enter higher education she should be warned 'that she is entering upon one of the most dangerous occupations of life'. While disclaiming 'the remotest hostility to the highest possible degree of female education', and stating that he had not opposed women students at Manchester, his lecture on 'Female education in its physiological aspect' in reality supplied heavy artillery against women's aspirations. He forecast a 'future life of complete unhappiness' if female students did not rest during their periods. Since he was addressing a professional audience, he was able to be less reticent than Clouston had been. Thorburn suggested not only that menstruation was 'subversive of close mental attention' but that the female pupil or student should not 'be subjected to the same kind of educational strain as their male compeers' or serious nervous consequences could ensue. Few physicians 'have not seen bright careers of mental work and usefulness cut short, never to be resumed, after a few days of hard mental strain during a menstrual period.' The physical price might be even higher because pathological departures at these times, if confirmed from month to month, became chronic 'future diseases of the gravest character'. If young women persisted in working at the same intensity regardless of their periodic function, then they did so 'at the peril of mental or physical disablement, perhaps for life. No physician will deny this for a moment.' The solution was therefore for special degrees and universities to be created for women which would cater for their particular needs. Elsewhere in his lecture he revealed his true preference: a reversion to a simple, homely role for women.[81] In the following year, Thorburn repeated much of this material in *A Practical Treatise on the Diseases of Women*, but came to even more alarmist conclusions, since he suggested that unremitting study might result in 'the unsexing of the girl'.[82]

Dr Elizabeth Garrett Anderson's professional authority was again used in this controversy on overwork, which was then being debated by increasing numbers of teachers, parents, doctors, and school inspectors. In letters written to *The Times* in 1880 and 1881[83] she took a moderate stance in suggesting that for high-school girls under the age of 18 some precautionary measures were advisable, since their organisms were still 'engaged in the process of self-construction. The machine is not ready for use because it is still itself in the workshop.' Parents had a responsibility to stop girls spending overlong periods on their home preparation, and schools had an equal one in restricting their curriculum to prevent overload. Having said that, she saw no reason why girls should not tackle junior and senior local examinations before the ages of 16 and 18. And at university young women over 18 or 19 could 'work hard, not only without harm to their health, but with very great advantage to it'. This last comment was aimed strategically at Cambridge dons, who were then debating the entrance of Girton and Newnham students to Tripos examinations.

To Garrett Anderson's medical expertise was added Sophie Bryant's voice of educational expertise. Bryant was an experienced high-school teacher who later became headmistress of North London Collegiate School. Like Garrett Anderson she had earlier scored an educational 'first' in being the first woman to gain an academic doctorate at the University of London. In *Over-Work from the Teacher's Point of View*, a lecture delivered in 1885, Bryant stated that the schoolmistress's conclusions on 'the over-work panic' were fit to challenge those of the male doctor:

> We believe that we see aspects of the questions which the doctor as doctor merely, could hardly be expected to imagine; and we found our opinions on a knowledge of children who are well, no less than of children who are ill, whereas the medical man knows only the latter.

She agreed that doctors drew their examples not from normal schoolgirls but from emotionally excited or thoroughly idle girls whose testimony was biased. It needed the corrective of information from the school, 'with a view to the diagnosis of moral as well as physical character in the cases of over-work that come before them', if doctors were to avoid 'mistaken medical diagnoses'. Bryant emphasized that in girls' schools a sensible control of the curriculum, good pastoral care, and the opportunities for physical activities avoided overwork and overstrain.

In Bryant's book was a warning about 'the evil effects of the vague over-work panic which has possession of so many minds'. This was soon to be reinforced by the pervasive formulations of Social Darwinism, with its stress on motherhood and the reproduction of a healthy race as women's highest function and calling. It was predictable in this intellectual climate that in 1896 W. S. Playfair should attack girls' education on the grounds that

> The one great fault of those who manage these educational establishments is that they have too often started on the absolutely untenable theory that the sexual factor is of secondary importance; and that there is little if any real distinction between a girl between the ages of 14 and 20, and a boy of the same age. I know of no large school for girls where the absolute distinction which exists between boys and girls as regards *the dominant menstrual function* is systematically cared for and attended to. The feeling of all schoolmistresses seems to be antagonistic to such an admission. . . . [But] every physician of experience sees many cases of anaemia and chlorosis in girls, accompanied by amenorrhoea or menorrhagia, headaches, palpitations, emaciation, and all the familiar accompaniments of breakdown, an analogous condition in a schoolboy is so rare that we may doubt if it is even seen at all.[84] (my italics)

That it was only twenty years since Garrett Anderson had established that not only girls but also boys faced problems during puberty indicated the way in which allegations were revived so as to reconstitute old grounds of contention as fresh battlefields.

The Victorian era ended, but these issues refused to die. In 1906 T. S. Clouston asked 'why should we spoil a good mother by making an ordinary grammarian?'[85] While unconvincingly disclaiming opposition to women's higher education *per se*, he wished to 'emphasise the fact that this higher education has often been carried out at the peril of losing something higher still. It must be made compatible with the motherhood of the race.'[86] Five years later, the logical conclusion of this whole debate was reached when women's collective biological destiny was held to override her individual choice. Clouston argued in a public lecture that

> Woman cannot fulfil her destiny if her maternal instincts are impaired. The ideals which would exalt culture above motherhood are suicidal and should be abandoned. It will not do to say that

213

women should have a choice either to take up culture and intellectual work, whether it has a lessened capacity for motherhood or not.[87]

PERSPECTIVES

Clouston's statement revealed the extent to which medical pronouncements could be conditioned by their social context; it provided a fitting crescendo to a century and a half of medical orchestration on the theme of the incommensurability of the sexes. A cultural construction – or, more accurately, reconstruction – of the female was a response to wider changes in society. Liberal assumptions of the Enlightenment required that evidence was needed to justify an inegalitarian denial of social and political rights to women. The constructs of eighteenth-century anatomists and nineteenth-century craniotomists *appeared* to show that fundamental gender differences were due not to nurture but to nature, and that women were permanently below men in the hierarchy of species.[88] It is in this wider context that we can interpret gynaecologists' and psychiatrists' work in Georgian and Victorian Britain – that of providing a biological rationale for gender differentiation in society.[89] By a revealing irony, not only did women not participate in formulating these allegedly scientific judgements, but they also found their access to the medical profession obstructed because of them. And the cultural bias within this allegedly objective writing was further shown by its blatant class discrimination; a continuing need for the hard physical labour of working-class women made their exclusion from the 'female equals frailty' equation socially desirable but physiologically implausible. It was patently absurd that working-class women were effectively relegated to a neuter category by their absence from the subject-matter of medical debate.

The character of much of this medical discourse reflected specialists' investment in it – in both social and economic terms. Investment in the social conservatism that I have discussed, meant that there was reluctance to subject to critical scrutiny the 'self-evident' truths of received wisdom, as, for example, in cases of female hysteria or of nervous diseases. Equally significant was an associated failure to correlate quantitative evidence on the incidence of such illnesses with qualitative rhetoric on its social significance. While there was recognized to be a low rate of peculiarly 'female' insanities, for instance, there was no reluctance to make general inferences from them, and so derive misleading 'insights' into female personality. Such perceptions could soon achieve plausibility because fundamental physiological and therapeutic advances came particularly late in gynaecology and psychiatry – most of them outside our period. Paradoxically, such translation of assumption into fact seems to have been encouraged by the positivistic ethos of the age. Practitioners in our low-status medical specialisms sought scientific legitimation through the construction of elaborate classifications – as in those on the causation or varieties of mental illness. And, since female medicine offered – with paediatrics – the main opportunity for expanded practice in an overcrowded medical profession, there were built-in incentives to make one's reputation in this field through original ideas or distinctive manuals on treatment. Indeed, a tendency towards more extreme or simplistic views in some medical texts may be partly attributable to a change in those to whom the doctors were addressing their thoughts; from an audience that was small and specialist to one that included students, practitioners, and, on occasion, members of the general public.

Statements to that general audience by certain members of the medical profession showed a further qualitative change from earlier medical discourse. A close correlation existed between their lectures and publications on women's suitability for secondary, higher, or medical education, and the timing of contemporary initiatives to expand female opportunities in these fields. While this made it obvious that individual doctors had adopted a political stance towards these developments, their pronouncements were purportedly value-free and delivered as objective, scientific truths. Although there does not seem to have been a conspiracy (if this is defined as involving organizational co-ordination), yet these publicists expressed shared masculine prejudices in expounding partisan views, and made little attempt to provide anything other than their own authority and professional prestige as the basis for their contentious statements. Just as the democratic challenges of the Enlightenment had earlier resulted in a medically based construction of gender dichotomy, so the 'feminist' challenges of the mid- and late nineteenth century produced in gynaecology and psychology a more intensive dualism. If these views had been accepted, it would have meant that the world of the intellect was construed as a male preserve while women were confined within their biological straitjacket.

ANNE DIGBY

NOTES

This paper has benefited from the very helpful suggestions made by members of a workshop at the University of York and those at a seminar at Harvard University. Financial support from the Wellcome Trust is gratefully acknowledged.

1   See *Representations*, 14, 1986; H. Smith, 'Gynecology and ideology', in B. A. Carrol (ed.), *Liberating Women's History*, Urbana and Chicago, University of Illinois Press, 1976, 97–114; B. Ehrenreich and D. English, *For Her Own Good*, New York, Anchor Press, 1979, 33–68; E. Cohen, 'Medical debates on women's "nature" in England around 1700', *Society for the Social History of Medicine*, 39, 1986, 7–11.
2   D. H. Tuke (ed.), *A Dictionary of Psychological Medicine*, London, 1892, vol. 1, 234. The writer was Dr Robert Barnes, Consulting Physician at St George's Hospital, Chelsea Hospital for Women, and the Hospital for the Diseases of Women and Children.
3   Smith, op. cit., 95–8, 101, 104, 106.
4   Cohen, op. cit., 9–10.
5   M. Poovey, ' "Scenes of an indelicate character": the medical "treatment" of Victorian women', *Representations*, 14, 1986, 146.
6   E. Shorter, *A History of Women's Bodies*, New York, Basic Books, 1982, 268–81.
7   E. Showalter, *The Female Malady: Women, Madness, and English Culture 1830–1980*, New York, Pantheon, 1985, 72–3.
8   P. Jalland, *Women, Marriage and Politics*, Oxford, Oxford University Press, 1986, 135.
9   N. and J. McKenzie (eds), *The Diary of Beatrice Webb 1873–92*, London, Virago, 1982, 22, 121; Parkes Papers, Girton College, Cambridge, letters from B. Rayner Parkes to B. Bodichon, in box V/62 dated 15 April 1852, in box V/106 dated August 1861, in box V/108 dated 8 December 1871, in box V/114 dated 1 April 1862, and in box V/129 dated 16 March 1864. I am indebted to Jane Rendall for these references on Parkes.
10 Quoted in Sir H. D. Rolleston, *The Rt Hon. Sir Thomas Allbutt: A Memoir*, London, Macmillan, 1929, 87. Allbutt (1836–1925) was Physician at Leeds Infirmary, and later the Regius Professor of Physic at Cambridge University, and a Commissioner in Lunacy.
11 E. Showalter, 'Victorian women and insanity', in A. Scull (ed.), *Madhouses, Mad-Doctors and Madmen*, London, Athlone, 1981, 329; M. Handfield Jones, 'The development of modern gynaecology', in T. C. Allbutt and W. S. Playfair (eds), *A System of Gynaecology*, London, 1896, 1–2, 11. Handfield Jones was Obstetric Physician and Lecturer on Midwifery at St Mary's Hospital.
12 A. J. Skene, *Treatise on the Diseases of Women*, London, 1889, 930. Skene was Professor of Gynaecology at Long Island College Hospital, New York, and his opinions were influential in Britain.
13 M. Mears, *The Pupil of Nature or Candid Advice to the Fair Sex*, 1797, 4–6. Mears had read many of the standard Georgian gynaecological treatises

and was prepared to criticize them on the basis of her own extensive practice in London.

14 The best account of this process is given in J. Donnison, *Midwives and Medical Men: A History of Inter-Professional Rivalries and Women's Rights*, New York, Schocken Books, 1977. See also M. C. Versluysen, 'Midwives, medical men and "poor women labouring of child": lying-in hospitals in eighteenth-century London', in H. Roberts (ed.), *Women, Health and Reproduction*, London, Routledge & Kegan Paul, 1981, 18–49.

15 R. Gooch, *An Account of Some of the Most Important Diseases Peculiar to Women*, London, 1829, xv.

16 'Preface' to Allbutt and Playfair (eds), op. cit. W. S. Playfair was Physician for the Diseases of Women and Children at King's College Hospital in London.

17 L. D. Longo, 'The rise and fall of Battey's operation: a fashion in surgery', *Bulletin of the History of Medicine*, 53, 1979, 244–67; Showalter, 'Victorian women', 327–9.

18 Quoted in Smith, op. cit., 101.

19 T. Denman, *An Introduction to the Practice of Midwifery*, 2nd edn, London, vol. 1, 163. Denman was a Licentiate of the College of Physicians in London.

20 A. Hamilton, *A Treatise on the Management of Female Complaints*, 7th edn, Edinburgh, 1813, 46–7. (This had been published first in 1780.)

21 J. Burns, *The Principles of Midwifery including Diseases of Women*, 2nd edn, London, 1811, 100–1. (This work had gone through nine editions by 1837.)

22 J. Thorburn, *A Practical Treatise on the Diseases of Women*, London, 1885, 157.

23 T. S. Clouston, *Clinical Lectures on Mental Diseases*, 4th edn, London, 1896, 521. This book first appeared in 1883 and had reached its sixth edition by 1904. Sir Thomas Clouston was Physician-Superintendent of the Royal Edinburgh Asylum, and the first Lecturer on Mental Disease in the University of Edinburgh.

24 Denman, op. cit., vol. 1, 179–80.

25 C. Smith-Rosenberg, *Disorderly Conduct: Visions of Gender in Victorian America*, New York, Knopf, 1985, 182–91.

26 'Insanity produced by insanity', 1866, quoted in Poovey, op. cit., 146.

27 Thorburn, op. cit., 192.

28 ibid., 192–3.

29 D. Davis, *Elements of Obstetric Medicine*, 2nd edn, London, 1841, 339. This had first appeared in 1836 as *Principles and Practice of Obstetric Medicine*, Davis had been on the staff of the General Lying-In Hospital and had attended the birth of Queen Victoria.

30 T. Bull, *Hints to Mothers for the Management of Health during the Period of Pregnancy etc.*, London, 1837, 55.

31 J. Leake, *A Lecture Introductory to the Theory and Practice of Midwifery*, London, 1782, 25–6.

32 Denman, op. cit., vol. 1, 305.

33 W. S. Playfair, *A Treatise on the Science and Practice of Midwifery*, London, 1876, 226.

ANNE DIGBY

34 L. J. Rather, 'Pathology at mid-century: a reassessment of Thomas Willis and Thomas Sydenham', in A. G. J. Debus (ed.), *Medicine in Seventeenth-Century England*, Berkeley, University of California Press, 1974, 106.
35 W. Battie, *A Treatise on Madness*, London, 1758, 48–9.
36 W. Falconer, *A Dissertation on the Influence of the Passions upon Disorders of the Body*, London, 1788, 54.
37 W. Cullen, *First Lines of the Practice of Physic*, vol. 4, Edinburgh, 1789, 97, 103.
38 *The Domestic Guide in Cases of Insanity*, London, 1805, 26–7.
39 J. Haslam, *Observations on insanity*, London, 1798, 108.
40 *Domestic Guide*, 26.
41 J. M. Cox, *Practical Observations on Insanity*, 2nd edn, London, 1806, 24–6; W. Pargeter, *Observations upon Maniacal Disorders*, Reading, 1792, 48.
42 Quoted in J. C. Prichard, *A Treatise on Insanity*, London, 1835, 312. Ferriar published his three-volume *Medical Histories and Reflections* between 1792 and 1798.
43 ibid., 311–12.
44 T. Denham, *Observations on the Rupture of the Uterus and on Mania Lactea*, London, 1810, 37.
45 Showalter, *The Female Malady*, and 'Victorian women'.
46 J. Thurnam, *The Statistics of the Retreat 1796–1840*, London, 1841, tables 13 and 14; *Reports of York Lunatic Asylum*, York, 1872 and 1885.
47 H. Maudsley, *The Pathology of Mind: A Study of its Distempers, Deformities and Disorders*, London, 1895, 388–9. (This was effectively the third edition of part of the *Physiology and Pathology of Mind* of 1867.) Henry Maudsley had been Medical Superintendent of Manchester Lunatic Hospital, Professor of Medical Jurisprudence at University College, London, and Editor of the *Journal of Mental Science*.
48 See C. Smith-Rosenberg, 'The hysterical women: sex roles and role conflict in 19th century America', *Social Research*, 39, 1972 (now reprinted in Smith-Rosenberg, *Disorderly Conduct*), for a different interpretation.
49 J. C. Bucknill and D. H. Tuke, *A Manual of Psychological Medicine*, 3rd edition, London, 1874, 347. (This had first appeared in 1858.) Thomas Laycock's *A Treatise on the Nervous Disorders of Women* had appeared in 1840. Laycock became Professor of Medicine and also Lecturer on Medical Psychology and Mental Disease at Edinburgh.
50 Clouston, op. cit., 528–9.
51 Showalter, *The Female Malady*, 74.
52 Tuke (ed.), op. cit., 627.
53 Maudsley, op. cit., 398.
54 Skene, op. cit., 933.
55 W. S. Playfair, 'The nervous system in relation to gynaecology', in Allbutt and Playfair (eds), op. cit., 220–5. See also B. Sicherman, 'The uses of a diagnosis: doctors, patients and neurasthenia', *Journal of the History of Medicine*, 32, 1977, 33–54, for comparative American experience.
56 Maudsley, op. cit., 422.

57 C. Mercier, *A Textbook of Insanity*, London, Macmillan, 1902, 157. (This went through a second edition in 1914.) Mercier had been Senior Medical Officer at the Leavesden Asylum, and also at the City of London Asylum, and became Physician for Mental Diseases at Charing Cross Hospital.

58 Clouston, op. cit., 526–7. See also C. Smith-Rosenberg, 'Puberty to menopause', in *Feminist Studies*, vol. 1, 1973, for similar views in American literature.

59 Tuke (ed.), op. cit., 235.

60 Bucknill and Tuke, op. cit., 346. Sir John Bucknill was Medical Superintendent of Devon County Asylum (1844–62) and the Lord Chancellor's Visitor in Lunacy from 1862 to 1876. D. H. Tuke had been Assistant Medical Officer at the York Retreat, Lecturer on Psychological Medicine at the York School of Medicine, and then became a Consultant Psychiatrist.

61 Maudsley, op. cit., 420.

62 Mercier, op. cit., 153.

63 Tuke (ed.), op. cit., 1,035. The extreme hostility to alcohol expressed here is probably related to Tuke's Quaker faith.

64 Prichard, op. cit., 310. James Cowles Prichard was Physician to St Peter's Hospital, Bristol, and a Commissioner in Lunacy from 1844 to 1848.

65 Mercier, op. cit., 155.

66 Playfair, *A Treatise on the Science and Practice of Midwifery*, 287.

67 Maudsley, op. cit., 416.

68 Mercier, op. cit., 155–6.

69 J. C. Bucknill and D. H. Tuke, *A Manual of Psychological Medicine*, London, 1858, 236–7.

70 *53rd Report of the Commissioners in Lunacy*, Parliamentary Papers, 1899, XL, table XXV. These data on causation of insanity are so ambiguously presented that little precision can be attached to them.

71 Bucknill and Tuke, *A Manual of Psychological Medicine*, 1874, 360.

72 I am most grateful to Charlotte Mackenzie for so generously allowing me to use this unpublished material. Her doctoral thesis will shortly be presented to the University of London. Comparable material is presented in M. S. Thompson's study of the Royal Edinburgh Asylum, where an even higher proportion of poor and middle-class women had gynaecological dysfunctions: 'The mad, the bad, the sad: psychiatric care in the Royal Edinburgh Asylum (Morningside) 1813–94', University of Boston PhD thesis, 1984, 222.

73 Mercier, op. cit., 154–5; Clouston, op. cit., 544.

74 *Domestic Guide*, 28.

75 Bucknill and Tuke, *A Manual of Psychological Medicine*, 1874, 595. See also V. Bullough and M. Voght, 'Women, menstruation, and nineteenth-century medicine', *Bulletin of the History of Medicine*, 1973, 66–82.

76 C. Dyhouse, 'Social Darwinistic ideas and the development of women's education in England 1880–1920', *History of Education*, 5, 1976, 41–58; S. Delamont and L. Duffin (eds), *The Nineteenth-Century Woman*, London,

Croom Helm, 1978, chs 3–4 *passim*; J. Burstyn, *Victorian Education and the Ideal of Womanhood*, London, Croom Helm, 1980, ch. 5 *passim*; A. Digby and P. Searby, *Children, School and Society in Nineteenth-Century England*, London, Macmillan, 1981, 49–52, 219–24.

77 H. Maudsley, 'Sex in mind and education', *Fortnightly Review*, 21, 1874, 475–6.
78 J. Manton, *Elizabeth Garrett Anderson*, London, Methuen, 1987, 236–7.
79 E. Garrett Anderson, 'Sex in mind and education: a reply', *Fortnightly Review*, 21, 1874, 585–6.
80 T. S. Clouston, *Female Education from a Medical Point of View*, Edinburgh, 1882, 26–42.
81 J. Thorburn, 'Female education in its physiological aspect', in *Six Introductory Lectures*, Manchester, 1884, 95–6, 102.
82 Thorburn, *Practical Treatise*, 102.
83 *The Times*, 15 April 1880, 17 February 1881.
84 Playfair, 'The nervous system', in Allbutt and Playfair (eds), op. cit., 221.
85 T. S. Clouston, *The Hygiene of Mind*, 3rd edn, London, Methuen, 1906, 581.
86 ibid., 157.
87 T. S. Clouston, 'The psychological dangers to women in modern social developments', in *The Position of Women, Actual and Ideal*, London, James Nisbet, 1911, 109–10.
88 See T. Laqueur, 'Orgasm, generation and the politics of reproductive biology', and L. Schiebinger, 'Skeletons in the closet: the first illustrations of the female skeleton in eighteenth-century anatomy', *Representations*, 14, 1986, for a more detailed exploration of these points.
89 For a discussion of the way in which other 'scientific' work of the period was unduly influenced by contemporary gender roles, see F. Alaya, 'Victorian science and the "genius of woman"', *Journal of the History of Ideas*, 38, 1977, 261–80; S. S. Mosedale, 'Science corrupted: Victorian biologists consider "the woman question"', *Journal of the History of Biology*, 11, 2, 1978, 1–55.

Chapter Seven

PRIVILEGE AND PATRIARCHY: FEMINIST THOUGHT IN THE NINETEENTH CENTURY

MARY MAYNARD

This chapter is an attempt by someone trained as a sociologist to understand the ideas, beliefs, and assumptions of nineteenth-century feminists. It has arisen from my experiences of teaching on an interdisciplinary MA in Women's Studies and from my growing awareness of the academic and personal benefits which can be obtained from breaking out of one's own particular disciplinary mould. With this in mind I began to turn my longstanding interest in feminist thought away from simply a study of its 'second-wave' characteristics, to its earlier manifestations in the Victorian period. It increasingly seemed important to ascertain whether an understanding of the thinking of 'first-wave' feminists could throw any light on the ways in which more contemporary forms have developed. In doing this I wanted to discover whether the issues with which nineteenth-century feminists had grappled were similar to those agonized over today. I hoped to reveal what elements they had identified as being at the root of their subordinate position, how they viewed gender relationships, and what kinds of visions they held for the future. In short, I was anxious to learn what kinds of intellectual heritage had been left to us by our Victorian sisters.

Over the past few years a vast amount of rich and detailed literature has been produced on women's experiences and situation in the nineteenth century, and a considerable proportion of this has been devoted to the feminist movement. I assumed, therefore, that my goal of becoming acquainted with the nature of Victorian feminist thought would be relatively easy to attain, as I expected the subject to have received substantial treatment. The more I read, however, the more it became apparent that this was by no means the case. The secondary source material (both feminist and non-feminist) tends to focus on events and on factual descriptions of the activities and campaigns in which feminists took part. Less readily available is the systematic review of what these women believed they were doing and the terms in which they discussed and tried to understand their predicament. This is in direct contrast to the literature on contemporary feminism, which emphasizes theoretical analysis and ideas but has paid less attention to documenting the history of a movement. The aim of this chapter, therefore, is to begin to consider the various modes of thinking which lay behind the activities and struggles of feminists in the Victorian period. In the first part it will be argued that much of the secondary literature concerned with these women gives us a distorted image of their concerns, which are presented as having little theoretical or analytical foundation. Not only is this a misrepresentation of Victorian feminism, but it also inaccurately reflects the images the women involved held of themselves. These, as will become apparent, while being the product of nineteenth-century ideology and morality, are often startlingly perceptive and of contemporary relevance.

The second part of the chapter focuses on some of the issues and themes relating to women's lives with which nineteenth-century feminists were concerned. It emphasizes the contradictions and tensions in these, indicating the range of thinking and positions which existed during the period.

The third section of the chapter argues that one line of thought which seems to concern and unite a lot of nineteenth-century feminists is a developing critique of sex privilege. Sometimes this involved a critique of the social construction of masculinity. Sometimes it meant blaming and criticizing particular types of men. At other times it was the system of patriarchal privilege, regarded as having been developed by men to support and extend their own interests, which was the focus of attention. It will be argued that we are mistaken to see Victorian feminism only as a series of piecemeal reform-oriented activities and that much is to be gained from a careful examination of the patterns of thought which lay behind the various campaigns. Indeed, only by doing so can we properly comprehend these early writers and activists as feminist sisters.

At this point, before beginning the main discussion, several caveats need to be made. First, the approach adopted here is woman-centred. It is about women's views about women and is not concerned with what men thought about them. This may be regarded as contentious, particularly since some of the most prolific writers on women's position in the nineteenth century were male – J. S. Mill and William Thompson, for example. Nevertheless the view held to here is that such authors have been afforded fairly detailed space elsewhere, whereas the thinking of women, although they poured forth a steady stream of books, pamphlets, journals, and broadsheets, has less often been subject to scrutiny.

A second issue to be noted is that of the definition of 'feminist' being employed. I do not intend to engage in a long discussion of this matter, although clearly it is highly important. However, other writers have already raised it as a problem, particularly in the context of the nineteenth century, where the term itself was not in use.[1] Here the term 'feminist' will be used not just to refer to a 'systematic campaigning for women's rights' but also to include 'sensitivity to their needs, awareness of their problems and concern for their situation'.[2] Such a definition involves acknowledging that Victorian feminism was concerned not just with 'women's rights' but also with their 'emancipation'. Gerda Lerner has described this as 'freedom from oppressive restrictions imposed by sex; self-determination; autonomy'.[3]

A further point to be made is that the focus of this chapter is Britain, that the discussion spans only the second half of the nineteenth century, and that, broadly speaking, it is concerned with middle-class, so-called 'equal rights' feminism. Of course, it would have been interesting indeed to have included other material, particularly from America, where the books of Charlotte Perkins Gilman and of Margaret Fuller are generally regarded as containing the most comprehensive theoretical accounts by women of women's position in the period. Further, as Barbara Taylor and others have clearly demonstrated, a lot of feminist writing and activities existed prior to the 1850s.[4] But these additions must be left to future analyses. The point of this chapter is to examine the kinds of feminist thought which developed in Britain from the 1850s onwards, given the silence of most secondary sources on the subject.

THE DISTORTED IMAGE

There are three major ways in which historians have analysed nineteenth-century feminism. The first of these focuses on specific issues and the campaigns relating to them that were organized to bring about reform. An example here would be the work of Lee Holcombe, which focuses on the struggle for the reform of the married women's property laws.[5] A similar approach is to be found in Walkowitz's study of prostitution, with its analysis of the campaign against the Contagious Diseases Acts and exploration of the general fight against the sexual double standard, and the many descriptions of the battle for suffrage.[6] A second focus in the literature has been on documenting the history of the nineteenth-century women's movement, taken as a whole. Here the concern is to record in detail women's various struggles for personal, legal, political, and social liberties. The timing of events is noted, the involvement of particular individuals is described, and the outcome of their activities is evaluated.[7] A third source of information is to be found in the burgeoning biographical literature. Here the lives of those active in nineteenth-century feminist politics are told. Their family backgrounds, friendships, and interests are traced, and their contributions to pioneering changes in the Victorian period are explored.[8]

It goes without saying, of course, that these three categories of work have given us an enormous amount of detailed and rich data, and have in many ways transformed our understanding of the period under consideration. However, it is my contention that they convey – sometimes explicitly, sometimes implicitly – a particular (and distorted) imagery of nineteenth-century feminists and their politics. For instance, this portrays the women concerned as being active in campaigns that were largely *unconnected* to each other. Even when it is acknowledged that many feminists involved themselves in a number of different causes, the relationship between these is hardly ever addressed. It is as though the Victorian women's movement was largely a disparate, piecemeal affair, composed of separate issues and activities in which people chose to take part on the basis of personal whim. Another picture conjured up of the feminists' position is that it is mainly a *reactive* one. This is to say that those involved appear to be simply responding to particular events which act as triggers to a specific bout of campaigning. Caroline Norton's outcry against her treatment at the hands of both husband and state is often taken in this way to have 'set off' the call for reform of the married women's property laws.[9] Similarly, events such as the passage of the first two Contagious Diseases Acts in 1864 and 1866 are regarded as signalling the need to organize to promote changes in attitudes to sexual immorality and vice.[10] Of course, the actions of an individual like

224

Norton and the introduction of anti-woman laws such as the Contagious Diseases Acts obviously aroused public feeling and drew attention to some particularly disquieting aspects of women's position at the time. The issue at stake here, however, is how far feminists simply responded to such triggers, or to what extent they were actively creating and constructing, throughout the second half of the nineteenth century, analyses and explanations of their subordinate position which then enabled them to make sense of the various 'triggering events' when they occurred? It seems to me highly likely that they were developing theories in this way, as is clear when we begin to explore the rich sources of primary material, the articles, pamphlets, and letters, in which nineteenth-century women themselves speak and which have only recently begun to be redisovered by feminist scholars. However, very little of this thinking has made its way into the history of the period, as currently available. Instead, Victorian feminists appear as *doing* rather than as developing ideas. They are busy organizing meetings, drafting the odd piece of propaganda, drawing up petitions, and, of course, campaigning. They are not often shown to have much of a coherent view of women's position *as women*. The whole image constructed of their politics is that it is one directed at achieving reforms, not at trying to understand or explain why, as women, such reforms needed to be sought in the first place. It is because of the lack of focus on such matters that I refer to our image of Victorian feminists as being *distorted*.

Now clearly, in focusing on only three main types of source material on nineteenth-century feminism, I am in danger of overstating my case. For, in recent years, other kinds of discussions on the subject have begun to emerge. One of the most important of these has charted the intellectual traditions deriving from the Enlightenment, evangelicalism, and various kinds of socialism, and the ways in which they led to feminism's birth.[11] A further development has been the growing interest in the politics of working-class women, and this has led to analyses of their role in the campaign for suffrage and their increasing clamour for trade-union representation, as well as to biographies of particularly influential individuals.[12] Most of this work, though, contains only passing reference to what the women involved, be they middle class or working class, thought they were doing and why they were doing it. In other words, it does little to correct the piecemeal, reactive, unreflective image of nineteenth-century feminism described above.

In fact, only a small number of texts actually do address the general issue of feminist thought. These either take the form of biographical descriptions of particular feminists' views and ideas or comprise volumes of selected extracts from women's writing on a wide range of subjects.[13] Neither of these kinds of literature attempts to draw out themes or relate the ideas of different authors on different subjects to each other. Indeed, for Britain, Olive Banks's *Becoming a Feminist* contains the only direct discussion I have found, as yet, about the beliefs lying behind feminists' more practical goals.[14] In a chapter entitled 'Feminist ideology' Banks draws on data obtained from the writing of a sample of Victorian 'feminist' women and men to categorize their ideas and views about the relationships of men and women. She argues that the resulting 'ideology' she is able to describe should be regarded as 'both the cause and the justification for the campaigns themselves'.[15] In other words, she suggests that the activities of nineteenth-century feminists cannot be properly understood without also considering the ideas about gender relationships and women's position generally which were current at the time.

FEMINIST THOUGHT: ISSUES AND THEMES

Olive Banks identifies nine different positions 'which appear to represent different aspects or facets of feminist ideology'.[16] In some respects the approach adopted here is similar, but it does differ in significant ways. It is based on an analysis of various kinds of publications produced by feminists from the 1850s onwards. The emphasis is on the ways in which feminist thought operates at different levels of analysis. By this I mean that, first, I have identified a range of substantive issues, to do with such matters as equal rights and the family, which concerned feminists and which, broadly speaking, are predicated either on their own experiences or on the experiences of other women for whom they were concerned. As will be seen, feminists did not always agree on their position in regard to such issues, and often contradictory views about them were expressed. Nevertheless, despite this confusing lack of consensus, opposing views can still be regarded as feminist in nature if they can be seen to be held with the hope of freeing women from oppressive relationships and allowing them a degree of self-determination. Perhaps it should be added in parenthesis here that contemporary feminist thinking is itself not immune from the kinds of contradictions that will be described.

Behind this range of substantive issues, however, lies a different order of thinking which operates in a rather different way. Here I identify a number of themes – concerning, for instance, the nature of the sexual division of labour, or whether it is freedom or protection which nineteenth-century women require – which inform the ways in which the substantive issues are addressed but which cannot be reduced entirely to them. Many of these are couched in terms of polar opposites, for example, the acceptance of separate spheres for men and women versus the challenging of such a distinction. A further, third level of thought for analysis is discussed in the section of the chapter on 'Feminist thoughts or feminist theory?'. This deals with feminist views on male privilege and the possible existence of systematic theorizing on the subject.

Issues in feminist thought

There are four broad issues in my categorization of feminist thought, each of which contains a number of emphases within it: equal rights; women and the family; employment and economic dependency; and sexuality and the threat from male lust.

Equal rights

Obviously the question of equal rights was highly prominent in the nineteenth century, and the rights that women sought were thought to be obtainable in civil society as well as in law. Women of the period wrote of their 'rights' to education, to the custody of their children, to access to the medical profession, and to ownership of property, as well as their 'rights' to be treated as persons in law and to be given the vote. However, it is not the claim to rights *per se* which concerns me here. Rather it is the way in which the language of the arguments was couched which reveals something about how Victorian feminists viewed women. There were several differing aspects to this. The first discusses women's position in terms of their *inalienable rights as human beings*. This derives in part from the liberal philosophy of individualism, which, since it has been well covered by Susan Mendus in chapter 5, will not be treated in any detail here. Its main points, however, follow from the argument that in the beginning man and woman were created equals by God, their differences having being designed to complement each other and form a harmonious unity. But man has usurped his role as protector of woman and established arbitrary rule over her. She has been degraded to the position of slave, for men have taken upon themselves the right to dictate to women what they should and should not do. This is both unjust and insulting. Yet the fact that women are protesting and demanding their inalienable rights shows they are not simply the natural appendages of men. As Helen Taylor proclaimed, woman

> claims the right to belong to herself, as a self-contained individual existence . . . in short her right to live up to the full measure of her capacities to reach up to the highest and most useful standard she can attain. . . . As her interests are co-extensive with human interests, wherever they extend her voice should be heard.[17]

The message here is that *all* human beings should be allowed to attain the most of which they are capable. The nature of those capabilities cannot be discerned without complete freedom and liberty of choice. Note that this is not an argument which necessarily implies that men and women are the same, simply that they resemble each other more than they differ and thus should be afforded equal civil and legal rights.

Not all advocates adhered to this view of rights, however, and, particularly as the century progressed, more women began to advocate them on the grounds of what Kraditor calls *expediency* rather than natural justice.[18] Both positions were represented in feminist circles well into the twentieth century and were sometimes both embraced by a particular writer. The expediency argument suggests not that woman should be given rights because she is in some sense man's equal but that certain benefits are to be gained by allowing women access to areas previously denied to them. Sometimes it is the benefits likely to accrue to *women themselves* which are highlighted. For instance, one of the arguments for educating girls was constructed in terms of the moral and mental training and development this would provide, enabling them to become better people.[19] It was also said that, since only women could understand women's experiences and interests, only they were capable of properly representing them-selves.[20] On other occasions the gains which extending certain rights to women would bring to the *sphere of the family* were highlighted. Many advocates of girls' schooling, for instance, also employed this tack, claiming that, among other things, educating women would make them better wives and mothers.[21] Millicent Garrett Fawcett, along with others, used it to suggest that it was women's *duty* to work for suffrage, stating that 'we want to have the ennobling influence of national responsibility brought into their lives'.[22] She argued that the wife and mother in a family should be more than just a housekeeper, or nurse, and that she would be better able to care for her husband and children if she was able to cater for their mental as well as physical needs.[23] A further argument for rights on the grounds of expediency claimed that women's participation in the *public sphere* would *improve the quality of the activities and decision-making* which occurred there as they were affected by women's particular abilities and strengths.[24] Such ideas were put forward in support of suffrage at both national and municipal levels, to support women's public service in prisons, public health, the workhouse, etc., and to encourage participation in pressure groups such as the Women's Industrial Council. An additional idea often put forward was that single women, variously referred to as 'superfluous' or 'redundant', should be allowed to engage in employment that was currently denied to them, not just enabling them to support themselves but also 'converting them into useful members of society'.[25]

Women and the family

There were several ways in which women's role in the family was discussed. The first, and most challenging, of these was the suggestion by certain feminists that *marriage did not necessarily have to be women's main or only vocation*. Barbara Bodichon, for example, observed that it was absurd to treat women as if they existed only in and for marriage, when significant numbers of adult women did not in fact live in this state.[26] Josephine Butler suggested that society had a lot of work to be done which required men and women to be detached from domestic ties, and she proclaimed: 'I cannot believe it is every woman's duty to marry, in this age of the world.'[27]

A second aspect of feminists' views on the family can be found in the *criticisms which they levelled at nineteenth-century marriage*. These consisted of: an attack on women's lack of financial resources and their enforced dependency on men; the suggestion that a wife's economic dependence on her husband put marriage on a par with prostitution; criticism of many nineteenth-century laws which were regarded as designed to keep women subordinate to men; and analyses of domestic violence, and man's general roughness to woman, which it was claimed helped to confirm men's power and authority over their wives.[28]

It is small wonder, then, that many Victorian feminists advocated a *positive role for single women* in the second half of the nineteenth century. This was not, as Martha Vicinus has suggested, simply because the statistics indicated the likelihood that there would not be enough men to go round, or an attempt by those without a husband to make the best of a bad job.[29] Rather, several women described how marriage gave wives little time for other things and how, as unmarried women, they had been free to pursue different forms of fulfilment and happiness.[30]

Yet, despite this strong awareness of the difficulties which marriage and family life presented to women, it would be very far from the truth to imply that nineteenth-century feminists were against the institution altogether. In fact marriage and motherhood were still regarded as women's primary roles. They were seen as the normal, but not inevitable, aspect of most women's lives. Rather, it was the wife's *subordination* in marriage with which they disagreed, and their challenge was largely to its patriarchal, authoritarian, and hierarchical form. In contrast, they emphasized the need for an *egalitarian relationship*, where marriage was a partnership and the wife equal to the husband.[31] Yet closer scrutiny of the literature suggests that, for most writers, it was not equality so much as *complementarity* which was being suggested.[32] Many, for instance (including J. S. Mill), seemed to accept that men and women would have different roles to play in the home and that these would be premised on the wife's maternal and domestic skills.[33] Indeed, it is precisely these aspects of women's duties, household management and servicing the comfort of others, which were held to be the qualities which women should take with them from the private into the public sphere. Certainly, when it came to motherhood, it was a concern with improving the conditions under which childcare took place which was discussed, rather than any suggestion that women should necessarily limit their families.[34] For in the context of the nineteenth century few were brave enough to raise the delicate issue of family planning. In summary, then, the nineteenth-century feminists, while being highly critical of the way in which the realities of family life treated women, tended to argue for elements of its internal reconstruction rather than either its transformation or its abolition.

Employment and economic dependency

There were a number of ways in which Victorian feminists addressed the issue of female employment. The first of these was to argue that paid work for women was *normal, desirable, and would make them into better human beings*. For example, both Bodichon and Butler pointed out that women had worked prior to industrialization, but that social and economic changes had taken economic activity away from them.[35] This must now be reversed. It was also suggested that women required employment to keep their minds and bodies active and healthy. Bodichon, for instance, attacked the notion that the feminine woman necessarily had to be 'frivolous, ignorant, weak and sickly' rather than gainfully occupied. She urged mothers to persuade their daughters not to pursue an idle life, proclaiming that 'No human being has the right to be idle'.[36]

A second argument advanced as to why women should have employment was to do with their need for an *independent income*. As we have seen, part of the critique of marriage at that time often centred around the way in which it forced women to be economically dependent on their husbands. It was also pointed out that, for those women who were not asked, or who chose not to marry, there was often little to look forward to in life other than destitution, particularly if their fathers or brothers objected to providing support. This was because the employment opportunities were very restricted for women, partly because of the expectation that they would be dependent on a man. Further, a woman whose husband died, or refused or was not able to maintain the family, would generally end up living in poverty. The resolution to all this, it was claimed, was to get rid of the stigma which prevented 'genteel' women from working, and to *expand the numbers and kinds of jobs* which it was acceptable for them to do. The corollary argument here was the need for women to be given adequate education and training, for, even when they were allowed into the job market, they tended to be disadvantaged because of their lack of skills.[37]

The latter decades of the nineteenth century saw some of the first deliberate and consistent attempts to organize women workers in Britain. Very few women were members of trade unions in the 1870s, and even where they were accepted into mixed unions, as in the textile industry, little had been done for them as a special group. The major issues for the members of the Women's Protective and Provident

League, which was set up in 1874, as for those involved in the Women's Industrial Council, which was founded in 1889, related to women's appalling working conditions, especially in occupations where they were not in competition with men, their very low pay, and the question of *protective legislation*. Protection was designed to limit the number of hours women could work, prevent them from taking on night work, and exclude them from certain types of jobs. The early women trade-unionists were against such laws, seeing them simply as an attempt to restrict women's employment.[38] This position was supported by those feminists who were arguing for the extension of work opportunities for women. For example, the *Englishwoman's Review* published the following in favour of allowing women to continue their pit-brow work:

> It seems to us that if legislation has any right to legislate at all about the labour of adults, it should do so impartially, and if it interferes to shut women out from work which they probably would not enter upon if they could get better paid for other kinds of labour, should prohibit men from undertaking light and easy employments, adapted to feminine strength.[39]

Some feminists held on to this view until the end of the century.[40] However, among women trade-union leaders, protective legislation gradually came to be seen as a major vehicle for improving the working conditions of women in industry, and, as Banks and Mappen have noted, the issue became a divisive one for feminism on many fronts.[41]

Sexuality and the threat of male lust

Nineteenth-century feminist thinking on sexuality is usually portrayed as developing as part of the hostile response to the Contagious Diseases Acts of the 1860s. While the campaign against these Acts highlighted a number of sexual and moral issues, it is important to remember that these were surfacing *before* the advent of the campaign itself and were still causing controversy at the beginning of the following century. The issues which were most significant centred around the double standard, the sexual economics of prostitution, the abuse of women's bodies, and women's need for protection from men.

Opposition to the *double standard* informed feminists' views on the other three issues. It involved a critique of male sexual hypocrisy whereby two different standards of sexual morality – one for men, the other for women – were in existence.[42] This hypocrisy, it was said, had led to the passing of the Contagious Diseases Acts, which punished prostitutes at the same time as protecting men and legitimizing their sexual misdemeanours. All women were affected by male immorality, since 'Any woman can be dragged into court, and required to prove that she is not a common prostitute'.[43] Feminists identified the double standard as an important element in the sexual exploitation of women. This could be seen not only in the legal system, which protected men while prosecuting their victims, but also in the general toleration of male sexual indulgence and in the actual physical and sexual abuse of women by men.[44]

Prostitution tended to be viewed as part of women's overall sexual and economic exploitation. Since women's entry to employment was restricted, feminists argued that it was quite often sheer economic necessity which put women on to the streets and forced them to become the victims of male lust. Indeed, for writers such as Bodichon and Butler, whether women 'traded' their bodies as prostitutes, mistresses, or wives made no difference, since they were all using sexual means in order to receive material support.[45]

Concern about the *abuse of women's bodies* was expressed in different ways. There was growing feeling, for instance, against the notion that a woman's body belonged to her husband, and there were increasing demands that men should learn to be chaste and be governed by the same standards of sexual morality as women, and for sexual intercourse only to take place when conception was intended.[46] Behind some of the writing appears to have been the view that the male sexual urge was a social, not a biological phenomenon, which could and should be controlled. There was also concern at the way in which women's bodies were examined, particularly during the period when the Contagious Diseases Acts were in force. Butler, for instance, referred to examinations as 'instrumental rape', with the speculum described as a 'steel penis', and several feminists argued for the necessity of women doctors, magistrates, and even police to be on hand to deal with women in sensitive ways.[47]

Nineteenth-century feminists' thinking about and work with prostitutes and those who had been raped, assaulted, and sexually harassed led to demands that women should be *protected* from male sexual abuse, primarily through male restraint, though later, in the first decades of the twentieth century, such measures as women-only parks, girl-only playgrounds, and women-only carriages in trains were advocated.[48] It has been customary in the past for commentators to see such measures as reactionary and puritanical and for those who called for a restriction on men's sexual behaviour to be regarded as prudes. Yet, as has recently been argued, behind the call for female protection lay a positive view of womanhood and the image of women's bodies as under attack.[49] It is not surprising that, in an era when contraception was not easily available, women should want to play down sex and sexuality. For many feminists, therefore, the threat from unbridled male lust was a core issue for both their thinking and their political agenda.

Themes in feminist thought

The above discussion has focused on some of the substantive issues which lay at the heart of nineteenth-century feminist thinking. It has indicated that many of these issues were approached from differing views and assumptions about the relationship between the sexes and the nature of womanhood. Further, it highlights some of the complexities and differences of idea which were developing at the time and which are hidden by only talking about campaigns and practical political activity. Many of these issues are still at the forefront of feminist discussion today.

Behind these substantive issues, however, lay certain key themes. These themes, which are to do with women's legitimate place and role in society, informed and helped to articulate the ways in which the substantive matters were discussed, although the one cannot be deduced directly from the other. The themes identified are not necessarily straightforwardly or unambiguously addressed in feminists' thinking. Rather, they constitute the backdrop against which matters of a more day-to-day significance were considered. The themes highlight some of the tensions underlying feminists' views. They can be seen as a series of continua, with different positions being adopted by different feminists.

The first major axis of debate concerned whether women were asking for improved rights (be these claimed on the grounds of either natural justice or expediency) or whether they were seeking new and improved opportunities for fulfilling their womanly duties. The theme of rights versus duties was significant in many areas of feminist thinking, and not just when the question of equal rights as a general issue was being discussed. For instance, discussions of the need for improved relationships in the family could centre on the justice of woman's equality with her husband or the need for more favourable conditions to facilitate the proper performance of her role.[50] Opening up education and medical training to women could be advanced either in terms of its natural justice or as a means of helping women to be better at their caring and servicing duties.[51] It can be seen, therefore, that one's view as to whether rights or duties were at stake could have profound implications for one's position on other issues. Nineteenth-century feminists disagreed on this matter, as they did on many others.

A second theme focused on the nature of womanhood and what this implied for the relationship between the sexes. Some feminists, for example, clearly saw men and women as equal human beings.[52] Others adopted the view that the roles of the two sexes were complementary: the 'different but equal' stance.[53] There was, as we have seen, a lot of support for the position that women were *naturally* equal to men. Also espoused, however, were arguments to the effect that equality was not naturally given, but had to be *attained*, and that social and cultural restrictions were preventing women from reaching that goal.[54] Others, of course, held that woman's natural *differences* from man should be the basis of the demand for wider opportunities. A further and related issue here was whether women should 'make much of their sex' by asserting their femininity in their favour or whether they should make little of it, playing down any differences with men.[55] As will have become apparent, there were differing attitudes to this dilemma. For some, feminism obviously involved minimizing sex differences in the course of arguing for equal treatment. But for others it was woman's special qualities as woman which were to be emphasized, sometimes to the point of asserting the moral superiority of women over men.

The third area of tension centred on the sexual division of labour. It was concerned with whether feminists consented to the current reality and ideology relating to acceptable activities and roles for women, whether there were arguments for these to be extended, or whether the division between male and female roles, as then prescribed, should be challenged. Again we can find feminists adopting a range of positions in relation to this, with some accepting the sexual division of labour, others arguing for its transformation, and many taking a more middle-of-the-road position. A related concern here was the

235

relationship between the public and the private spheres and the assumption that they were gender-specific. While some feminists were prepared to accept the public/private distinction, others were not. Arguments ranged form the assertion that the boundaries of woman's sphere should be extended to allow her female qualities to influence aspects of public life, to attacks on the very existence of separate spheres for men and women.[56] Once again a full spectrum of opinion on the theme of legitimate activities and roles for women exists in their writings.

At first glance, a final tension to be found in the thinking of Victorian feminists is that between advocacy of the need for women's protection on the one hand and the assertion of the demand for their independence and autonomy on the other. We have seen, for example, that feminists wanted women to be afforded protection on one issue, that of male sexuality, while arguing against it in another sphere, that of employment. Further, an important crux of some feminists' thought was woman's need to be treated as autonomous from man, both legally and economically, in order for her to be a properly independent and 'free' human being. Yet, while this was clearly a tension in their thinking, it is not necessarily the contradiction that some commentators have claimed.[57] For it could be argued that freedom from being treated as continually sexually available to men is an important aspect of developing autonomy and freedom. Indeed, can one have the latter without the former? While this may sound too much like the voice of contemporary feminism speaking, there is evidence from the writings of women like Butler, Swiney, and Wolstenholme Elmy that such an analysis was very much at the heart of their campaigns around sexuality.[58] The matter of protection versus autonomy was, therefore, a fairly complex one in the context of nineteenth-century feminist thinking.

The existence of contradictory themes in Victorian feminist thought led to the development of many different views on the nature of both feminism and femininity. Yet this should not blind us to the inherent radicalism in their analyses. For, while it was obviously challenging for women to demand equality with men and entry to the world of public issues, it was also, in the context of the nineteenth century, equally daring to be asking for increased opportunities, even if the arguments used were based on fairly conservative assumptions about women's duty and role in life. Nineteenth-century feminists are often taken to task by twentieth-century commentators for being reformist and not developing their politics further. But not only does this ignore the very restrictive context in which these women were working; it also overlooks the radicalism inherent in what they thought they were doing. In the following section I shall take this point further by considering who and what feminists thought they were fighting and how they perceived themselves in relation to this.

FEMINIST THOUGHTS OR FEMINIST THEORY?

The previous discussion has identified certain issues and themes in the thinking of Victorian feminists. These have been referred to as different elements in their 'thought', a term used to signify that they were engaged in serious reflection on both their own experiences and those of other women during the period. Yet, as presented so far, nineteenth-century feminist thought appears to be as piecemeal and as disparate as the usual characterizations of their political actions. What seems lacking is any sense of an overall coherent critique of women's position and possible explanations for it. Did feminists regard their activities as simply fighting for an abstract right, such as 'the vote', or challenging a non-human agent, such as 'vice', or did they operate with a more detailed understanding of the politics in which they were engaged? On the basis of their writings I believe that it is possible to suggest that they did have a more comprehensive view.

One aspect of this is the questioning of gender relations which pervades their thought. This can be seen in all the issues previously discussed, whether the focus is on equal rights, the family, employment, or sexuality. For it is not simply woman's position which is addressed but woman's position *in relation to man's*, and it is the relationship between the two as much as a concern with woman herself which is discussed. Even when the conventional view of woman's role is accepted, it is the contemporary relation between the sexes, taken to demean this role, which is the focus of attention.

A further point is that once we consider these feminists' views on gender relations, rather than simply concentrating on issues, it becomes possible to identify embryonic theorizing in their work. Here I am making a distinction between thought and theory. I take feminist theory to comprise the act of systematically connecting various aspects of women's subordinate position to reach an interrelated framework of explanations. On the basis of such a framework, the origins of, reproduction of, and possibility of changes in women's

237

position can be explored. Although rooted in women's experience, the purpose of such theory is to be able to generalize about particular aspects of womanhood, without necessarily having to reduce everything to the individual experience of a particular woman. I refer to nineteenth-century feminist theory as 'embryonic' not to dismiss their ideas as immature or undeveloped, nor because I do not recognize the important contribution of those who did publish theoretical treatises. For many writers, however, it is a very difficult task systematically to bring together articles and papers written on different subjects for different audiences over a period of many years. Feminist theorists, unlike the founding fathers of many academic disciplines, tended not to present their work in large, authoritative-like tomes.

What it is possible to do, though – and this is my third point – is to acknowledge the considerable preoccupation of nineteenth-century feminists with men. A constant theme in their writings on women's condition was the role of *men* in creating and perpetuating particular sources of subordination for women, whether this was in the public or the private arena. Since this aspect of their thinking is seldom discussed in the literature, the subject deserves further attention. It should be added that even women with husbands and male friends who gave them positive political support were critical of men in their analyses. Yet agreement on this issue did not necessarily signify consensus on other matters, and we find adherents to many political persuasions – some conservative, like Cobbe – among these feminist critics.

If we return to the topic of equal rights it is clear that feminists considered the beliefs and actions of men to be crucial in preventing them from achieving their goals. Regarding the law, for instance, a common theme to be found in the *English Woman's Journal* during the 1850s and 1860s was the fact that the legal system had been created by men to protect their interests. Because men were in positions of power, it was argued, they were able to ensure that the system was retained, in the face of all the evidence that it was unjust. It was, therefore, *men* who were claimed to be denying women their inalienable rights and *men* who had to be challenged.

Other feminists also advanced this form of analysis. Frances Power Cobbe, for instance, attacked the male legal system in a provocative pamphlet with the title 'Criminals, idiots, women and minors: is the classification sound?' (1868). In this she argued that men made laws on the basis of their own limited experiences, and that in doing so they thought only of themselves and were mainly concerned with strengthening their own positions of power. She pointed out that on marriage it was entirely legal for men to take all of their wives' possessions, but they did not have any legal responsibilities towards them in return. Cobbe writes:

> The legal act by which a man puts his hand in his wife's pocket, or draws her money out of the savings bank, is perfectly clear, easy, inexpensive. . . . the corresponding process by which the wife can obtain food and clothing from her husband when he neglects to provide it, where may it be? Where is it described?[59]

Cobbe forces her point home by describing women's situation in nineteenth-century society, through the eyes of a 'visitor' from a distant planet who comes with different cultural assumptions. The subject is the law's attitude to marriage, and, having rehearsed the visitor's increasingly incredulous questions about what it entails, she finishes her parable with the following lines:

> Pardon me; I must seem to you so stupid! Why is the property of the woman who commits Murder, and the property of the woman who commits Matrimony, dealt with alike by your law?[60]

The argument from the feminists is clear: men make laws which treat women as their property. Men make such laws because, in rendering women dependent on them, they can then treat women how they like, keep their resources, use their bodies, even physically abuse them.

That men place women in such a double bind is argued in writings on many subjects. For example, nearly all those who campaigned for women's education shared the assumption that a basic reason why women were not treated seriously as intellectuals was because they were not being educated. But whose fault was this? Why, men had constructed the education system and decreed that only those who received certain kinds of instruction were serious and rational human beings. *De facto*, then, women were regarded as other than serious and rational because men denied them access to learning. They then became what men intended, frivolous creatures, and easy for men to control.[61]

It is possible to find equally strong views from nineteenth-century women on marriage. Several of them, as already noted, wrote severe indictments of the position in which man-made laws placed married women. They also pointed out that marriage gave women very limited horizons that would never have been accepted by men.[62] A further argument, made particularly powerfully, focuses on woman's economic dependence on her husband and the ways in which this serves to safeguard man's authority and power in the home. The language used time and time again is of woman as victim – victim of man's superior position, power, and control. The point is brought home very poignantly in nineteenth-century feminists' discussion of wife-beating. Cobbe, for example, highlights two particular aspects of what she calls 'wife torture': the way in which it is considered as a source of humour, and its foundation in a man's perception of his wife as his property. In an article very reminiscent of feminist writing on domestic violence today, Cobbe says:

> The assault on a wife by her husband seems to be surrounded by a certain halo of jocularity which invites people to smile whenever they hear of a case of it . . . and causes the mention of the subject to conduce rather than otherwise to the hilarity of a dinner party. . . . Probably the sense that they must carry with them a good deal of tacit sympathy on the part of other men has something to do in encouraging wife-beaters, just as the fatal notion of the good fellowship of drink has made thousands of sots. . . . The general depreciation of women *as a sex* is bad enough, but in the matter we are considering, the special depreciation of *wives* is more directly responsible for the outrages they endure. The notion that a man's wife is his PROPERTY . . . is the fatal root of incalculable evil and misery. Every brutal-minded man, and many a man who in other relations of life is not brutal, entertains more or less vaguely the notion that his wife is his *thing*.[63]

Cobbe and others saw violence against women not as the pathological behaviour of a few 'sick' men but as an extension of a system of practices and laws which sanctioned men's rights to regard women as their property and, therefore, keep them under their control.

Women's lack of economic independence is also discussed in terms of their poor education and training and their supposed reliance on men, leading to what Martineau referred to as an 'artificial depreciation of women's work'.[64] Again the view is expressed that women's improved access to the world of work and of skills and knowledge is denied to them by men, whose laws, customs, and behaviour are an obstacle to women's greater achievement. Indeed, as Matthews has suggested,[65] Bodichon even expressed the germ of an idea that women's work is regarded as inferior and is badly paid because it is done by women and not because the women themselves are unskilled: 'So long as nearly every remunerative employment is engrossed by men only, so long must the wretchedness and slavery of women remain what is it.'[66]

Clearly, however, one of the severest indictments of the nineteenth-century male was to be found in the arguments around the sexual double standard. Whether it was sexuality, over-indulgence, sexual harassment, or the Contagious Diseases Acts which were the focus of attention, an attack on male standards and behaviour was at the forefront of the analyses. For instance, writing about the plight of prostitutes, J. Ellice Hopkins asks, rhetorically, who is responsible for their sorry state, and replies:

Men; men who ought to have protected them instead of degrading them; men who have taken advantage of a woman's weakness to gratify their own selfish pleasure, not seeing that a woman's weakness was given to call out man's strength. Ay, I know that it is often the woman who tempts; these poor creatures must tempt or starve. But that does not touch the broad issue, that it is men who endow the degradation of women; it is men who, making the demand, create the supply.[67]

A similar point was made by Josephine Butler, quoting one of the victims of the Contagious Diseases Acts:

I recall the bitter complaint of one of these poor women: 'It is *men, men, only men*, from the first to the last. . . . To please a man I did wrong at first, then I was flung about from man to man. Men police lay hands on us. By men we are examined, handled, doctored. . . . In the hospitals it is a man again who makes prayers and reads the Bible for us. We are had up before the magistrates who are men, and we never get out of the hands of men til we die."'

And Butler recalls:

as she spoke I thought, "And it was a Parliament of men only who made this law which treats you as an outlaw. Men alone met in committee over it. Men alone are the executives."[68]

In drawing attention to nineteenth-century feminists' critique of men, I have, of course, cited only a few examples of the many available to make my point. I am not suggesting that *all* feminists

241

wrote about men in this way, nor am I claiming that such an emphasis is the only existing undercurrent in their thought. What I *am* arguing, however, is that the problematic of men and maleness as a way of opening up the question of gender relations, as a vehicle for trying to explain woman's subordinate situation, and as an indication of the need for possible social changes constitutes an attempt by feminists to place their particular concerns within an overall theoretical framework. This involves a perspective which critiques maleness: men, masculinity, and male power. There appear to be three positions relating to this. Different writings focused upon whether the root of women's inferior position was the behaviour of men, the construction of their gender, or the institutionalization of their privilege.

First, there is the understanding of woman's position as the result of the behaviour of men as *individuals*. Here we find the critique of males as wife-beaters, as poor providers for their families, or as involved in sin and vice. It is the men who act in this way who are the agents through whom women's lives are made a misery and who provide the key to understanding how best these may be improved. Such men must be controlled rather than condoned. A second level of understanding focuses on the more general *social construction of masculinity*, and sometimes of femininity as well. For instance, many of those involved in the fight against the sexual double standard clearly asserted that men were not naturally and inevitably sexually aggressive and indulgent. Rather, these aspects of male identity had been socially constructed and were, therefore, open to change – if men themselves could be persuaded to give up this aspect of their power. We have also seen that some feminists argued that female qualities such as frivolity, ignorance, and a weak constitution were not innate but culturally learnt, to women's disadvantage.

A third level at which the feminist critique of men works is in terms of the existence of a *system* of male power, authority, and sex privilege. Indeed, inasmuch as these notions all imply men's subordination and control of women, they clearly operate at the two previous levels also. Here, however, it is the idea of *systemness* which is emphasized. This implies that there is something about man's power over woman which is not just arbitrary and individualized. Rather, such power should be understood as a complex whole with a range of interconnected parts. Such an approach is to be found in feminists' analyses of their lack of rights, of the law, and in some of their critiques of marriage and the sphere of paid work.[69] In such writings we find the clear understanding that men have historically created a system of patriarchal privilege, that they maintain such a system in their own interests, and, further, that they are not likely to deliver up their stake in such a system without a struggle. Such a position is clearly resonant with that of some feminists today.

If, as I have argued, underlying the concern of nineteenth-century feminists lay a diagnosis of women's position as being determined by men's behaviour and a system of male privilege, then we should also expect to find that diagnosis manifested in the ways in which some worked together as friends, political allies, and intellectual companions. Evidence elsewhere bears considerable testimony to precisely this state of affairs.[70] The importance of women's friendship, as discussed by Jane Rendall in chapter 4 of this volume, the formation of women's organizations and activities, and the significance of having other women's support are all addressed with feeling in the literature and lend weight to the idea of considerable pro-woman sympathies. Eisenstein has argued that there is a real difference between nineteenth-century liberalism and its liberal-feminist variant, 'in that feminism requires a recognition, however implicit and undefined, of the sexual-class identification of women as women'.[71] This suggests that Victorian feminists viewed women not simply as individuals but as individuals differentiated from men in terms of the power men held. They therefore had some sense of women's collective existence and an understanding that it was time 'that women should arise and demand their most sacred rights in regard to their sisters'.[72]

CONCLUSION

This chapter has involved the excursion of a sociologist into historical material. For the author this has proved to be both a challenging and exciting exercise. The analysis presented here depicts Victorian feminists as attempting to explore the reasons for women's subordinate position rather than as simply involved in reactive and disparate activities. It has suggested that behind the campaigns and apparent reforming zeal existed a developing pattern of thought which should be of considerable interest to historians and contemporary feminists.

Despite the social, economic, and political upheavals of the second part of the nineteenth century, the feminists stoically fixed their attentions on *women*. They discussed how the changes taking place at the time would affect their sex and what opportunities needed to be extended to them, and they argued, both in campaigns and in their writing, for an overall improvement in women's position. Behind all these activities, as I have suggested, existed an emerging critique of maleness, male privilege, and male power, signalling systematic condemnation of men's position in society and the ways in which this disadvantaged women. This critique extended to challenging male advantage under the law, male 'rights' within the family, male control of the public sphere, and the hypocrisy of male morality in sexual relations. Indeed, there are many similarities between the issues and ideas put forward by feminists in the nineteenth century and those still discussed by feminists in the 1980s. Not least of these was the argument that part of the explanation for female subordination and 'oppression' was the existence of 'patriarchy' and male power. We are not generally accustomed to seeing such a radical image of our Victorian sisters. In this respect, one of the aims of this chapter has been to set the record straight.

NOTES

1   For example: John Charvet, *Feminism*, London, Dent, 1982; Zillah Eisenstein, *The Radical Future of Liberal Feminism*, New York, Longman, 1981; Richard J. Evans, *The Feminists*, London, Croom Helm, 1977; W. O'Neill (ed.), *The Woman Movement*, Chicago, Quadrangle Books, 1971; Jane Rendall, *The Origins of Modern Feminism*, London, Macmillan, 1985; Katherine M. Rogers, *Feminism in Eighteenth Century England*, Brighton, Harvester, 1982.
2   Rogers, op. cit., 4.
3   Ellen DuBois, Mari Jo Buhle, Temma Kaplan, Gerda Lerner, and Carroll Smith-Rosenberg, 'Politics and culture in women's history: a symposium', *Feminist Studies*, 6, Spring 1980.
4   Barbara Taylor, *Eve and the New Jerusalem*, London, Virago, 1983.
5   Lee Holcombe, *Wives and Property: Reform of the Married Women's Property Law in Nineteenth Century England*, Oxford, Martin Robertson, 1983.
6   See, for example: Paul McHugh, *Prostitution and Victorian Social Reform*, New York, St Martin's Press, 1980; David Morgan, *Suffragists and Liberals: The Politics of Women's Suffrage in England*, Oxford, Blackwell, 1975; Constance Rover, *Women's Suffrage and Party Politics in Britain 1866–1914*, London, Routledge & Kegan Paul, 1967; Judith R. Walkowitz, *Prostitution and Victorian Society*, Cambridge, Cambridge University Press, 1980.
7   For example: Olive Banks, *Faces of Feminism*, Oxford, Martin Robertson, 1981; Evans, op. cit.; O'Neill (ed.), op. cit.; Sheila Rowbotham, *Hidden from History*, London, Pluto, 1973; Ray Strachey, *The Cause*, London, Virago, 1978.

8   For example: Nancy Boyd, *Josephine Butler, Octavia Hill, Florence Nightingale: Three Women who Changed the World*, Macmillan, 1982; Doris Nield Chew, *Ada Nield Chew*, London, Virago, 1982; Margaret Forster, *Significant Sisters*, Harmondsworth, Penguin, 1986; Sheila Herstein, *A Mid-Victorian Feminist: Barbara Leigh Smith Bodichon*, New Haven and London, Yale University Press, 1985; Jill Liddington, *The Life and Times of a Respectable Rebel*, London, Virago, 1984.

9   Holcombe, op. cit.

10 Constance Rover, *Love, Morals, and the Feminists*, London, Routledge & Kegan Paul, 1970.

11 See, for example: Banks, op cit.; Evans, op. cit.; Rendall, op. cit.

12 For instance: Chew, op. cit.; Sheila Lewenhak, *Women and Trade Unions*, London, Ernest Benn, 1977; Liddington, op. cit.; Jill Liddington and Jill Norris, *One Hand Tied Behind Us*, London, Virago, 1978; Norbert C. Soldon, *Women in British Trade Unions 1874–1976*, Dublin, Gill & Macmillan, 1978.

13 See, for example: Patricia Hollis, *Women in Public: The Women's Movement 1850–1900*, London, George Allen & Unwin, 1979; Janet Horowitz Murray, *Strong-Minded Women*, Harmondsworth, Penguin, 1984; Eleanor S. Riemer and John C. Fout (eds), *European Women: A Documentary History 1789–1945*, Brighton, Harvester, 1983; Dale Spender, *Women of Ideas*, London, Ark, 1983; Dale Spender (ed.), *Feminist Theorists*, London, The Women's Press, 1983.

14 Olive Banks, *Becoming a Feminist*, Brighton, Wheatsheaf, 1986.

15 ibid., 73.

16 ibid., 73.

17 Helen Taylor, reported address to the third annual meeting of the Edinburgh branch of the National Society for Women's Suffrage, 1872.

18 Aileen S. Kraditor, *The Ideas of the Woman Suffrage Movement 1890–1920*, New York, Anchor Books, 1971.

19 See, for instance, the *Englishwoman's Review*, April 1876.

20 For example: Frances Power Cobbe, 'Criminals, idiots, women and minors: is the classification sound?', *Fraser's Magazine*, 8 December 1868.

21 See Josephine E. Butler, *The Education and Employment of Women*, London, 1868.

22 Millicent Garrett Fawcett, speech delivered to the Women's Debating Society, Manchester, 1899.

23 Henry Fawcett and Millicent Garrett Fawcett, *Essays and Lectures on Social and Political Subjects*, London, 1872.

24 For example: Barbara Bodichon, *Reasons for the Enfranchisement of Women*, London, 1866; Josephine E. Butler (ed.), *Women's Work and Women's Culture*, London, 1869; Ellen Mappen, *Helping Women at Work*, London, Hutchinson, 1985.

25 For example, Jessie Boucherett, 'How to provide for superfluous women', in Butler (ed.), *Women's Work and Women's Culture*.

26 Barbara Bodichon, *Women and Work*, London, 1857.

27 Josephine Butler (ed.), *Women's Work and Women's Culture*.

28 Barbara Bodichon, *A Brief Summary, in Plain Language, of the Most*

Important Laws Concerning Women, London, 1854; Bodichon, *Women and Work*; Butler, *The Education and Employment of Women*; Butler (ed.), *Women's Work and Women's Culture*; Mona Caird, 'Marriage', *Westminster Review*, 130, 1888; Cobbe, op. cit.; Frances Power Cobbe, 'Wife torture in England', *Contemporary Review*, April 1878; Frances Power Cobbe, *The Duties of Women*, London, 1888.

29 Martha Vicinus, *Independent Women*, London, Virago, 1985.

30 For example: Frances Power Cobbe, *Life of Frances Power Cobbe as Told by Herself*, posthumous edition, Swan and Sonnenschen & Co., 1904; Maria Grey and Emily Shirreff, *Thoughts on Self Culture*, London, 1850; Harriet Martineau, *Autobiography: with Memorials by Maria Weston Chapman*, London, 1877.

31 See, for example, Butler (ed.), *Women's Work and Women's Culture*.

32 See Banks, *Becoming a Feminist*.

33 Bodichon, *Women and Work*; Fawcett and Fawcett, op cit.

34 Banks, *Becoming a Feminist*.

35 Bodichon,   Women and Work; Butler (ed.), *Women's Work and Women's Culture*.

36 Bodichon, *Women and Work*.

37 Bodichon, *Women and Work*; Butler (ed.), *Women's Work and Women's Culture*; Caird, op. cit.; Cobbe, 'Criminals, idiots, women and minors'; Dinah Mulock Craik, *A Woman's Thoughts about Women*, London, 1862; Harriet Martineau, 'Female industry', *Edinburgh Review*, 109, 1859; Julia Wedgwood, 'Female suffrage', in Butler (ed.), *Women's Work and Women's Culture*.

38 Lewenhak, op. cit.; Soldon, op. cit.

39 *Englishwoman's Review*, February 1886.

40 See Jessie Boucherett and Helen Blackburn, *The Condition of Working Women and the Factory Acts*, London, 1896.

41 Banks, *Becoming a Feminist*; Ellen F. Mappen, 'Strategies for change: social feminist approaches to the problems of women's work', in Angela V. John (ed.), *Unequal Opportunities*, Oxford, Blackwell, 1986.

42 Josephine E. Butler, *Personal Reminiscences of a Great Crusade*, London, 1896; J. Ellice Hopkins, *A Plea for the Wider Action of the Church of England in the Prevention of the Degradation of Women*, London, 1879; Walkowitz, op. cit.

43 *The Shield*, 14 March 1870.

44 Banks, *Becoming a Feminist*.

45 Bodichon, *Women and Work*; Caird, op. cit.; Butler (ed.), *Women's Work and Women's Culture*.

46 See, for example: Lal Coveney, Margaret Jackson, Sheila Jeffreys, Leslie Kay, and Pat Mahony, *The Sexuality Papers*, London, Hutchinson, 1984; Ellis Ethelmer, *Woman Free*, Congleton, 1893; Sheila Jeffreys, *The Spinster and her Enemies*, London, Pandora, 1985; Francis Swiney, *The Bar of Isis*, London C. W. Daniel, 1907.

47 See, for example: Coveney *et al.*, op cit.; Jeffreys, op. cit.; Jenny C. Uglow, 'Josephine Butler: from sympathy to theory', in Spender (ed.), *Feminist Theorists*; Walkowitz, op. cit.

48 See Jeffreys, op. cit.
49 Coveney *et al.*, op. cit.; Jeffreys, op. cit.
50 See: Cobbe, 'Criminals, idiots, women and minors'; Fawcett and
    Fawcett, op. cit.
51 See *Englishwoman's Review*, December 1876; Elizabeth Wolstenholme,
    'The education of girls, its present and its future', in Butler (ed.),
    Women's Work and Women's Culture.
52 See Harriet Taylor, 'Enfranchisement of women', *Westminster Review*, 55,
    1851.
53 Butler (ed.), *Women's Work and Women's Culture*.
54 Bodichon, *Women and Work*.
55 Maggie MacFadden, 'Anatomy of differences: towards a classification of
    feminist theory', *Women's Studies International Forum*, 7, 6, 1984.
56 Emily Davies, 'Ideals', *The Higher Education of Women*, London, 1866;
    Englishwoman's Review, December 1876.
57 Banks, *Becoming a Feminist*.
58 Butler (ed.), *Women's Work and Women's Culture*; Ellis Ethelmer, *The Phases
    of Love*, Congleton, 1897; Swiney, op. cit.
59 Cobbe, 'Criminals, idiots, women and minors', 11.
60 ibid., 5.
61 See: Bodichon, *Women and Work*; Maria Grey, *On the Education of Women*,
    London, 1871; Harriet Martineau as quoted in *Englishwoman's Review*,
    April 1876.
62 Bodichon, *A Brief Summary in Plain Language*; Bodichon, *Women and Work*;
    Butler (ed.), *Women's Work and Women's Culture*; Cobbe, 'Criminals,
    idiots, women and minors'.
63 Cobbe, 'Wife torture in England'.
64 Martineau, 'Female industry'.
65 Jacquie Matthews, 'Barbara Bodichon: integrity in diversity', in
    Spender (ed.), *Feminist Theorists*.
66 Bodichon, *Women and Work*, 46.
67 J. Ellice Hopkins, *The Roles of Death*, London, n.d.
68 Josephine E. Butler, contribution to *The Shield*, 9 May 1870.
69 Bodichon, *A Brief Summary in Plain Language*; Bodichon, *Women and Work*;
    Butler (ed.), *Women's Work and Women's Culture*; Cobbe, 'Criminals,
    idiots, women and minors'; Cobbe, 'Wife torture in England'; Taylor,
    reported address, London, 1872.
70 Lillian Faderman, *Surpassing the Love of Men*, London, The Women's
    Press, 1985; Jeffreys, op. cit.; Vicinus, op. cit.
71 Eisenstein, op. cit., 6.
72 Butler, *Personal Reminiscences of a Great Crusade*.

POSTSCRIPT

In October 1984 the University of York registered its first students for the MA degree in Women's Studies. The introduction of the degree course marked, for those of us teaching on it, the fruit of several years of planning and preparation. Prior to this, courses such as women's history, women and politics, and feminist philosophy had been taught at undergraduate level in individual departments. There had, however, been very little interdisciplinary teaching of women's studies, and none at graduate level. The MA degree began with an interdisciplinary course on Victorianism, and this collection of essays reflects the spread of topics which that course has covered since its inception in 1984.

Teaching staff on the MA course are drawn from a variety of disciplines: history, philosophy, sociology, economics, literature. The choice of Victorianism as a central theme seemed appropriate both to these disciplines and as an introduction to women's studies. As feminists, we need to understand our historical roots, and the Victorian era was one in which feminism as a movement became increasingly prominent. Through the activities of the suffrage movement, women began to claim their political rights. Through literature, they reflected upon their positions of powerlessness, and upon the sexual double standards which perpetuated that powerlessness. Through (predominantly male) philosophy, they analysed the theoretical basis on which citizenship and enfranchisement were denied them. Most importantly, active feminists and their supporters came together from a wide variety of intellectual backgrounds. The Victorian feminist movement was itself 'interdisciplinary' and therefore seemed to us to be an appropriate starting-point for an interdisciplinary course.

All teaching is fraught with difficulties, but interdisciplinary teaching more so than most, and the study of an age as stereotyped as the Victorian period is a minefield of potential problems: not only was there an uncertain, and sometimes slender, background of shared knowledge for those coming from different disciplines, but there was also a divergence of approach to topics which span disciplines. However committed to feminist politics, and to women's studies we may be, as literary critics, philosophers, and historians, we have, through our collective teaching and research, become more rather than less conscious of the different languages and different priorities that divide us. The meditative, free-flowing, allusive prose of the literary critic *is* at a distance from the rigorous analysis of the philosopher and the sociologist. The historian can be so bound fast to her evidence and the specific context in front of her that she may miss the broader picture suggested by such analyses.

Despite these difficulties, however, feminists search for theoretical formulations which will cross the boundaries of the disciplines. We need to be able to analyse gender differences, the cultural construction of the appropriate roles of men and women, and the languages of sexuality, and these tasks may be illuminated by bringing a variety of disciplines to bear upon them. Thus, for example, it is fruitful to analyse orientalist painting as an example of the close interaction of the politics and language of gender and race. Fuller understanding may be obtained by bringing together cultural representations and historical specificity. Similarly, a philosophical analysis of Mill's *The Subjection of Women* can help the historian to recognize new layers of argument – to understand more clearly the discourse of sexuality within and against which Mill wrote. In our teaching and in our research, our aim was to bring together these different considerations, gleaned from different academic areas. But in order to do that it was essential that we pool our intellectual resources. The interdisciplinary nature of the course therefore presented us with a learning experience as well as a teaching experience. In teaching our students, we were also, and at the same time, learning from one another. The language of sexuality and of subordination was one language to the historian, another to the philosopher, yet another to the literary critic. Through discussion we came to understand that they were also, in a sense, dialects of the same language. Just as, for the Victorians, there were many languages of sexuality, so for us there were many languages through which to understand Victorianism.

One literary critic writes:

'The Lady of Shalott' has a veil of narrative between the Lady and the world which evokes her consciousness.

> But who hath seen her wave her hand?
> Or at the casement seen her stand?
> Or is she known in all the land
> The Lady of Shalott?

Such questions suggest other positions, other consciousnesses than the Lady's.

These essays, and the collaborative work which produced them, are an attempt to recognize and come to terms with 'other consciousnesses': to understand the many layers of discourse which may contribute to an understanding of poetry, of history, or of philosophy. Like the Lady, we are each compelled to view the world through a mirror, which sometimes distorts. But, by using many different mirrors, we hope, eventually, to construct a truer reflection and a better understanding of Victorian society.

NAME AND TITLE INDEX

Numbers in italic denote main references.

251

Les Illusions perdues 39, 53
In the Artist's Studio 83
In Memoriam 82
Ingres, Jean Auguste Dominique 12, 102, 107, 114–15, 121, fig. 3.3
L'Interdiction 38

Jacobi, Mary Putnam 12
Jaggar, Alison 187–8
Jalland, Patricia 6
James, Gilbert 81
Jameson, Anna 156, 159, 162
Jan, Laurent 46
Jane Eyre 63, 82, 99, 108, 121–2
Jourda, Pierre 104
Journey to the Orient 101, 102
Jouve, Nicole Ward 3, 21, *25–59*
Judah and Tamar 118, fig. 3.5
Jung, Carl Gustav 83

Kent, Susan Kingsley 7
Kiernan, V. 112
Killham, John 72, 81
King Cophetua 63
Kingsford, Philip 143
Kipling, Rudyard 97, 122–3
Kossuth, Louis 147
Kraditor, Aileen S. 228
Kucuk Hanem 107, 110

Laclos, Pierre Choderlos de 28
The Lady of Shalott 22, *60–88*, 247–8, fig. 2.1, fig. 2.2, fig. 2.3, fig. 2.4, fig. 2.5, fig. 2.6
Lamartine, Alphonse de 97, 102–5, 109, 114
Lamb, Lady Caroline 43
'Lancelot and Elaine' 60–1, 65, 69, 75, 78, 79
Lane, Edward 101, 104, 106, 121
Laqueur, Thomas 12
Lawrence of Arabia 103
Layamon 62
Laycock, Thomas 202
The Leader 150
Leake, John 199
Leçons de littérature 35
Leighton, Robert 110
Lerner, Gerda 223
Letters edifiantes 35
Lévi-Strauss, Claude 12, 44
Lewes, George 153

Lewis, John Frederick 102, 103, 110, 112, 113, 121, fig. 3.1
Lewis, Sarah 11
Liberty, Equality, Fraternity 132
'Lilian' 83
Liszt, Franz 31
Little Dorrit 29
Locke, John 145
Lost Illusions 39, 53
Loti, Pierre 110
Lowell, Sarah 30
Lowndes, Marie Belloc 138
Lubbock, Sir John 133
Le Lys dans la vallée 29, 38

The Mabinogion 62
Mackenzie, Charlotte 207
Mademoiselle de Maupin 46
Maffei, Cavaliere 48
Maffei, Clara 47–8, 50
Magasin pittoresque 120
Maine, Henry 134
La Maison Nucingen 38
Maistre, Joseph de 35
Malleson, Elizabeth 154–5
Malory, Sir Thomas 22, 62–3, 69, 74
Malthus, Thomas Robert 147
The Man Who Would Be King 122
Manilow, Barry 185
Manners and Customs of the Modern Egyptians 101
Mappen, Ellen F. 232
Marsh, Jan 60, 84
Martineau, Harriet 121–2, 150, 238
Marx, Karl 88
Matthews, Jacquie 240
Maudsley, Henry 202, 204, 208–10
Mauss, Marcel 45
Maynard, Mary 11, 15, 88, 133, *221–47*
Mazzini, Giuseppe 147
Mears, Martha 195–6
Memoirs of Two Young Brides 32
Mendus, Susan 10, 132, *171–91*, 225
Mercier, Charles 204
Merryweather, Mary 157–8
Meteyard, Sidney Harold 73, 76, 78
Michel, Arlette 36–7
Michel Strogoff 120
Mill, Harriet Taylor 132
Mill, James 95
Mill, John Stuart 9, 10, 11, 23, 69, 121–2, 132–4, 146–7, 150, 159, 162–3, *171–92*, 223, 230, 249

SUBJECT INDEX

adultery 28, 32–3, 41, 45, 49
animals 9, 177–9, 182–5
anthropology 23, 94, 132–4
aristocracy 39, 41, 43
art 81, 83, 122, 131, 153; orientalist 13, 93, 101–3, 106, 109, 111, 119–21
artists 13; male 21–128; power of 118, 120

baths 110–12
biology 12, 23, 94–5, 132–3, *192–220*
bourgeoisie 3, 5, 38–9, 41
Britain 164, 209–10, 223; and France 3, 5, 13–14, 22, 26, 93, 100, 206

childbirth 193, 196, 199, 201, 205–8
children 97–8, 189, 227
class 3, 45; and gender 2, 9, 90–2, 135; middle 1–4, 10, 192, 223; and race 2, 90–2; working 3, 210, 214, 225
clitoridectomy 195, 197
complementarity 184–90, 230, 235
construction: of femininity 242; of masculinity 222
Contagious Diseases Acts 224, 232–3, 241
courtesan 53–6
cultural differences 88, 91, 94, 104, 110

Darwinism 213
divorce 189–90
doctors 133, 192–216
domesticity 4–5, 23, 38, 108, 189
dominance 23, 91–2, 107, 110
double standards 156, 224, 232–3, 241–2
dualism 7–9, 156, 163, 216

economic inequalities 1, 173, 186, 189, 231–3
education 159, 162, 179–80, 231; girls' 10,
34–8, 132, 154–5, 228; higher 133–4, 193, 208, 210–11, 213, 215; and marriage 28, 43; medical 215, 235; and medical profession 204, 208–14; secondary 134, 193, 208, 210, 215; women's 95, 161, 198, 208–14, 227, 235, 239–40
emotion 184–5, 187–8
employment 4, 159–62, 231–3, 236, 240–1
Enlightenment 133, 214, 216, 225
equal rights 223, *227–9*, 234, 238
eroticism 22–3, 64, 81
evangelicalism 10, 225
experience of women 7, 78, 89, 101–2, 131, 238

family 4–5, 10, 32, 94; women in 132–4, 161, 229–30, 235
female: autonomy 236; friendship 136–70, 243; passivity 8, 10, 21, 51, 112; purity 10, 160; rationality 8; sexuality 3, 11, 133, 203; stereotypes 60, 94, 104, 193; subordination 1–3, 15, 91–3, 107, 120–2, *131–247*; vulnerability 148–9, 201; writers 14
femininity 21–2, 51, 193, 235; concepts of 2, 5, 95, 118, 187, 234–6; images of 82–3, 94; oriental 109, 118; social construction of 242
feminism 131–247; and friendship networks 163; language of 135, 227, 240; see also: women's movement
feminists 221–47; contemporary 222, 226, 236, 243–4; definition of 223; politics of 224, 237; Victorian 2, 7, 11, 15, 134, 188, 216
France 10, 148; and Britain 3, 5, 13–14, 22, 26, 93, 100, 206

257

orientalism 22, 100; in art and literature 13, 93, 100–3, 106, 108–9, 111, 120–2; and femininity 55, 109, 118; and Otherness 23, 100, 103–5
Otherness 115, 122; oriental 23, 100, 103–5; in sex, race, and class 92, 99, 108, 110
overwork 194, 210, 212–13

painting 81, 83, 122, 131, 153; orientalist 13, 93, 100–3, 106, 109, 111, 120–1
passivity 8, 10, 21, 51, 112
patriarchy 44–5, 134, *221–47*
perfectability of character 174–83
philanthropy 149, 154, 158–9, 162–3
poetry 43–4, 187
political economy 147, 161
politics 136–70, 208, 215, 225; feminist 224, 237; of gender relations 131–247
power 98, 110, 114; artistic 118, 120; male 7, 99, 106–7, 120–1, 239–40
pregnancy 193–6, 199–201, 205–6, 208
Pre-Raphaelites 22–3, 60–1, 70, 78–9, 83, 153, 161
private and public spheres 5, 38, 131, 136, 236, 238
privilege 221–47
property 227, 240; laws 137, 140–1, 156–7, 172, 223–4
prostitution 55, 155–6, 162, 224, 232–3, 241
Protestantism 10, 162
psychiatry 133, 192–3, 195–6, *200–8*, 209, 214–15
psychological medicine 200, 206, 208, 216
puberty 198–203
public and private spheres 5, 38, 131, 136, 236, 238
purity 10, 160

race: and class 2, 90–2; and gender 2, 23, *89–128*
radicalism 159, 186, 236–7
rationalism 8–9
rationality 6, 8–10, 95; Mill's view on 177–8, 184, 187–8
reading 145–6, 160
reformism 186, 237
representations of women 6, 8–9, 12–13, *21–128*
reproductive system 12, 133, 213; and mental illness 193, 197, 201–5, 208
rights of women 133, 214, 223, 234–5;

equal 223, *227–9*, 234, 238; legal 228, 238
Roman Catholicism 10, 162–3
romanticism 51, 108, 146

science 8–9, 94–5, 132
sensuality 75, 183, 190
sex *see* gender
sexuality 1, 5–9, 99; bisexuality 49–50, 56; double standards of 156, 163, 224, 232–3, 142–3; female 3, 11, 133, 203; and feminism 131–247; language of 1, 12, 131; male 11, 15, 106–8, 178–9, 189–90, 232–4, 236; and marriage 182; and medicine 11; oriental 106, 108, 118; public and private 5, 38, 131, 136, 236, 238; representations of 13, 21–128; and subordination 1–2, 15, 23, 88, *131–247*; suppression of 4–5, 9–10
slavery 113–14, 121, 186
social change 2, 90, 162, 214, 242
social construction: of femininity 241; of masculinity 222
social economy 161
socialism 225
source materials 6; feminist 224–5; medieval 60–4; orientalist 109
stereotypes 60, 94, 104, 193
subordination of women 3, 15, 122, 237; and feminism 131–247; and male dominance 91–2, 107, 120–1, 238, 242–3; in marriage 230; and political action 137; and sexuality 1–2, 15, 23, 88, *131–247*
suffrage 163, 224–5, 229

trade unions 225, 231–2
travel 93, 101–3, 105, 120–2

unitarianism 138–40, 155–6, 184
uterus 195, 199–206
utilitarianism 132, 175, 177

Victorian feminists 2, 7, 11, 15, 134, 189, 216, 221–47
Victorianism 1, 4, 9, 60, 81, 83, 248
virginity 7, 71–3

wives 34–7, 40, 230
women: abuse of 233, 240; and biology 192–220; and children 97–8, 189, 227; doctors 209; and double standards 156, 163, 224, 232–3, 241–2; education of